MW01616473

Growing up in the Baptist South, we always spoke of revival in terms of meetings placed on the church schedule in the spring and fall. Once I began to wrestle with the doctrines of grace, one of my immediate questions was, "How does revival square with theology built upon the meticulous sovereignty of God?" Here, Tom Nettles shows that Reformation theology has always undergirded genuine revival, a reality shown to be true in America, where revivalism replaced revival and largely went to Arminian seed after the rise of Charles Finney. Do we have the means to secure revival, is it entirely a work of God, or is it something in between? Nettles, one of America's pre-eminent church historians, is a trusted guide who knows how to answer these questions compellingly by a journey through the primary sources. This work can help us recover genuine revival in an age that desperately needs it.

Dr. Jeff Robinson,
President and Editor in Chief,
The Baptist Courier, Greenville, SC
Adjunct Professor of Church History,
North Greenville University

America has a rich heritage of revival(s). In this survey of American awakenings, Tom Nettles traces the course of revival in America from the post-Reformation era to the Great Awakening, and from the 1858 revival in New York to the revivals of the twentieth century. Using the historical record to show both the roots and fruits of Spirit-worked revival, Nettles provides a balanced evaluation of the revivals that have defined American church and society, as well as of controversial revivalists like Charles Finney and Billy Sunday. May God be pleased to use this book to renew and revive the hearts of His people today, just as He did in centuries past!

Dr. Joel R. Beeke,
Chancellor and Professor,
Systematic Theology and Homiletics,
Puritan Reformed Theological Seminary
Pastor, Heritage Reformed Congregation,
Grand Rapids, MI

Seeking revival is seeking God. The more we are content to live without revival, the more we need reviving. But it's not manufactured emotionalism that is needed. What is needed is for the Word of God to be preached faithfully with the supernatural power of the Holy Spirit. What is needed is the spiritual and eternal fruit that comes from our hearts being renewed by a fresh visitation of God's presence. What is needed is for God to be experientially magnified in our hearts, churches, and communities. The stories in this book are remarkable because they are nothing less than supernatural. Tom Nettles has a way of making history come alive. He not only identifies the true and false marks of revival in this excellent history of reformation and revival in America, but He also installs within the reader a greater longing to see the true fruits of revival in our day. By observing the wonderful works of God in the past, we learn what is greatly needed today. I pray that God uses this book to inspire His people to long and pray for a fresh visitation of His divine power in our day.

Jeffrey D. Johnson,
Pastor, Grace Bible Church
President, Grace Bible Theological Seminary,
Conway, AR

IN THE MIDST
OF THE YEARS

IN THE MIDST
OF THE YEARS

A HISTORY OF REFORMATION
AND REVIVAL IN AMERICA

THOMAS J. NETTLES

IN THE MIDST OF THE YEARS

A History of Reformation and Revival in America

Published by Founders Press

P.O. Box 150931 • Cape Coral, FL • 33915

Phone: (888) 525-1689

Electronic Mail: officeadmin@founders.org

Website: www.founders.org

Printed in the United States of America

ISBN: 978-1-965810-18-7 (Hardback)

ISBN: 978-1-965810-04-0 (Paperback)

ISBN: 978-1-965810-05-7 (eBook)

ISBN: 978-1-965810-06-4 (Audiobook)

Library of Congress Control Number: 2024949934

TABLE OF CONTENTS

FOREWORD

Any book that contains substantive scholarship, along with brevity and readability, is quite a task to accomplish. Dr. Tom Nettles has blended well all three qualities in his new book, *In the Midst of the Years: A History of Reformation and Revival in America,* which summarizes and analyzes American revival history from the middle of the eighteenth century into the first half of the twentieth century.

There have been many books written on the subject of revival in the last hundred years, and the publication of such literature continues to this day. Revival—what an important subject! But most professing Christians today are generally grossly ignorant of or indifferent to the word itself. It has lost all of its historical meaning in the twenty-first century. Yet what does our country lack more right now than a massive turning to Christ again across the land? Is it not the most important need America has in this hour? Therefore, a new and quality work on the subject of reformation, revival, and spiritual awakening in the context of American history is very timely for today if it is well sourced and well written. This book is both.

In the Midst of the Years is a quality and timely addition to the genre of revival literature. Dr. Nettles, a noted Baptist historian and author, reveals himself here also as an exceptional writer on the subject of revival, which requires the scholarship of a true historian, the accurate thinking of a trained theologian, and the kind of spiritual heart that sees the pastoral and moral importance of what revival would mean in our day.

The opening chapter is worth the price of the book, as Nettles develops a solid historical and theological foundation in defining the meaning of reformation and revival. Drawing from numerous historical authorities, the author provides not only a substantive definition of both realities, but shows their proper relationship one to another.

Beginning with the eighteenth century, Nettles provides a summary of the First Great Awakening, primarily connected with the names of Jonathan Edwards and George Whitefield during the 1740s in New England. He then proceeds to the Second Great Awakening fifty years later, which began in the 1790s and proceeded into the first half of the nineteenth century under the ministries of Asahel Nettleton and Charles G. Finney, including the phenomenon of the 1858 Prayer Revival which swept the nation. In addition, the lesser known but inspiring movements of God's Spirit on both sides of America's Civil War is accurately presented here as part of the Second Great Awakening.

Proceeding to the Third Great Awakening in the mid-nineteenth century, the names of Dwight L. Moody and Billy Sunday ring a bell for many Christians. They were very significant evangelists who labored in the more modern technique of crusade-like evangelistic meetings, both in America and in Great Britain. Rather than seeing significant outpourings of the Holy Spirit, as Edwards, Whitefield, and Nettleton witnessed, Moody and Sunday saw thousands brought into the kingdom through the basic fundamental preaching of Christ crucified. This period of awakening saw the formative beginnings of contemporary evangelism in the early stages of American evangelicalism, which had already departed from its formative roots of Calvinistic experiential theology.

The words of A. W. Tozer are more applicable today than when he first spoke them over sixty years ago: "True revival changes the moral climate of the community." If this is true, a genuine outpouring of the Holy Spirit, producing widespread moral reformation and spiritual change, is the primary need of America today. This book deserves a wide reading. I heartily recommend it to any Christian leader or believer who not only wants to increase their understanding of revival and spiritual awakening, but also longs to see God rend the heavens again and come down in reviving power for His glory in America in the midst of our years.

Mack Tomlinson
Providence Chapel
Denton, Texas

PREFACE

The title of this book, *In the Midst of the Years*, comes from a prayer of Habakkuk as he sees the holy purpose of God in the discipline of Judah by Babylon. Based on what he now senses about God's purpose with His people, and how the Lord has shown His faithfulness in the past, Habakkuk prays for a revival of that same kind of powerful and purposeful intervention in light of the coming disaster. "O LORD, revive your work in the midst of the years" (Hab. 3:2) seems to imply that he desires to see these things happen before the culmination of the ages. God's manifestation of His glory now, before the rolling up of all things at the final conflagration, is at the heart of Habakkuk's prayer. He knows that wrath is the proper response to evil, injustice, and idolatry, but mercy is a surprising display of wisdom and power and gives a marvelous symmetry to the revelation that God gives of Himself in this age. "In wrath remember mercy."

We have seen the perfect fulfillment of this prayer in the crucifixion of Christ (Rom. 3:26) and the historical verification of it in the resurrection (Rom. 4:25; 5:10). We know of the full application of its benefits because Jesus the Christ was received back into heaven, where He is our Mediator and our Advocate with the Father, "Jesus Christ the righteous" (1 John 2:1). We have found in Scripture, in history, in our churches, and in our lives that times of spiritual declension and confusion may arise. We also know, in these same spheres of experience, that God's gracious extension of life-giving power can revive us and revive our churches from these struggling, almost-smothered frames. Though we await the "glorious appearing of our great God and Savior Jesus Christ" (Titus 2:13) for the consummate manifestation of glory, we can pray, "In the midst of the years" make Your life-giving, transforming, sanctifying power operate in an accelerated and expansive way. Lord, give us hearts that seek You more purely and lives that reflect Your holiness more fully.

CHAPTER 1

INTRODUCTION TO AMERICAN REVIVAL

Martyn Lloyd-Jones defined revival as "an experience in the life of the Church when the Holy Spirit does an unusual work. He does that work, primarily, amongst the members of the Church; it is a reviving of the believers. You cannot revive something that has never had life, so revival, by definition, is first of all an enlivening and quickening and awakening of lethargic, sleeping, almost moribund Church members." He went on to describe a sudden work of the Spirit that "comes upon them and they are brought into a new and more profound awareness of the truths that they had previously held intellectually, and perhaps at a deeper level too." Such a work brings humility, conviction of sin, and terror at any notion of self-sufficiency. "Many of them feel that they had never been Christians. And then they come to see the great salvation of God in all its glory and to feel its power." This quickening and enlivening power brings prayer. Also, "new power comes into the preaching of the ministers, and the result of this is that large numbers who were previously outside the Church are converted and brought in."[1]

In W. B. Sprague's *Lectures on Revival*, he noted that he gave these lectures to his congregation to "vindicate the cause of genuine revivals of religion; and in doing this . . . to distinguish between a genuine revival and a spurious excitement." He began by defining

---

[1] Martyn Lloyd-Jones, "Revival: An Historical and Theological Survey," in *The Puritans: Their Origins and Successors: Addresses Delivered at the Puritan and Westminster Conferences 1959–1978* (Edinburgh: Banner of Truth, 1987), 1–23.

religion in general and showed how the Christian religion fits that pattern but with peculiar distinctives.

> Religion consists in a conformity of heart and life to the will of God. It consists in a principle of obedience implanted in the soul, and in the operation of that principle in the conduct. Religion is substantially the same in all worlds; though the religion of a sinner is modified, in some respects, by his peculiar character and condition. In common with the religion of the angels, it consists in love to God—to his law, to his government, to his service; but in distinction from that, it consists in repentance; faith in the merits of a crucified Saviour; resignation under trials; opposition to spiritual enemies. Moreover, religion in the angels is an inherent principle; it begins with their existence; but in the human heart it is something superinduced by the operation of the Spirit of God. Wherever there exists a cordial belief of God's truth, and submission of the will to his authority, and the graces of the heart shine forth in the virtues of the life, there is true religion.[2]

Sprague than gave a brief definition supported by an extended analysis. "Now, if such be the nature of religion," he surmised, "you will readily perceive in what consists a *revival* of religion. It is a revival of scriptural knowledge; of vital piety; of practical obedience." He went on to defend the use of the word, revival, when it included in its meaning the element of conversion. "The term," he noted, "is to be applied in a general sense, to denote the improved religious state of a congregation, or of some other community. And it is moreover applicable, in a strict sense, to the condition of Christians, who, at such a season, are in a greater or less degree revived; and whose increased zeal is usually rendered instrumental of the conversion of sinners." He then summarized

---

[2] W. B. Sprague, *Lectures on Revivals*, (Edinburgh: Banner of Truth, 1958 [first published 1832]), 6–7.

his observation into an expanded definition: "Wherever then you see religion rising up from a state of comparative depression to a tone of increased vigor and strength; wherever you see professing Christians becoming more faithful to their obligations, and behold the strength of the church increased by fresh accession of piety from the world; *There* is a state of things which you need not hesitate to denominate a revival of religion."[3]

In his introductory chapter to *Revival and Revivalism*, Iain Murray posits two historical phenomena concerning this subject. One was present in American evangelicalism from about 1620 through 1858—this period he views as the period of revival. The second dominates the last of the nineteenth century through the first half of the twentieth century—this period he calls revivalism. After that, as Murray puts it, "the opinion became widespread that such revivals did more harm to the churches than they did good. In the outcome, revival was for many years a discredited subject and the study of it fell into abeyance."[4] He also looks at the historiography of revival.

One historical method seeks to discern the difference between those two approaches to revival. A second type of history does not discern any distinctive difference but sees all the phenomena of revival culture as the same. A third and more recent approach sees all so-called revival as explicable in purely sociological terms. Among these histories are the ones written by Bernard Weisberger (*They Gathered at the River*) and William McLoughlin (*Modern Revivalism: Charles Grandison Finney to Billy Graham*).

Murray's thesis, in light of these other approaches to revival, sought a more carefully developed integration of belief and skepticism, based on an acceptance of the reality of truly Holy Spirit-wrought revival as well as the reality of contrived, humanly generated excitements and religious confidence based on false

---

[3] Sprague, *Lectures on Revivals*, 7–8.

[4] Iain Murray, *Revival and Revivalism* (Edinburgh: Banner of Truth Trust, 1994), xviii.

doctrine. He stated his thesis this way: "American history was shaped by the Spirit of God in revivals of the same kind as launched the early church into a pagan world." Before 1858, a univocal understanding of revival sounded clearly by the untrained preachers of the frontier and those trained in Eastern universities. Murray argued that these men were "equally opposed to what was merely emotional, contrived or manipulated. They believed that strict adherence to Scripture is the only guard against what may be wrongly claimed as the work of God's Spirit." They saw within some aspects of revival the tendencies to revivalism "long before it became a respected part of evangelicalism, and they would have had no problem in agreeing with the criticism which has since discredited it."[5]

More recently, Jon Butler has argued in *Awash in a Sea of Faith* that the Great Awakening did not occur but might be thought of as "an interpretive fiction and as an American equivalent of the Roman Empire's Donation of Constantine."[6] Earlier he had written "Enthusiasm Described and Decried: The Great Awakening as Interpretive Fiction," in which he called the Great Awakening merely a "short-lived Calvinist revival in New England during the 1740's." It became a grandiose idea with massive historiographical power through the work of Joseph Tracy's *The Great Awakening*, written in 1845 to establish a pattern of divine visitations in the history of American Christianity. Frank Lambert also believed that the Great Awakening was a historical fiction, but a fiction invented on the spot, not a century later. Lambert wrote,

> Revivals are not timeless universals; they are historically contingent. They are cultural formations constructed by persons who believe in and expect periodical outpourings of divine grace that supersede the ordinary means of salvation found in the Christian church. The

---

[5]   Murray, *Revival and Revivalism*, xx.

[6]   Jon Butler, *Awash in a Sea of Faith* (Cambridge: Harvard University Press, 1990), 165.

4

eighteenth-century Great Awakening was the creation of a particular group of evangelicals who viewed themselves as, first, discoverers of a "Work of God" and, second, instruments in promoting that work. They preached with fervor and prayed with expectation for an effusion of God's Spirit. When scores of men and women came under "conviction" for their sins and seemed to undergo "conversion," the revivalists declared the existence of revival. Then, they spread the news of local awakenings from community to community inspiring similar occurrences throughout America. By the early 1740's, the revivalists, viewing events from the inside—that is, as active participants within a revival culture—declared that an extraordinary Work of God had overspread America.[7]

Lambert then crafts a story from the variety of publications of the day, driving his point that the "revival" is the conglomerate product of all the publicity, self-promotion, newspaper accounts, journals, periodical magazines, correspondence (including localized, inter-colonial, and trans-Atlantic), theologically driven historical analysis, and personal testimonies. From this interesting conglomeration of texts, Lambert infers that the Great Awakening was a literary promotion in which the defenders of the movement were able to overwhelm its opposers in affirming the genuineness and substantiality of the movement on a grand scale.

However, Lambert points to the "contestation" as evidence that the reality was only literary and not undeniably substantive. "Every assertion promoters advanced met with a counterassertion argued with logic as convincing and evidence as compelling."[8] Lambert drew three conclusions. "First, the colonial American revival was both regional and intercolonial." It happened in two areas prone

---

[7] Frank Lambert, *Inventing the Great Awakening,* (Princeton: Princeton University Press, 1999), 6.

[8] Lambert, *Inventing the Great Awakening,* 252.

to revival expectation and rich in revival tradition. The progenitors knew how to "pray down" as well as "preach up" a revival. This event became known throughout the colonies with only sporadic movements outside the two areas of New England and the Middle Colonies. Second, "the Great Awakening was a religious invention." In other words, it was a "fabrication," developed by the use of means that were expected to produce it, and then given reality by reporting the success of the means. "Third, the Great Awakening was a contested event, part of a colonial culture war." Some saw it only as "rank enthusiasm" generated among the "vulgar masses."[9]

This generated a war of interpretation and counterinterpretation about the revival and its effects. Jonathan Edwards, according to Lambert, became moderate in his estimations of the extent of it, but still asserted its genuineness in many cases. Thomas Prince, in *Christian History*, believed that his own accounts had not done full justice to the extent of it but had only given a "specimen of the wondrous Work of God which has been in the midst of these years."[10]

My own view will gradually unfold in the flow of this historical narrative. I do, however, want to set forth a major assumption about this issue and then attempt some definitions. I believe that reformation and revival go together. One is preparatory and the other executes. One establishes truth and the other breathes life into it. Michael McClymond generally endorses this observation in stating, "There is no way to disentangle the descriptions of revival experiences from Christian ideas and teachings." After a description of Finney's experience of justification by faith, he made the general judgment, "This sort of interplay between doctrine and experience, cognitive content and affective response, is common in the narratives within the documentary history."[11]

---

[9] Lambert, *Inventing the Great Awakening*, 253–256.

[10] Lambert, *Inventing the Great Awakening*, 257.

[11] Michael McClymond, ed., *Encyclopedia of Religious Revivals in America* (Westport, CT: Greenwood Press, 2007), Vol. 1, xx–xxi.

Martyn Lloyd-Jones rejected the idea that reformation had any *necessary* connection as a prerequisite to revival. He believed that connection lapsed into "Arminian terminology and thinking," and was "to deny the fundamental tenet of the Reformed position." He went on to say, "If you truly believe in the sovereignty of God, you must believe that whatever the state of the Church, God can send revival." He illustrated it by showing that the apologetic efforts of Butler, Warburton, and others did not effect any rescue of the church from its destitution in the opening decades of the eighteenth century. He pointed to the preaching of Whitefield, who "received his baptism of power" in 1737 before he adopted Calvinism as a theological system, and to the Wesleys, whom God used mightily in reviving large segments of the Church of England in spite of theological muddleheadedness in some vital areas.[12]

I have questions about the accuracy of the good doctor's thinking in this matter.

Reformation and revival follow the Puritan pattern of preparation and conversion. Just as the mind must be fitted with certain perceptions and perspectives on human existence, sin, and destiny and certain views of God's law, holiness, and mercy before faith can come, so revival assumes some degree of fitness—conformity of mind—to pivotal truths conformed to the Spirit's work of glorifying Christ. In a very distilled fashion, Hebrews, in its discussion of faith, shows this connection clearly in pointing to Enoch as a man of faith, based on the biblical assertion that he "pleased God" (Gen. 5:24, LXX; in Hebrew "walked with God") by saying, "And without faith it is impossible to please him, for whoever would draw near to God must believe that he exists and that he rewards those who seek him" (Heb. 11:6). Certain spheres of cognition are necessary as ordained means for the infusion of faith. This is why Peter tied Christian faith, growth, and zeal to the operation of the Spirit through the Word, specifically the preached gospel:

---

[12] Lloyd-Jones, *The Puritans: Their Origins and Successors*, 15.

> Having purified your souls by your obedience to the truth for a sincere brotherly love, love one another earnestly from a pure heart, since you have been born again, not of perishable seed but of imperishable, through the living and abiding world of God; for "All flesh is grass, and all its glory like the flower of grass. The grass withers and the flower falls, but the word of the Lord remains forever." And this word is the good news that was preached to you. (1 Peter 1:22–25 ESV)

Note particularly such phrases as "obedience to the truth" as a synonym for faith; note the affective parts of the response intrinsically tied to the cognitive—sincere, love one another, earnestly, pure heart—as an assumption of what the entire transaction of truth, proclamation, Spirit (the "imperishable" seed), new birth, and continued growth in love necessarily involves. Just as conversion assumes the truth, so growth in fervency of love—certainly a component of revival—depends on the right negotiation of truth to the soul.

In general, I define reformation as the recovery of biblical truth that leads to the purifying of one's theology. It involves a rediscovery of the Bible as the judge and guide of all thought and action; it corrects errors in interpretation and gives precision, coherence, and courage to doctrinal confession; and it gives form and energy to the corporate worship of the triune God. Though it should be an ongoing enterprise in all churches and in the body of Christ throughout the world, the most poignant displays of reformation come at times of great theological, moral, spiritual, and ecclesiological declension in the church.

This involves a recovery of the formal principle of the Reformation, the principle of *sola Scriptura*, and it reasserts the material principle of justification by faith with all the necessary attendant doctrines to that view of salvation. Among these are the doctrine of human sinfulness resulting in both condemnation and corruption and, in its most thoroughly biblical form, the doctrine of the bondage of the will. The doctrine of the new birth is important to understand one's existential reliance on the intervention of God for the genesis of real spiritual life. The doctrine of imputed righteousness is necessary, not only as a matter of clear biblical teaching but as a part of the doctrinal coherence that eliminates the contribution of any human work to justification.

How then does revival relate to this concept of reformation? Revival is the application of reformation truth to human experience, It occurs one person at a time and may appear in individuals who become somewhat isolated from the more general apathy around them; or it may appear on a relatively massive scale, radically altering the spiritual face of an entire church, community, or even nation. Normally, therefore, revival involves three things: the presence of reformation doctrine either preached, read, or otherwise known; the experiential application of that doctrine accompanied by loving but careful investigation of the experience; and the extension of such an experience to a large number of people.

In Revelation, we find the church at Thyatira having good experience but in need of great doctrinal perception They must work to maintain the purity of what they know. The church at Ephesus is doctrinally sound and mature and courageous in the application of truth against the specific threats in the church. They, however, stand in need of increased experience, that is, a heightened conformity of affection for the God of truth. A proper grasp of doctrinal truth always implies the reality of the experiential element in it. To have a true doctrine of Christ implies a heart that consents to the biblical exclamation, that "in everything he might be preeminent" (Col. 1:18). A biblical doctrine of sin implies that we sense the despair into which it brings its perpetrator so that in embracing its truth we also cry out, "Wretched man that I am!" (Rom. 7:24). The doctrine of faith cannot be grasped apart from the cordiality of our consent to the truths of the gospel, a personal sense of trust in Christ, and abandonment of soul to Him, all infused with a hope of future glory and a sense of the perfection of life only within the sphere of divine love.

Revival means to make live again. A person formerly alive in Adam before the fall, but now dead in trespasses and sin because "as in Adam all die" (1 Cor. 15:22), is raised from death to life. This is revival. A person who has true spiritual life has drifted in discipline and cooled in affection for biblical truth and the Lord Jesus Christ. But then he has an intensification of love, devotion, holy living, and intentional biblical orientation. This is revival.

Both of these examples arise from the consistent application of the biblically revealed use of means to propagate the Christian faith and promote its utterly transforming effect on individual lives and corporate harmony. This use of means is graced by a period of intensive and pervasive operations of the Spirit of God that gives rapid maturing of the goals pursued through these means. Thus, sanctification rapidly increases, and community life has substantial healing of remaining jealousies and divisions. Conversions occur at a more rapid pace, a vision for gospel expansion is given clarity, and means for its execution are developed.

McClymond, from his observation of the phenomena of various revival traditions, gives seven characteristics of revivals. Only the first, he noted, is essential to all revival, and it generally corresponds to my description above. The other characteristics may or may not be present or will be present in differing combinations and intensity.

1. Revival involves "intensified experience." Participants in revival share a "vivid sense of spiritual things, great joy and faith, deep sorrow over sin, a passionate desire to evangelize others, and heightened feelings of love for God and fellow human beings."[13]

2. Bodily manifestations often characterize these times of the intensification of feeling. The documentary history is quite profound on this. From sobbing, to

---

[13] This list is derived from McClymond, *Encyclopedia of Religious Revivals*, Vol. 1, xxii–xxiii.

jumping for joy, to a sense of warmth and electrical impulses in the body, to fainting, to various impulses to speak in testimony, to prayer, to prophecy, to dancing or shouting, the effect of deeply moving spiritual and emotional perceptions frequently has a somatic effect.

3. Many revival expressions have resulted in, or even focused on, "extraordinary occurrences." This is particularly true in many of the twentieth-century movements related to the rise of Pentecostal and Charismatic revival.

4. They give rise to the need for "spiritual discernment"—to distinguish between the true and the false in spiritual experience, between the merely natural human response to stimuli and the divine intervention in a person's soul, between the operations of the Spirit of God and the counterfeiting activity of Satan, and between the true hortatory gift in preaching and evangelism and the manipulative techniques of a well-schooled tactician.

5. Revivals frequently lead to issues of "lay and clerical authority." How freely should those who are immature in biblical knowledge and doctrine be allowed to testify and exhort others? How much guidance should trained and ordained clerics exert? Will a church body genuinely moved by spiritual truth in a powerful way turn on its leaders as unspiritual because they naturally approach such a phenomenon with a greater sense of critical interaction due to the particular stewardship that is on them?

6. Sometimes this gives rise to "conflict and division in church and community." That tends to happen in the latter stages of a revival period as interpretations

have solidified and often have pivotal points of difference.

7. We find, therefore, the development of different associations, denominations, benevolent organizations, and educational institutions that emerge from the positive energy of a revival, as well as differences that emerge in the intensification of thought and emotion and the emphases that consolidate in the process of discernment.

In this book, I will propose that Charles Finney set in motion ideas and methods that greatly altered the American evangelical understanding of revival and, consequently, of Christian experience and truth. His emphases, which began to emerge in the late 1820s, had matured by 1835 and were published in a systematic theology in 1846. I will argue that there is a logical trajectory from the leading ideas of his thought into the silly narcissism of much that poses as evangelical religion today. Joel Osteen can be explained in terms of Charles Finney. In 1832, Sprague pointed to the reason for his lectures and for obtaining letters from many of his brethren of theological like-mindedness: "If the volume should, by the blessing of God, be instrumental, even in a humble degree, of promoting such revivals as those for which Edwards, and Dwight, and Nettleton, and a host of others among the living and the dead, have counted it an honor to labor, the best wish of the author . . . will be answered."[14]

Before we start our historical journey into these storms of controversy and change, however, I want to point to several assumptions that Finney *shared* with those who initially opposed him.

First, in times of declension revival is needed. From Solomon Stoddard to Billy Graham, a commitment to a harvest of souls and the escalation of spirituality among Christians has been seen as a

---

[14] Sprague, *Lectures on Revivals*, xiv–xv.

desideratum, except from those who oppose revival in principle. Lloyd-Jones noted, in an introduction to Sprague's *Lectures on Revivals*, "I am profoundly convinced that the greatest need in the world today is revival in the Church of God. Yet, Alas! The whole idea of revival seems to have become strange to so many good Christian people. There are some who even seem to resent the very idea and actually speak and write against it." Though revival was seen as a sovereign work of God in the earlier period while later it was viewed as the rational result of the employment of proper methods, both groups believed that it was legitimate to work for and pray for revival. In the Minutes of the Charleston Association for November 1825, after resolving to pray for the work in Burmah and among the Creek Indians, the Association, conscious of its depressed state due to the recent loss of Richard Furman, set aside a day for "fasting, humiliation, and prayer" for several objects, one of which was that God "may revive his work with power in the bounds of this Association, in our country generally, and throughout the world."[15] This was then followed by a separate resolution on revival.

> Resolved, While we greatly rejoice to hear of the many precious revivals of religion, which have been lately experienced in many parts of our country, and feeling earnestly desirous of witnessing similar gracious effusions of the Holy Spirit among ourselves, and being at the same time deeply sensible that extraordinary exertion on the part of the friends of Zion, are absolutely necessary: we do, therefore affectionately, earnestly and solemnly recommend to our brethren, that as far as practicable, they should set apart every Lord's evening as seasons of special prayer: that on these evenings they exert themselves to meet together as often as possible; but when this is impracticable they should then in their

---

[15] *Minutes of the Charleston Association, 1825* (W. Riley; 125 Church Street, Charleston), 5–6.

families and in their closets supplicate Almighty God for the special out-pourings of his Holy Spirit on our churches and on the rising generation.

Second, Finney asserted, in the same energetic conviction of Jonathan Edwards, that spiritual life and the quest for eternal life infinitely exceeds in importance any status, comfort, or power one might pursue and achieve in this life. One must lay everything aside and press into the kingdom. Edwards enjoined his listeners to "count the cost of a thorough, violent, and perpetual pursuit of salvation, and forsake all, as Ruth forsook her own country, and all her pleasant enjoyments in it. Do not do as Orpah did; who set out, and then was discouraged, and went back. But hold out with Ruth through all discouragement and opposition."[16]

In a sermon called "The Doom of those who Neglect the Great Salvation," Finney pressed the conscience of his hearers with their lack of fitting seriousness about the task of seeking salvation.

> This salvation is life's great work. If not made such, it had best be left alone. To put it in any other relation is worse than nothing. If you make it second to anything else, your course will surely be ineffectual—a lie, a delusion, a damnation! . . . It is infinite folly to make the matter of personal salvation only a secondary matter; for to do so is only to neglect it after all. Unless it has your whole heart, you virtually neglect it, for nothing less than your whole heart is the devotion due. To give it less than your whole heart is truly to insult God, and to insult the subject of salvation.[17]

And in a sermon on "The Loss when a Soul is Lost," Finney preached concerning this same urgency to those who would give

---

[16] Jonathan Edwards, *The Works of Jonathan Edwards* (Edinburgh: Banner of Truth, 1976), 1:668.

[17] Charles Finney, *The Way of Salvation*, (London: R. D. Dickinson, 1896), 214–215.

their energies to anything other than the task of saving souls from eternal perdition.

> What is really worth living for but to save souls? You may think it is worth living for to be a judge or a senator but is it? Is it, if the price must be the loss of your soul? How many of our American presidents have died as you would wish to die? If you should live to gain the object of your ambition, what would be your chance of saving your soul? The world being what it is, and the temptations incident to office and worldly honor being as they are, how great would be your prospects of saving yourselves? Would it be wise of you to run the hazard? What else would you live for than to save souls? Would you not rather save souls than be president of this union? "He that winneth souls is wise." "They that turn many to righteousness shall shine as the stars forever." Will this be the case with the ungodly presidents who die in their sins? What do you propose to do, young man, or young woman, with your education? Have you any higher or nobler object to live for than to save souls? Have you any more worthy object upon which to expand the resources of a cultivated mind and the accumulated powers gained by education? Think, what should I live for but the gems of heaven, for what but the honor of Jesus, my master?[18]

Third, "excitements" without proper understanding were detrimental to revival. As Edwards called for light in the understanding commensurate with heat in the affections, so Finney felt that lack of sufficient instruction in converting doctrines was a fault of many revival preachers. He criticized them, as well as local church pastors, by observing, "They have failed to present the objects of faith, and to hold them before the mind until the

---

[18] Charles Finney, "The Loss When a Soul is Lost," from *The Oberlin Evangelist*, July 2, 1851 (Lecture 1).

mind believes. They philosophized, perhaps correctly about the nature of faith, but they have not so forcibly arrayed before their minds the truth to be believed as to beget faith." We will show, in fact, that though some contrivances seemed to present a false stimulation to the conscience in Finney's methods, the real danger of his view was that it was too "rational."

Although Finney had a robust philosophy of the human affections in relation to the mind and the will, his rearrangement of this relationship constituted one of the major points of his departure. Even on this, however, Finney moved more toward previous views of the theology of revival in some of his mature reflections on this issue. He believed that he had failed to emphasize human depravity with sufficient strength and, therefore, had a corresponding de-emphasis on the necessity for a work of the Spirit. He stated that "true Christianity is the law of love written on the heart by the Holy Spirit and of course necessarily acted out in practical life." His explanation of each of the terms implied in this statement is not what Jonathan Edwards would mean by them, but it at least shows that, in his doctrinal perception, the work of the Spirit is vitally connected with the production of genuine Christian affections.

Fourth, like revival preachers before him and contemporary with him, Finney filled his sermons with doctrine. He set in motion certain ideas that gradually diminished the doctrinal content of messages, but for himself, the insistence on doctrine was a key element of his assault on the will of sinners to convince them to change their ultimate intention. Like those before him, he staunchly opposed Unitarianism, universalism, and any denials of the deity of Christ or of the doctrine of eternal punishment. The exclusivity of Christ and that His death constituted the only way in which God could remain just and justify the sinner were also themes that he shared in common with his predecessors among Reformed revivalists. We receive salvation only by means of repentance and faith—he shared this view with those from whom he departed. Though we will point to many details of these doctrines that were altered significantly, it is important to see the elements of truth in order not to dismiss all response to his message as built on a faulty perception of gospel reality.

Fifth, another point of agreement, though harboring details of disagreement, was Finney's commitment to persuasion. One cannot read the sermons of Edwards, Whitefield, and Nettleton without being impressed with their persuasive passion. Whitefield, in a sermon called "The Folly and Danger of Parting with Christ," after aiming several thrusts at the sinner to persuade him to "open the door of your hearts and the King of Glory shall enter in," made a last urgent attempt:

> What shall, I say, my brethren, unto you? My heart is full, it is quite full and I must speak, O I shall burst. What, do you think your souls of no value? Do you esteem them as not worth saving? Are your pleasures worth more than your souls? Had you rather regard the diversions of this life, than the salvation of your souls? If so, you will never be partakers with him in glory. But if you come unto him, he will give you a new nature, supply you with his grace here and bring you to glory hereafter. And there you may sing praises and Hallelujahs to the Lamb forever.[19]

Finney, though aligning it differently with the work of the Spirit and the place of the human will, still saw persuasion as one of the major elements of revival preaching and chastened ministers who did not seek to do so with sufficient tenacity. "They have made men understand what faith is," Finney noted, "but have not persuaded them to exercise faith." Only those who make a "lucid and forcible exhibition of appropriate truths such as makes its

---

[19] George Whitefield, *The Sermons of George Whitefield.* ed. Lee Gattis (Wheaton: Crossway, 2012), 1:382.

appeal to the heart" will ever "be instrumental in begetting true religion."[20]

In the personal persuasion of sinners, he was vivid and forceful for the necessity of immediate decision:

> How many times have you been called to decide, but have decided all wrong? You have been pressed earnestly with God's claims, and many a time have prayers and groans gone forth from the Christian heart of this whole community; but ah! Where are you still? Not yet safe; and, in greater peril than ever! Often reproved, hardening your neck; and what next? Suddenly destroyed, and that *without remedy.* Suppose now the curtain should drop— *you are dead!* And whither, then goes the undying, guilty soul?[21]

Sixth, because he was committed to a doctrinal approach and to persuasion, he shared with the previous generations a deep commitment to rigorous thinking as a necessary aspect of arriving at original knowledge of truth. "It will do you good to think," Finney proclaimed, "to develop your powers by study." Because there was a complementary rather than a contradictory relation between matters of faith and a full engagement of the mind with the power of truth, Finney insisted, "I do not pretend to so explain theology as to dispose with the labor of thinking." Neither a lost person nor a saved person should think that he will receive benefit from God's truth apart from considering it a subject worthy of serious reflection. A person who would not *think*, so as to understand his doctrinal arguments, had no right to contradict, Finney posited, as he foreknew objections that might come his way. He professed to have little patience with mere cavilers but would welcome any honest inquiry. Previous generations of

---

[20] Charles Finney, "Letter 5: Erroneous Revival Preaching," *Letters on Revival,* SermonIndex.net, https://www.sermonindex.net/modules/articles/index.php?view=article&aid=15984.

[21] Finney, *The Way of Salvation*, 162.

pastor-theologians who prayed for and promoted revival also made strong mental demands on those who heard them preach, and they expected sincere engagement with their arguments for truth.[22]

In light of these and other points of agreement, in seeking to sort out the wheat from the chaff in the religious development through the nineteenth century, one should labor with sincerity to discern the errors of a system without condemning its fruit. Much good fruit grows from systems that entertain some, or much, error. The fruit should not be identified with the error of the system or seen as developing from it. Rather, any good fruit should be seen as the result of those parts of a system that are vitally related to truth in general, and blessed by the Spirit of truth, much of which would be shared with those who opposed the distinctive departures Finney had made from his ostensible confessional heritage.

---

[22] Charles Finney, *Finney's Systematic Theology*, ed. J. H. Fairchild (Minneapolis: Bethany Fellowship, INC.,1976), xi.

CHAPTER 2

HISTORICAL AND THEOLOGICAL FOUNDATIONS FOR AMERICAN EXPECTATIONS OF REVIVAL

"God is not bound to change your heart. God is absolutely free. He may help you but, if He will not, He is blessed forever. It is true, He may help you without any wrong to Himself, but that lays Him under no necessity. It is His choice whether He will glorify His justice or His mercy on you."

—Solomon Stoddard[1]

The theological foundations for true spiritual awakening extend into the earliest corpus of biblical truth. Moses warned against idolatrous apostasy for the children of Israel but paralleled that warning with a promise: "But from there you will seek the LORD your God, and you will find Him if you seek Him with all your heart and with all your soul. When you are in distress, and all these things come upon you in the latter days, when you turn to the LORD your God and obey His voice (for the LORD your God is a merciful God), He will not forsake you nor destroy you, nor forget the covenant of your fathers which He swore to them" (Deut. 4:29–31). A short summary of the need and the means of revival we find in Christ's words to the church at Ephesus: "Nevertheless I have this against you, that you have left your first love. Remember therefore from where you have fallen, repent and

---

[1] Solomon Stoddard, "To Preach the Gospel to the Poor," in *A Guide to Christ* (Ligonier, PA: Soli Deo Gloria Publications, 1993), 96.

do the first works" (Rev. 2:4–5). We find a final picture of spiritual restoration that we call revival in Revelation 22:14–17:

> Blessed are those who do His commandments, that they may have the right to the tree of life, and may enter through the gates into the city. . . . "I, Jesus, have sent my angel to testify to you these things in the churches. I am the Root and the Offspring of David, the Bright and Morning Star." And the Spirit and the bride say, "Come!" and let I who hears say, "Come!" and let him who thirsts come. Whoever desires, let him take the water of life freely."

From the first writer to the last, and all in between, the purpose of God is to bring His people along toward the goal of godliness in accord with His covenant. So the idea of revival—a continual renovation of the human affections toward godliness—permeates Scripture. If it were not so, we would be wrong to pursue it.

REFORMATION PRINCIPLES

The Reformation, in differing degrees, rejected the sacramentalism of the Roman Catholic Church. Its rejection of the efficacy of *ex opere operato* (done in the doing), and its consequent dependence upon *fides ex auditu* (faith comes by hearing), focused on the effectual converting operations of the Holy Spirit upon the preaching of Scripture and the saving work of Christ.

Martin Luther (1483–1546) rocked the epistemological and soteriological foundation of Roman Catholicism. The doctrine of *sola Scriptura* and unwavering confidence in the inspiration, infallibility, and sole authority of Scripture changed the entire structure of Christendom. No longer could popes, councils, and tradition dominate as the referees for developing the propositions of revealed truth, but confidence in the inerrancy, clarity, sufficiency, and unadorned authority of Scripture had sole prerogative for the Christian. The church would no longer grovel in captivity to Babylon but could find freedom in the captivity of mind and heart to the Word of God. Dependence on merits would not suffice for right standing before God but would, in fact, aggravate condemnation. Only in the righteousness of Christ could a sinner stand free in the world and justified before God.

Ulrich Zwingli (1484–1531), in his book *On the Clarity and Certainty of the Word of God*, argued not only for Scripture's infallibility propositionally, but for its invincible power in infallibly accomplishing its purpose. "Thus we see," Zwingli reflected on God's announcing of the virgin birth, "that the whole course of nature must be altered rather than the Word of God should not remain and be fulfilled."[2] Geoffrey Bromiley presented Zwingli fundamentally as a preacher of the Bible. "At bottom," he summarized, "the practical measures were simply an outworking of the inward revolution accomplished by the preaching of the divine Word." This unadorned method arose from Zwingli's dual convictions of the "supremacy of the divine revelation in Holy Scripture, and the sovereignty of God in his election and grace."[3]

Though several circumstances endemic to sixteenth-century politics and ecclesiastical power conspired to limit Zwingli's influence to a restricted geographical area, along with leading to his untimely death, his bibliocentric evangelical theology found a powerful proponent in the Genevan Reformer John Calvin. In this way, Zwingli's vision of a Word-centered community "exercised a wider influence in and through the ever-extending Reformed communities of the later part of the century."[4] These biblical ideas are central to any theology of and reification of revival.

John Calvin (1509–1564) highlighted the doctrines of the Word and of calling, which are fundamental to one's confidence that God will grant revival through the faithful and fitting use of means. Calvin pointed out that only by the Spirit do the elect

---

[2]   G. W. Bromiley, ed., *Library of Christian Classics: Zwingli and Bullinger*, (Philadelphia: Westminster Press, 1953), 70.

[3]   Bromiley, *Library of Christian Classics*, 29, 31.

[4]   Bromiley, *Library of Christian Classics*, 30–31.

achieve faith in Christ. "The Holy Spirit is the bond by which Christ effectually unites us to himself."[5] Only by the Word of God does the Spirit generate faith. Calvin called faith "the principal work of the Holy Spirit." Since "by faith alone he leads us into the light of the gospel," one's embracing of the gospel and subsequent conformity to its spiritual beauty is an extension of the Spirit's work. "Paul shows the Spirit to be the inner teacher by whose effort the promise of salvation penetrates into our minds, a promise that would otherwise only strike the air or beat upon our ears."[6]

He referred to the biblical ideas of the Spirit as the "Spirit of adoption" and the "guarantee and seal of our inheritance"; He is called "life" because of righteousness, and He is likened to water because of His "power to cleanse and purify" and to satisfy one's spiritual thirst. "From that fact that he restores and nourishes unto vigor of life those on whom he has poured the stream of his grace, he gets the names 'oil' and 'anointing.'" Also, the Holy Spirit is called "fire" in light of His "persistently boiling away and burning up our vicious and inordinate desires" and His enflaming "our hearts with the love of God and with zealous devotion."[7] All of these aspects of the work of the Spirit, so cogently and consistently set forth by Calvin as integral to his theology, were the fuel of truth that ignited revival in eighteenth-century America.

On the other hand, Calvin's doctrine of the church, with his retention of infant baptism along with Zwingli and Luther, has some elements that are discouraging to the possibility of the revival of a local congregation. As the state-church is a body mixed with regenerate and unregenerate, God alone "knows who are his." He encloses them under His seal, which is the Spirit, as taught in Ephesians 1:13. When Calvin said that "they bear his insignia by which they may be distinguished from the reprobate,"

---

[5]   John Calvin, *Institutes of the Christian Religion,* III.1.1.

[6]   Calvin, *Institutes*, III.1.4

[7]   Calvin, *Institutes*, III.1.3.

he probably referred to the second part of 2 Timothy 2:19—"Let everyone who names the name of the Lord depart from iniquity."[8] In Calvin's ecclesiology, this departure from iniquity related only to the individual deportment of the believer, not to his church relations or even to the goal of a congregation as a whole.

This arose from Calvin's lack of any theology for constituting a church of believers only, for "a small and contemptible number are hidden in a huge multitude and a few grains of wheat are covered by a pile of chaff." It does not fall to our stewardship, therefore, to seek the purity of membership in a church—an impossible task in state churches established by law—for "we must leave to God alone the knowledge of his church, whose foundation is his secret election."[9] Since the true church is not visible, and our faith must recognize a church "beyond our ken," Calvin argued that "we are not bidden to distinguish between reprobate and elect—that is for God alone, not for us, to do." Instead, our duty is more singularly personal, that is, "to establish with certainty in our hearts that all those who by the kindness of God the Father, through the working of the Holy Spirit, have entered into fellowship with Christ, are set apart as God's property and personal possession; and that when we are of their number we share that great grace"[10]

In any single congregation, those who have this confidence that they share such grace are mingled with "many hypocrites who have nothing of Christ but the name and outward appearance. There are very many ambitious, greedy, envious persons, evil speakers, and some of quite unclean life." In this condition, it is obvious that "a vigorous discipline does not always flourish as it ought." There is a pure church of the elect seen only by God's eyes, but we must function in this church visible to our eyes, for we are "commanded to revere and keep communion with the latter."[11]

---

[8]   Calvin, *Institutes*, IV.1.2.

[9]   Calvin, *Institutes*, IV. 1.2

[10] Calvin, *Institutes*, IV. 1.3.

[11] Calvin, *Institutes*, IV.1.7

This attempt to justify the moral corruption of many "church members" in state-supported-and-mandated "churches" led Calvin to an aggravated attack on the Anabaptists. While he wrote against some of the Anabaptist doctrines that were marginally heterodox, he was particularly agitated by their attempt to found pure churches built on Word-induced regeneration followed by baptism. For example, drawing a conclusion from Paul's testimony in Acts 22:14–16, Felix Manz wrote, "From these words we clearly see what baptism is and when it should be practiced. One should be baptized who has been converted through God's Word, who has changed his heart, and now henceforth desires to live in newness of life—as Paul clearly shows in the sixth chapter of his Epistle to the Romans"[12] The Schleitheim Confession included as its first article this discussion of baptism:

> First. Observe concerning baptism: Baptism shall be given to all who have learned repentance and amendment of life, and who believe truly that their sins are taken away by Christ, and to all those who walk in the resurrection of Jesus Christ, and wish to be buried with Him in death, so that they may be resurrected with Him and to those who with this significance request [baptism] of us and demand it for themselves. Mt 28, M. 16, Acts 2, 8, 16, 19. This we wish to hold simply, yet firmly, and with assurance.[13]

Calvin's crippling consent to the state church held no possibility for an invigorated church purity by revival, but only for deeper holiness and knowledge of a single individual. The attempts of the Anabaptists, therefore, to establish bodies of believers only, through incorporating believers' baptism as the initial mark of the church, led him to judge them severely. They sinned "out of ill-advised zeal for righteousness," as well as out of "insane pride";

---

[12] W. R. Estep, Ed. *Anabaptist Beginnings* (Nieuwkoop: B. De Graaf, 1976), 57.

[13] Estep, *Anabaptist Beginnings*, 101.

they "wish to appear advanced beyond other men"; "they give themselves over completely to immoderate severity"; "they depart out of hatred and wickedness from the lawful church, while they fancy themselves turning aside from the faction of the wicked."[14]

Calvin recognized that "our cursed sloth is not to be excused," and that these tender consciences are wounded and provoked by "such dissolute and criminal license." Nevertheless, those immoderate pursuers of righteousness "sin in that they do not know how to restrain their disfavor." When they pointed out Paul's admonition for discipline and separation in 1 Corinthians 5, he admitted that "it is a great disgrace if pigs and dogs have a place among the children of God," and even greater if the Lord's Supper "be prostituted to them." This condition reflected that pastors are not always on the watch, or are "sometimes more lenient than they should be," or are hindered from exercising due severity so that "even the openly wicked are not always removed from the company of the saints."[15] Though Calvin argued a good case that an individual should not separate from the body because he makes assumptions about its imperfect holiness, but rather should pursue both truth and unity in love and deference, the Anabaptists contended that the very foundation of the state church was faulty. Proper New Testament discipline, as well as New Testament unity, was impossible, they argued, with such an uncertain and corrupt first principle. They contended that one of the marks of revival should be a reinvigorated church purity.

In New England, Roger Williams's objections to the established church, and to this idea of the chaff covering the wheat, revealed the faulty starting point. He argued that the church should be formed only by the operations of the Spirit of God. In his *Christenings Make Not Christians,* Williams discussed the true meaning of the word "heathen," which was regularly applied to the Native Americans. He pointed to the danger of the concept

---

[14] Calvin, *Institutes*, IV.1.13.

[15] Calvin, *Institutes*, IV.1.15

of Christendom. Having become purer in doctrine and precept by their separation from the abominations and humanly invented rites and righteousness of Rome, still, if so-called Protestant nations "remaine in an unrepentant, unregenerate, naturall estate, and so consequently farre from hearing the admonitions of the Lord Jesus, . . . I say they must sadly consider and know (least their profession of the name of Jesus prove at last but an aggravation of condemnation) that Christ hath said, they are but Heathens and Publicans." He earnestly sought to convince his countrymen that retaining the name of Christendom on the basis of Rome's pattern of a state church would not put them beyond the pale of the domination of the beast. They still could remain "unconverted and *un Christian Christians.*" They still would be devoid of "true Regeneration within" and remain strangers to "the true spirituall Jew from without amongst the Nations." The unregenerate among the nations are the true heathen (that is, Gentiles), separated from the covenant people of God. This is a truth into which each soul must search, particularly "such as profess to be Guides, Leaders, and Builders of the HOUSE of God."[16]

Williams believed that in the initial generation of the Reformation many experienced true conversion who had formerly been looked at as Christians because of their participation in the rites of Christendom. We should not, however, perpetuate the false state of Christendom and still expect God to honor with conversion our false dealing with the true power of the gospel and the true spiritual character of the church. Williams wrote, "I say then, woe be to me if intending to catch men (as the Lord Jesus said to Peter) I should pretend conversion and the bringing of men as mystical fish, into a Church-estate, that is a converted estate, and so build them up with Ordinances as a converted Christian people, and yet afterward still pretend to catch them

---

[16] Roger Williams, *The Complete Writings of Roger Williams* (Paris, Arkansas, 2005; originally by Russell & Russell, 1963), 7:34–35.

by an after conversion."[17] Treating unconverted men as converted and then hoping for eventual conversion is not a biblical way of proceeding and falls into the errors of Rome and its false boast of Christendom.

These differing views present us with two models of revival that we often find blending with each other, while also competing with each other. Sometimes the one becomes very negative toward revival as a kind of "enthusiasm" and Donatistic perfectionism. So we usually find three parties that develop in a time of revival. First, we find the anti-revival party that looks upon the entire movement as a false spirituality, assuming a condemning spirit toward the stable membership of the church. This view is similar to that held by Calvin toward the Anabaptists. Ironically, within this group, history reveals the development of liberal trends that minimized doctrines such as total depravity, substitutionary atonement, and the need for regeneration. Second, we find the pro-revival, pro-conversion contingent within the established church that believes that periodic "corrections" in church purity and genuine gospel clarity and conviction are needed. Solomon Stoddard (1643–1729) was an ardent advocate of this kind of awakening, as was his grandson, Jonathan Edwards. Third, history reveals a separatistic wing that believed revival and reformation come by conversions from the world and infusion of new and lively affections into the biblically warranted structures of the church. If they have become staid and formal, they become lively and effectual means of Christian discipleship. The Separate Baptist movement embodied this kind of revival conviction.

SPECIFIC PRECURSORS TO THE FIRST GREAT AWAKENING

The Cambridge Platform of 1648 presented a Calvinist, paedobaptist view of church life that gave energy to Calvin's desire for purity. It described church government, constitution, officers,

---

[17] Williams, *The Complete Writings*, 7:37.

admission of members, excommunication, and synods, as well as relations of churches to one another and the relation of church and state. On the admission of members into the church it is stated that the "doors of the Churches of Christ upon Earth, do not by God's appointment stand so wide open, that all sorts of People, good or bad may freely enter therein at their pleasure." They are to be examined as to whether they are spiritually qualified to enter church society. Requisite for church members was repentance from sin and faith in Jesus Christ. "The weakest measure of faith is to be accepted in those that desire to be admitted into the Church," for even weak but sincere Christians have the substance of repentance, belief, and holy desires required for union with Christ's church. Also, they most need the ordinances granted in church membership. Even if no public profession is made, they may give satisfactory communication of Christian faith and sensibility to elders who will make public statement to the church. Those weak persons then assent to the elders' public statement. Persons of more public competence should "make their relations and confessions personally with their own Mouth." Church members by virtue of covenantal infant baptism, when they reach years of discretion, must make a profession of their faith before they can be received to the Lord's Supper.[18]

The ambivalence of the situation was that they had formed expectations of a very predictable order and transfer of this order from generation to generation, while at the same time they were insistent upon true conversion. The acknowledgement of true conversion and thus readiness to participate in the Lord's Supper called for a deeply probing examination and a challenge to the confident civility of many citizens. It became harder to maintain a predictable generational replenishment of church membership as covenant infants became non-communing adults. On the

---

[18] "The Cambridge Platform," in *American Christianity*, eds. H. Shelton Smith, Robert T. Handy, Lefferts A. Loetscher, (New York: Charles Scribner's Sons, 1960) 1:136–137.

basis of the Puritan understanding of the covenant, the church consisted of true believers and "their seed" who were considered "federally holy." If they never professed to have had an experience of grace that constituted conversion, and thus never came to be communing members of the church, could they bring their own children to baptism?

A synod of churches in Massachusetts in 1662 adopted a policy that eventually was called the "Halfway Covenant." That name came from one of the provisions that stated, "Church-members who were admitted in minority, understanding the Doctrine of Faith, and publickly professing their assent thereto; not scandalous in Life, and solemnly owning the Covenant before the Church, wherein they give up themselves and their Children to the Lord, and subject themselves to the government of Christ in the Church, their Children are to be baptized."[19] These conforming and loyal but unconverted "members" could maintain the line of covenantal faithfulness by bringing their children to baptism. This led to continuing decline in orthodox Christian fervency, the unregenerate having the majority in many congregations, and eventually, under the provision of Solomon Stoddard, it led to pressing for the acceptance of the unconverted to the Lord's Supper.

On the relation of the civil magistrate to the church, the Cambridge Platform affirmed that the church could exist without government approval and even amidst government opposition. Churches do not oppose civil governments but encourage hearty obedience to them. Churches do not seek to usurp the duties of the magistrate nor the magistrate the work of church officers. They cannot make people members of the church nor require their partaking of the Lord's Supper. They are responsible, however, for enforcing both tables of the Law, thus making laws concerning idolatry, blasphemy, and heresy. They prohibit public statements of "corrupt and pernicious" opinions that create open contempt

---

[19] *American Christianity*, 1:204.

of the preaching of the Word. Magistrates should outlaw any profanation of the Lord's Day and regard schism from the communion of other churches a matter of creating civil instability. If churches, therefore, "walk incorrigibly or obstinately in any corrupt way of their own, contrary to the Rule of the Word," the magistrate has a coercive power to punish them and make them conform.[20]

Declining spirituality in the churches brought increased agitation for remedies. Movements of separation that had produced Baptist churches in Providence, Newport, and Boston brought about the growth of "Separate" churches, in the framework of traditional Congregationalism.[21] Opposition to them ran high both from the ministry and the magistrate and resulted in the hanging of Quakers and the public whipping of Baptists.

This decline of primitive fervency produced a series of activities on the part of ministers in efforts to halt the wave of mere nominalism in church membership. Apparent divine judgments increased the fervency and variety of warnings against spiritual laxness and infidelity. The devastation brought about by an Indian revolt known as "King Philip's War," combined with fires in Boston, led to a variety of attempts at stirring the flames of reformation. The lamentation of spiritual decline known as "the jeremiad" produced a long list of violations of divine law and profanations of divine worship.

A synod produced a document on the subject, called "God hath a Controversy with his New-England People."[22] Such a controversy was "undeniable," they contended, or such devastations as they had experienced would not have occurred. God was angry. The synod recognized "a great and visible decay of the power of Godliness amongst many Professors in these Churches." Pride, disorder, and

---

[20] *American Christianity*, 1:139–140.

[21] See Thomas Kidd, *The Great Awakening* (New Haven: Yale University Press, 2007), 174–188.

[22] *American Christianity*, 205–216.

violations of the second, third, and fourth commandments had created a profane, unstable, contentious society. Judgment could be seen partially in the rise of "Quakers and Anabaptists" fomenting "opposition to the churches of the Lord Jesus, receiving into their society those that have been for scandal delivered unto Satan." They observed a great decline in family government, leading to houses filled with "ignorance and profaneness" and giving rise to an increase of "inordinate passions, sinful heats and hatreds." They pointed to intemperance, breaches of the seventh commandment by "immodest apparel," mixed dancing, and "company keeping with light and vain persons." Promise breaking increased, and idolatry manifested in rampant covetousness in which "farms and merchandising have been preferred before the things of God," goods were sold at an "excessive rate," and day laborers were dealt with deceitfully and oppressively. Neither calls of the gospel nor judgments from God had brought repentance and reformation.

The document listed a large number of remedies to be pursued to avert further judgment and restore gospel spirituality. Leaders should be exemplary, and churches must reaffirm the Cambridge Platform and guard communion according to the old way. They must exercise discipline in the churches, maintain all the biblically warranted officers, and pay the magistrates a proper wage. Proper magistrates must be maintained fittingly, for "the magistrate is to be a keeper of both tables, which as a Magistrate he cannot be, if he do not promote the Interest of religion, by all those means which are of the Lord's appointment."[23] These included laws to promote the interest of reformation and enforcement of laws already made by the general court, particularly that the public houses should be run by people of piety and fidelity.

A most important measure for reformation was an explicit renewal of the covenant at a solemn assembly as exemplified in Ezra 8–10. Several of these were done in the 1670s and 1680s and were viewed as a means of experiencing the presence of God

---

[23] *American Christianity*, 214.

with them. At these assemblies a review of both judgments and blessings should be given, and specific sins of the times must be reprimanded. All this was but prerequisite to a renewing of covenant in such things as are clear and indisputably necessary. The assembled people should pray for the Lord to pour down His Spirit. "It doth concern us to cry mightily unto God," the promoters insisted, "both in an ordinary and an extraordinary manner, that he would be pleased to rain down righteousness on us."[24]

One of the most successful of these assemblies took place in the ministry of Samuel Willard (1640–1707). Willard led a covenant renewal in 1680 in immediate response to the document concerning "God's Controversy." It produced a great "harvest time," bringing more than a hundred to own their baptismal covenant and become full communicants of the church. It soon passed away, however, and in 1700 he preached about the renewed decline in *The Peril of the Times Displayed*. He listed numerous characteristics of decline, including denying the power of God, immoralities among professing Christians, little "cordial compliance" with gospel mandates and graces, contempt for the gospel ministry, and "grievous neglect of family worship." The younger generation forsook any spiritual ideals that had driven their fathers to seek pure religion instead of worldly pleasures and comforts. Despite the earlier reformation, "the life of religion is panting and gasping among us." Willard ended with instructions as to how the truly godly could preserve their cordial attachment to Christ and the gospel: "To those that are truly Godly: be you Exhorted to preserve the power of Godliness in times wherein there is little of it to be found. And to move you hereto, Consider . . . "[25]

---

[24] *American Christianity*, 215–216.

[25] Samuel Willard, *The Peril of the Times Displayed* (Boston: Printed by B. Green and J. Allen, 1700), 156–168. Accessed online: https://quod. lib.umich.edu/e/eebo2/A66108.0001.001.

The genre of "Election Day" sermons consistently reminded the people of the original ideals of the those who migrated from England. The people were reminded of the moral foundation of government and the necessity of earnest religious persuasion to sustain a hope, not only for eternity, but for stability, well-being, and favorable circumstances for spiritual prosperity in this life.

A prominent example of both the decline of the Puritan ideal of ecclesiology and the success of using measures for awakening was the grandfather of Jonathan Edwards, Solomon Stoddard. By 1700, Stoddard was advocating the Lord's Supper as a converting ordinance and was encouraging, maybe requiring, the confessedly unconverted to partake of the Supper. By 1704, it was practiced in his church with no internal dispute, though alarms were set off against the practice in the New England colonies. Integrated with this heterodoxy was an earnestness in preaching and zeal for conversion that led to five specific harvests under Stoddard's ministry at Northampton. His theology and practice of working for awakening influenced his grandson, Jonathan Edwards. Stoddard's writings were designed to instruct preachers in biblical principles in pursuing conversion, promoting spiritual health, and seeking revival. In the introduction to *A Guide to Christ,* Increase Mather wrote, "A man that knows there must be a work of preparation will be careful how he encourages others that they are in Christ. He will inquire how God has made way for their receiving of Christ; but another who is a stranger to it will be ready to take all for gold that glitters, and, if he sees men religiously disposed, will be speaking peace to them."[26] Stoddard gave detailed instruction in discerning the spiritual state of a soul in quest of salvation and what must be told at each stage. In *Defects in Preachers Reproved,* Stoddard discussed the elements of good preaching in the context of reprimanding bad preaching—bad in content, bad in delivery, bad in tone, and bad in diminished affections. *The Safety of*

---

[26] Solomon Stoddard, *A Guide to Christ*, (Ligonier, PA: Soli Deo Gloria Publications, 1993), xv.

Appearing in the Righteousness of Christ gave a detailed exegetical, polemical, and doctrinal discussion of justification by faith. Each of these issues—preparationism, the nature of good and earnest preaching, and justification by faith—would all appear as tools for revival as well as points of contention in the revival soon to come.

CHAPTER 3

JONATHAN EDWARDS AND REVIVAL: A SELECTIVE VIEW OF BIOGRAPHICAL DATA

"In the person of Christ do meet together, infinite glory, and lowest humility, . . . infinite majesty and transcendent meekness, . . . deepest reverence towards God and equality with God, . . . infinite worthiness of good, and the greatest patience under sufferings of evil, . . . an exceeding spirit of obedience, with supreme dominion over heaven and earth, . . . absolute sovereignty and perfect resignation, . . . self-sufficiency, and an entire trust and reliance on God."

—Jonathan Edwards[1]

Jonathan Edwards was born on October 5, 1703, in East Windsor, Connecticut. His father, Timothy Edwards, was a minister in the Congregational church in that town. His mother, Esther Stoddard Edwards, was daughter of Solomon Stoddard, a long-time pastor in Northampton, Massachusetts. Jonathan began the study of Latin at six years of age under the tutelage of his father and his sisters. He had four older sisters and six younger sisters.

During his early years, Edwards recalled two remarkable religious experiences. One, for several months the concept of prayer was riveted in his consciousness to the degree that he set up a booth for prayer in the woods. He "took much righteous

---

[1] Jonathan Edwards, "The Excellency of Jesus Christ," in *The Sermons of Jonathan Edwards,* ed. Wilson Kimnach, et.al. (New Haven: Yale University Press, 1999), 166–171.

pleasure in religious duties," praying five times a day. Two, during the last year of college, mortality and judgment gripped his mind and imagination strongly. During an illness, he remarked that God "shook me over the pit of hell."[2]

Edwards recalled an inexplicable change from seeking God in a miserable manner to seeking Him with a willingness to part with all other things "for an interest in Christ."[3] He described a transformation in spiritual perception that involved "sweet, inward delight in God and divine things" and "a new kind of apprehensions and ideas of Christ, and the work of redemption, and the glorious way of salvation by him."[4] Though, at the time, he did not conclude that these new apprehensions and sense were of a saving nature, his subsequent change in spiritual perception testify that they were.

He also revealed the transformation from having troubling and deep objections to the idea of the absolute sovereignty of God to having a quiet complicity in the doctrine and, finally, a "delightful conviction." He remarked, "The doctrine of God's sovereignty has very often appeared, an exceeding, bright and sweet doctrine to me; and absolute sovereignty is what I love to ascribe to God."[5] Edwards thus found a sensible apprehension of many truths of Scripture: Christ, heaven, divine majesty and meekness, and the "ravishingly lovely" beauty and amiableness of holiness. He saw God's wisdom and power in nature, prayer, Scripture, the conversion of others, the gospel, union with Christ, the "excellent fullness of Christ," the glory of the Holy Spirit, and "a vastly greater sense of my own wickedness."[6] These doctrines

---

[2] Jonathan Edwards, *Personal Narrative* in *A Jonathan Edwards Reader*, eds. John E. Smith, Harry S. Stout, Kenneth P. Minkema (New Haven; Yale University Press, 1995), 282.

[3] Edwards, *A Jonathan Edwards Reader*, 283.

[4] Edwards, *A Jonathan Edwards Reader*, 283–284.

[5] Edwards, *A Jonathan Edwards Reader*, 283.

[6] Edwards, *A Jonathan Edwards Reader*, 283–294.

filled his sermons with an undiluted sense of the full duty of the creature to love God, to worship Him, and to do all that the gospel sets before sinners as the conditions placed on them for salvation. Under regular intensification in his senses were the doctrines of sovereignty and the glory of Christ. "I have had a more full and constant sense of the absolute sovereignty of God, and a delight in that sovereignty; and have had more of a sense of the glory of Christ, as a mediator, as revealed the gospel."[7]

In 1716, Edwards entered Yale College before he was thirteen years of age. He participated in a student uprising against the tutor system of government and, particularly, the unpopularity of one of the tutors who had strong Anglican leanings. He joined others in leaving New Haven to go to Wethersfeld from 1717 to 1719. During that time, the young Edwards read John Locke's *On Human Understanding*. He remembered that he found greater pleasure "than the most greedy miser finds, when gathering up handfuls of silver and gold, from some newly discovered treasure."[8]

Around 1720, Edwards began his "Miscellanies." To begin recording his thoughts on a wide variety of ideas, he stitched together forty-four sheets of foolscap into a blank folio book. The first entry was entitled "Of Holiness." He began his ruminations by writing, "Holiness is a most beautiful and lovely thing. We drink in strange notions of holiness from our childhood, as if it were a melancholy, morose, sour and unpleasant thing; but there is nothing in it but what is sweet and ravishingly lovely."[9]

The second meditation was entitled "Of Christ's mediation and satisfaction." His final statement in this early entry said, "Now a loving of them so well as to be willing to undergo the punishment

---

[7]   Edwards, *A Jonathan Edwards Reader*, 295–296.

[8]   Jonathan Edwards, *The Works of Jonathan Edwards* (Edinburgh: Banner of Truth, 1974 [first published 1834]), 1:xvii.

[9]   Jonathan Edwards, *The Works of Jonathan Edwards, Volume 13: The "Miscellanies,"* ed. Thomas A. Schafer (New Haven: Yale University Press, 1957–2009), 163.

that they have deserved, as to be willing to stand in their stead in misery and torments, is to love them so well as that they may be looked upon as one."[10]

By 1758, these miscellaneous observations had filled nine such volumes and the number was 1,360, "some of them elaborate treatises."[11] The one on Hades (No. 60) is about 2,250 words long. The entry on "Sin against the Holy Ghost" (No. 475) runs about 2,800. Although from the beginning Edwards showed highly developed intellectual, theological, and philosophical sophistication, entries that recur on similar themes show a development of increasing profundity both in content and powers of analysis. It does not seem that he ever repudiated concepts developed early in this discipline but revisited some themes in light of increased perception of their importance or a more profound sense of spiritual power. His entry "On Being" established him in the field of ontology and showed the shape of his epistemology very early. "On the Mind" also was an important entry.[12]

In his letter to Princeton trustees in 1757 trying to show reasons he was not fit to be the president, Edwards explained his habit of writing and why he preferred a private use of gifts to the more public demands of such a position. He explained, "My method of study, from my first beginning the work of the ministry, has been very much by writing; applying myself in this way, to improve every important hint; pursuing the clue to my utmost, when anything in reading, meditation or conversation, has been suggested to my mind, that seemed to promise light in any weighty point."[13] This allowed a particular type of concentration so that his best thoughts were the result. The longer he pursued this method of study "the more habitual it became, and the more

---

[10] Edwards, *Works*, *Volume 13* (Yale University Press), 165.

[11] Perry Miller, *Jonathan Edwards,* (Cleveland and New York: The World Publishing Company, 1959), 127.

[12] Edwards, *A Jonathan Edwards Reader*, 9.

[13] Edwards, *A Jonathan Edwards Reader*, 322.

peasant and profitable I found it." This discipline continually widened his subjects of inquiry and contemplation. Therefore, his writing projects accumulated, and he found a desire to interact with "most of the prevailing errors of the present day, which I cannot with any patience see maintained (to the utter subverting of the gospel of Christ)." He mentioned in particular the "main points in dispute between the Arminians and Calvinists."[14]

In August 1722, Edwards began a regular preaching ministry at a Presbyterian church in New York. While there, he began his resolutions, which finally reached a total of seventy, thirty-four of them written before December 18, 1722. Through this highly specific discipline, his sense of divine things increased to a "much higher degree."[15]

Edwards left New York in April 1723, less than a year later. He received his MA degree and probably composed his observations about Sarah Pierrepont as well as his observations on spiders. Edwards did not consider any portion of creation or of philosophical, theological, and interpretive issues outside the sphere of thoughtful examination. "They say there is a young lady," Edwards began, "who is beloved of that almighty Being, who made and rules the world, and that there are certain seasons in which this great Being, in some way or other invisible, comes to her and fills her mind with exceeding sweet delight, and that she hardly cares for anything, except to meditate on him." Writing as if he could discern her internal thoughts, perhaps reflecting his own, Edwards wrote, "She expects after a while to be received up where he is, to be raised up out of the world and caught up into heaven; being assured that he loves her too well to let her remain at a distance from him always." Again, reflecting on his own increasingly intense sensibilities, Edwards continued, "There she is to dwell with him, and to be ravished with his love and delight forever." Nothing in the world, therefore, of all its

---

[14] Edwards, *A Jonathan Edwards Reader*, 322.

[15] Edwards, *A Jonathan Edwards Reader*, 286.

treasures and temporal advantages, had any attraction to her, and any pain or affliction gives her little concern. Given her "strange sweetness" of mind and "singular purity" in affections, her just and conscientious actions, none could "persuade her to do anything wrong or sinful." She possessed a "wonderful sweetness, calmness and universal benevolence of mind; especially after those seasons in which this great God has manifested himself." She sang sweetly, was always full of joy, "and seems to have someone invisible always conversing with her."[16]

Edwards's considerable powers of analysis, which were in evidence at this early age, prompted the twentieth-century scholar Vernon Parrington to reflect regret that Edwards's mentality was anachronistic and that a potentially great scientist was lost to religion. Parrington failed to appreciate the point that all of Edwards's scientific, philosophical, aesthetic, and psychological musings served as an entry point to a discussion of the larger invisible world where God dwells in infinite sufficiency, bliss, and beauty. All of these disciplines formed elements of general revelation and were the servants of God to reflect His wisdom power, and goodness. All such closely reasoned analyses and intense ruminations must be subdued to the assertions of divine revelation in the Scripture. This can be seen amusingly with Edwards's remarks in his treatise on insects and spiders, in which one of the corollaries said, "Hence the exuberant goodness of the creator, who hath not only provided for all the necessities, but also for the pleasure and recreation of all sorts of creatures, and even the insects and those that are most despicable."[17]

Edwards served briefly as pastor in Bolton, from November 1723 to February 1724. Apparently, he was pressured into this

---

[16] Edwards, *A Jonathan Edwards Reader*, 281.

[17] Edwards, *A Jonathan Edwards Reader*, 5; Jonathan Edwards, *The Works of Jonathan Edwards, Volume 6: Scientific and Philosophical Writings*, ed. Wallace E. Anderson (New Haven: Yale University Press, 1957–2009), 158.

pastorate by his father and it had an unpleasant appearance for Edwards. Some of his resolutions and diary entries at this time focus on minimizing the troubling nature of an affliction and thinking and speaking mainly of spiritual joys; this in itself would virtually eliminate the trial. While there, he preached a sermon entitled "The Pleasantness of Religion." Even repentance is pleasant, he taught, for "repentance of sin is a sorrow arising from the sight of God's excellency and mercy, but the apprehension of excellency or mercy must necessarily and unavoidably beget pleasure in the mind of the beholder."[18] Also, his theme of "sensibility" was prominent, as shown in a sermon entitled "A Spiritual Understanding of Divine Things Denied to the Unregenerate." The taste of honey cannot be reduced to propositions, but can only be known by the sense of taste. Both the empirical foundation of sensibility and his fascination with Sarah Pierrepont support this observation that explores the analogy between the senses and the development of human love and how the perception of divine love is, as it were, the giving of a new sense. "Thus with respect to earthly beauty," Edwards preached, "'tis not the hearing of elegant descriptions of a beautiful face that can ever make a person have a sense of the sweetness and amiableness of the beauty; 'tis not the slight notion of beauty by hearsay that causes love to burn in the heart: but it is the sight of the eye. One glance of the eye doth more than all the most particular descriptions that can be given."[19]

Eventually, a call from Yale released him from his reluctant stay in Bolton. In May 1724, he was elected to office of tutor. Yet this would turn into a greater trial than serving as pastor at Bolton. For two years, in the absence of a permanent president, Edwards had worries about students (not the least of which was his concern about their eternity) and his own spiritual frustration. He wrote

---

[18] Jonathan Edwards, *The Works of Jonathan Edwards, Volume 14: Sermons and Discourses, 1723–1729*, ed. Kenneth P. Minkema (New Haven: Yale University Press, 1957–2009), 76, 79.

[19] Edwards, *Works, Volume 14* (Yale University Press), 76, 79.

in his personal narrative, "After I went to New Haven, I sunk in religion; my mind being diverted from my eager and violent pursuits after holiness, by some affairs that greatly perplexed and distracted my mind."[20] In September 1725, he became ill and sought to go home to Windsor but could travel no further than North Village. He had to remain there around three months, convalescing and being cared for. He experienced some gracious visitations of the Spirit of God during this time.

In September 1726, Edwards received a call to Northampton to assist his grandfather, Solomon Stoddard. He settled in November 1726, and on February 15, 1727, he was ordained as a minister of the gospel. Stoddard was eighty-four years old and in his fifty-fifth year of ministry. Revivals of religion had occurred in 1679, 1683, 1690, 1712, and 1718. Stoddard had a profound and positive impact on Edwards in preaching and in his expectation of "surprising" works of God in revival. On July 28, 1727, Edwards married Sarah Pierrepont, she being seventeen. On August 25, 1728, their first child, Sarah, was born. They eventually had eleven children, eight daughters and three sons, one child about every two years.

While he served as Stoddard's assistant, Edwards preached periodically. Based on Revelation 21:18–21, remarking that on earth we know of nothing resembling "pure gold, like unto clear glass," Edwards entitled a message "Nothing on Earth can Represent the Glories of Heaven." It began with seven arguments from reason and ended with the scriptural demonstration. He introduced the latter section with this sentence: "*Second* place, to give those reasons and arguments drawn from the holy Scriptures which make it abundantly clear beyond manner of doubt that the happiness and glory of saints will be thus exceedingly great, even quite beyond all that reason without the Scriptures could tell us,

---

[20] Edwards, *A Jonathan Edwards Reader*, 290.

quite above all that we can speak or think, or anything on earth can represent."[21]

He also preached "All of God's Methods are most Reasonable," based on Isaiah 1:18–20: "Come let us reason together."[22] In this message, he defended reasonableness under six heads of thought. In the first, discussing sin, Edwards engaged the ideas of necessity and liberty and contingency, which he viewed as "the accidentalness of a thing." This served his later discussions related to the freedom of the will. He argued that nothing is unreasonable about God withholding sustaining grace in an estate of innocence in the context of clear commands. Second, concerning election and reprobation, he argued that "God deals most reasonably with men in choosing some to eternal life, and not others." Third, God's operation through making covenants—the covenant of works and covenant of grace—is entirely reasonable. Though in the fallen condition men are "utterly unable to believe in Christ without God's giving life to them, . . . neither are they willing." The inclination of their wills, their affections, "are opposite to the nature and person of the Mediator, and also the way of salvation." The refusal of sinners to comply with the covenant of grace is most unreasonable. In giving commands, God is exercising His absolute right over us as the one who gave and sustains our being. His sovereignty over us and our absolute dependence on Him make it most reasonable that we should obey whatever He commands. That He has the right to reward and punish according to His decrees, His prerogative of election, His covenants, and His commandments is eminently reasonable. "If we were but sensible of the majesty of God, and saw how great and glorious he is, we should not think it at all hard that he that sins against him should be tormented without hope forever and ever." Finally, God is most reasonable in His providential dealing with His children, often prospering the wicked while decreeing great difficulties for

---

[21] Edwards, *Works*, *Volume 14* (Yale University Press), 154.

[22] Edwards, *Works*, *Volume 14* (Yale University Press), 165–197.

His elect. "The chastening of children is better than the fatting of beasts for the slaughter."[23]

On February 22, 1729, Solomon Stoddard died. Edwards became minister. His salary doubled, from one hundred pounds to two hundred. At his installation, Edwards preached a message from 2 Corinthians 4:7, "Ministers Need the Power of God." He argued that the utter insufficiency of the minister serves as a means to magnify the absolute necessity of divine power. The removal of Stoddard, whose ministry was accompanied with such fullness of power, did not mean that the excellency of God's power could not be manifest even through the feeblest instrument.

Edwards's first public lecture, and first printed sermon, was "God Glorified in Man's Dependence," preached in the fall of 1730 and also delivered at the First Church of Boston on July 8, 1731. Jonathan Edwards was 28. The text 1 Corinthians 1:29–30. The doctrine was that "God is glorified in the work of redemption in this, that there appears in it so absolute and universal a dependence of the redeemed on him." He proposed two things: that there is an absolute and universal dependence of the redeemed on God for all their good, and that God thereby is exalted and glorified in the work of redemption.[24]

In August 1733, he preached "A Divine and Supernatural Light immediately imparted to the Soul by the Spirit of God shown to be both a Scriptural and rational doctrine." The text was found in Matthew 16:17: "Flesh and blood has not revealed this to you, but My Father who is in heaven." After a careful reworking, it was published in 1734. The sermon contained themes to which Edwards returned, both in preaching and in writing, throughout his ministry.[25]

---

[23] Edwards, *Works*, *Volume 14* (Yale University Press), 193.

[24] Edwards, *Works* (Banner of Truth), 2:3–7.

[25] Edwards, *Works* (Banner of Truth), 2:12–17.

In 1734, the initial energies of what is known as the First Great Awakening began in Northampton through a series of messages on the doctrine of justification by faith. According to Edwards's account, some three hundred persons seemed to have been savingly "wrought upon"—there were ten above ninety years old, fifty above forty years old, thirty between ten and fourteen, and one Phebe Bartlett, age four. This movement led to a series of writings involving both empirical analysis and theological/exegetical reasoning that constitute perhaps the most profound and integrated discussion of the phenomenon in English literature. These writings will be discussed briefly below.

The congregation at Northampton requested Edwards to publish some of the sermons that were instrumental in stirring such awakenings in the congregation. Justification by faith alone was preached in two public lectures. "At that time, while I was greatly reproached for defending this doctrine in the pulpit, and just upon my suffering a very open abuse for it," Edwards narrated, "God's work wonderfully brake forth amongst us, and souls began to flock to Christ, as the Saviour in whose righteousness alone they hoped to be justified."[26] He also saw this as a repudiation of Arminianism.

> Let the Arminian scheme of justification by our own virtue be as plain and natural as it will, if at the same time it is plainly contrary to the certain and demonstrable doctrine of the gospel, as contained in the Scriptures, we are bound to reject it, unless we reject the Scriptures themselves as perplexed and absurd, and make ourselves wiser than God, and pretend to know his mind better than himself.[27]

Edwards gave a detailed discussion of the character of faith and the necessity of imputed righteousness.

---

[26] Edwards, *Works* (Banner of Truth), 1:620.
[27] Edwards, *Works* (Banner of Truth), 1:621.

"Pressing Into the Kingdom" was based on Luke 16:16 and set forth the doctrine that "it concerns every one that would obtain the kingdom of God, to be pressing into it." Responding to the objection that "we cannot do this of ourselves," Edwards said, "Though strong desires and resolutions of mind be not in your power, yet painfulness of endeavours is in your power." In the context of natural ability, "it is in your power, with great diligence to attend the matter of your duty towards God and towards your neighbor. It is in your power to attend all ordinances, and all public and private duties of religion, and to do it with your might." Though a person cannot do a thing with *more* might than he has, it would be absurd to state that one "cannot do these things with all the might he has." It is no lack of natural ability to strive with great energy toward a goal. "Dullness and deadness of the heart, and slothfulness of disposition, do not hinder men being able to take pains, though it hinders their being willing." Human bondage to sin clearly did not mean a lack of power to heartily pursue one's desire, but it was a moral revulsion toward true righteousness, repentance, and holiness.[28]

Edwards explored the nature of a Spirit-given determination to be rightly related to God in a sermon entitled "Ruth's Resolution," based on Ruth 1:16. In speaking of the separation that will come if the unconverted do not follow their converted friends and family to Christ, Edwards warned,

> And what a wide separation will the sentence then passed and executed make between you and them! When you shall be sent away out of the presence of the Judge with indignation and abhorrence, as cursed and loathsome creatures they shall be sweetly accosted and invited into his glory as his dear friends, and the blessed of his Father![29]

---

28 Edwards, *Works* (Banner of Truth), 1:654–663.
29 Edwards, *Works* (Banner of Truth), 1:667–668.

Unrelenting in his depiction of the reality of plodding forward in a godless state, Edwards continued,

> When you, with all that vast throng of wicked and accursed men and devils, shall descend with loud lamentings, and horrid shrieks, into that dreadful gulf of fire and brimstone, and shall be swallowed up in that great and everlasting furnace; they shall joyfully, and with sweet songs of glory and praise, ascend with Christ, and all that beauteous and blessed company of saints and angels, into eternal felicity, in the glorious presence of God, and the sweet embraces of his love.[30]

In short, given the distinction between the respective destinations of the lost and the saved, "You and they shall spend eternity in such a separation, and immensely different circumstances!" Like Ruth, therefore, who forsook all she knew to make Israel's God her God, those who have heard must "count the cost of thorough, violent, and perpetual pursuit of salvation, and forsake all, as Ruth forsook her own country, and all her pleasant enjoyments in it. Do not do as Orpah did; who set out, and then was discouraged, and went back; but hold out with Ruth through all discouragement and opposition."[31]

Those who heard Edwards set forth with unabashed candor the reality of divine righteousness and divine wrath as fundamental to the entire question of "what is salvation and why is pursuit of it so urgent?" had no excuse for any lack of warning. In "The Justice of God in the Damnation of Sinners," based on Romans 3:19, Edwards asked, "How can you be willing to have Christ for a Saviour from a desert of hell, if you be not sensible that you have a desert of hell? If you have not really deserved everlasting burnings in hell, then the very offer of an atonement for such a desert is an imposition upon you." Edwards was unwilling to concede that

---

[30] Edwards, *Works* (Banner of Truth), 1:667–668.

[31] Edwards, *Works* (Banner of Truth), 1:667–668.

people actually desired to know Christ if they had not experienced "such a sense of your own sinfulness, and such a conviction of your great guilt in God' sight, as to be indeed convinced that you lay justly condemned to the punishment of hell." A true conviction of sin and a real coming to Christ necessarily involved one's being "convinced that you had forfeited all favour, and was in God's hands, and at his sovereign and arbitrary disposal, to be either destroyed or saved, just as he pleased." Sinfulness placed the sinner in the hands of pure divine sovereignty and eliminated objections arising from original sin, God's decrees, and the mercy received by others.[32]

Preached somewhat later than the initial surge of conviction and conversion, by request Edwards included in this publication a sermon entitled "The Excellence of Christ," based on Revelation 5:5–6. The reason for its inclusion was "that a discourse on such an evangelical subject would properly follow others that were chiefly awakening, and that something on the excellency of the Saviour was proper to succeed those things that were to show the necessity of salvation." The doctrine, based on the vision of a Lamb when John had looked to see a Lion, was this: "There is an admirable conjunction of diverse excellencies in Jesus Christ." Among the many memorable passages in this sermon, we find this tender and provocative invitation to embrace Christ for salvation:

> What is there that you can desire should be in a Savior, that is not in Christ? Or, wherein should you desire a Savior should be otherwise than Christ is? What excellency is there wanting? What is there that is great or good; what is there that is venerable or winning; what is there that is adorable or endearing; or, what can you think of that would be encouraging, which is not to be found in the person of Christ? . . . Would you not only have a Savior of high degree, but would you have him, notwithstanding his exaltation and dignity, to be

---

[32] Edwards, *Works* (Banner of Truth), 1:675.

made also of low degree, that he might have experience of afflictions and trials, that he might learn by the things that he has suffered, to pity them that suffer and are tempted? And has not Christ been made low enough for you? and has he not suffered enough? Would you not only have him possess experience of the afflictions you now suffer, but also of that amazing wrath that you fear hereafter, that he may know how to pity those that are in danger, and afraid of it? This Christ has had experience of, which experience gave him a greater sense of it, a thousand times, than you have, or any man living has. Would you have your Savior to be one who is near to God, that so his mediation might be prevalent with him? And can you desire him to be nearer to God than Christ is, who is his only-begotten Son, of the same essence with the Father? And would you not only have him near to God, but also near to you, that you may have free access to him? And would you have him nearer to you than to be in the same nature, united to you by a spiritual union, so close as to be fitly represented by the union of the wife to the husband, of the branch to the vine, of the member to the head; yea, so as to be one spirit? For so he will be united to you, if you accept of him. . . . What is there wanting, or what would you add if you could, to make him more fit to be your Savior?[33]

In 1739, Edwards wrote his "Personal Narration" and also preached a series of thirty sermons that constitute his *History of the Work of Redemption*—based on Isaiah 51:8: "For the moth will eat them up like a garment, and the worm will eat them like wool; but My righteousness will be forever, and My salvation from generation to generation." The doctrine was that "the work of redemption is a work that God carries on from the fall of man to the end of the world."[34] Almost twenty years later, in 1757, he had designs to

---

[33] Edwards, *Works* (Banner of Truth), 1:687.
[34] Edwards, *Works* (Banner of Truth), 1:533–534.

publish this volume and described it to the trustees of Princeton as "a body of divinity in an entire new method, being thrown into the form of an history, considering the affair of Christian theology, as the whole of it, in each part, stands in reference to the great work of redemption by Jesus Christ; which I suppose is to be the grand design of all God's designs, and the *summum* and *ultimum* of all the divine operations and degrees; particularly considering all parts of the grand scheme in their historical order."[35]

Pastoral difficulties at Northampton began in 1744 with "The Bad Book Controversy." A midwife's book came into the hands of some male youths. They used it to embarrass and intimidate the female youths. Edwards's handling, or mishandling, of the situation led to the beginning of division between him and the congregation, but it also increased his caution about the revival. Some of the youth involved had been "converted" during the earlier revival.

In 1747, David Brainerd (1718–1747) died in Edwards's home. Brainerd destroyed his health in evangelistic work among the North American Indians. His sponsoring organization was the Scottish Society for the Propagation of Christian Knowledge, and his work among these people lasted from April 1743 to November 1747. What he observed as a sovereign and mighty work of grace brought about close to 130 conversions among the Indians at Crossweeksung.[36] During that awakening "savages became civilized, murderers relented, drunkards reformed, adulterers became chaste, scoffers reverential.[37] Spent physically and emotionally, Brainerd went to live the final four months of his life in the home of Jonathan and Sarah Edwards. Jonathan observed the closing weeks of Brainerd's life carefully, during which time

---

[35] Edwards, *A Jonathan Edwards Reader*, 323.

[36] For a summary of this event see Mack Tomlinson, *The Indomitable Brainerds* (Grand Rapids: Reformation Heritage Books, 2023) 34–42.

[37] Tomlinson, *The Indomitable Brainerds*, 40, citing Thomas Brainerd's *Life of John Brainerd*.

he was "in an extremely weak and low state, often scarcely able to speak." Edwards commented biographically on the extraordinary vigor of Brainerd's spiritual life and his painful efforts to give the gospel to the Indians even while he looked on himself as "the meanest and least of saints, yea, very often, as the vilest and worst of mankind." To Edwards, this conscience-driven self-deprecation gave evidence of true repentance and true dependence on all-sufficient Savior. "We had the opportunity for much acquaintance and conversation with him," Edwards summarized, "to show him kindness in such circumstances, to see his dying behavior, to hear his dying speeches, to receive his dying counsels, and to have the benefit of his dying prayers."[38] The Edwards' seventeen-year-old daughter Jerusha took on the task of caring for Brainerd in his desperate condition. As George Marsden commented, "Jerusha, in turn, was ready to give herself to caring for this physically wrecked embodiment of her spiritual ideals."[39] As a result of these months, Edwards put several important writing projects aside in order to arrange and publish the journal and diary of Brainerd.

An increasing agitation was gently bubbling since 1744 over the midwife's book and Edwards's public exposure of the offending parties, and the gentle bubble came to a boil of serious proportions in 1748. The powerful awakening had raised Edwards's expectations of genuine spirituality in his congregation and had helped alter his views of the qualifications for partaking of the Lord's Supper. Whereas Solomon Stoddard had viewed the Supper as a means of grace aiding in the conversion of person, so that none should be excluded, Edwards had come to see it more in terms of a public testimony to the completed work of Christ and one's personal investment of mind, heart, and spirit in that saving work. The residual loyalty to Stoddard's ministry among the

---

[38] Tomlinson, *The Indomitable Brainerds*, 56–57.

[39] George Marsden, *Jonathan Edwards* (New Haven: Yale University Press, 2003) 323.

congregation became the undoing of the ministry of his grandson. Edwards had to go.

On June 22, 1750, Jonathan Edwards delivered his farewell sermon at Northampton. He based it on 2 Corinthians 1:14: "As also you have acknowledged us in part, that we are your rejoicing, even as ye also are ours in the day of the Lord Jesus" (KJV).

From that passage he deduced this doctrine: "Ministers and the people that have been under their care, must meet one another before Christ's tribunal at the day of Judgment." In one turgid statement, Edwards summarized the concern that generated this sermon and its doctrine. "Thus ministers and people" (Edwards identified the parties concerned), "between whom there has been the greatest mutual regard and strictest union" (he summarized past relations), "may not only differ in their judgments, and be alienated in affection" (he distilled the present consternation), "but one may rend from the other, and all relation between them be dissolved" (he summarized the immediate alienation), "the minister may be removed to a distant place, and they may never have any more to do one with another" (he lamented the rigidity of the separation). Edwards then applied the eternal to the temporal. "But if it be so, there is one meeting that they must have, and that is in the last great day of accounts."[40]

After some consideration as to what to do now with his call, his wife, and his children, Edwards settled at Stockbridge, Massachusetts, in 1751 as pastor to the local church and missionary to the Indians. Some had suggested he stay at Northampton to begin a new work. No! He was sought by Scots friends to minster there—but the move would have been too difficult for his "numerous and chargeable family."[41] Samuel Davies sought him for Virginia—but he learned too late of this possibility. Stockbridge was where his daughter, Sarah, lived with her husband

---

[40] Edwards, *The Sermons*, 214.
[41] Edwards, *Works* (Banner of Truth), 1:cxx.

Elihu Parsons. So Edwards was installed on August 8, 1751; his family did not join him until October.

Edwards preached regularly to the Stockbridge Indians. His first message was from Acts 11:12–13, on Cornelius praying and then having a gospel preacher sent to him. Edwards made this application: "Now I am come to preach the true religion to you and your children as Peter did to Cornelius and his family, that you and all your children may be saved. . . . Now therefore I'll tell you what true religion is." A sermon on 2 Peter 1:19, preached to the Mohawks, gave a brief summary of creation, fall, depravity, divine mercy in giving a revelation of the way of salvation, the progress of the Scriptures, and the necessity of the Scriptures and preaching the gospel to know the true religion. That they could not read the word of God was in the present due to the "shameful neglect of the white people, by which the great God has undoubtedly been made very angry." He told them, "Jesus Christ gave the command that the gospel should be preached to all nations" so that never before was there such "an opportunity for you to be brought into the light as there is now." The heart, however, will not receive the word without a special work of the Holy Spirit; it is "like a piece of dung in the light of the sun. It sends forth a stink but reflects no light."[42]

Edwards preached to the Indians with all the intensity and doctrinal clarity that he gave to his sophisticated Northampton congregation. Two sermons in one day on belief and unbelief showed why believing in Christ is the only way to be saved. Using images and even certain passages from "Sinners in the Hands of an Angry God," Edwards described what it is to be damned and showed why that is the fate for every man not believing in Christ. "There the soul shall be cast into a great fire and shall be tormented continually without any rest, day or night," Edwards preached. The bodies of unbelievers "shall be raised . . . and then the body and soul shall be cast into a great fire along with the

---

[42] Edwards, *The Sermons*, 105–110.

devils." So offensive to Him will they be that "God will have no pity on them. . . . They shall have no friends. . . . So that they will have no hope when they think of eternity before 'em." Coming closer in his application, Edwards pled, "If you are a great sinner, a wicked person, if you have done wickedness a thousand times, yet Christ is ready to receive you if you will come to him." His closing appeal showed the zeal of Edwards for the souls of all men: "Christ this day calls and invites you. I am his servant, and I invite you to come to him. Therefore make haste. Delay not. Give your heart to Christ and he will save you from hell, and all heaven shall be yours."[43]

The time at Stockbridge allowed Edwards to begin finalizing works that he had been developing for some years through his notebooks and even in sermons. His thoughts on the key differences between Arminianism and Calvinism were given compelling expression in 1754 in a work entitled *A Strict and Careful Enquiry into the Modern Prevailing Notions of Freedom of Will*. In that book he treated concepts of necessity, impossibility, inability, and contingence; he stated, "In some sense the will always follows the last dictate of the understanding." By *understanding* he meant "the whole faculty of perception or apprehension." The "will" itself he defined as "that view of the mind which has the greatest degree of previous tendency to excite volition." In other words, given any situation, the human acts according to what he most wants to do in light of intrinsic inclinations.[44] This means that fallen humanity never will choose the way of righteousness and holiness found in Christ apart from an effectual, supernaturally induced change of affections.

In 1755, Edwards brought to completion companion volumes entitled *The Nature of True Virtue* and *The End for which God Created*

---

[43] Edwards, *The Sermons*, 111–120.

[44] Jonathan Edwards, *The Works of Jonathan Edwards, Volume 1: Freedom of the Will*, ed. Paul Ramsey (New Haven: Yale University Press, 1957–2009), 148.

the World. In the first, he unfolded layer by layer the definition that "true virtue consists of benevolence toward being in general."[45] In the latter, he dealt with the implication of this clear assertion: "This one end is most properly and comprehensively called the glory of God."[46] These, however, were not published until 1765. In 1758, the year of his death, Edwards completed *The Great Christian Doctrine of Original Sin Defended.* The subtitle read, "Evidence of its truth produced, and arguments to the contrary answered." The publishing information included this in the author space: "By the late Reverend and Learned Jonathan Edwards, A. M. President of the College of New Jersey."

As that byline indicates, Edwards had been selected, in 1757, as president of the College of New Jersey, now known as Princeton University. He had objections to this and sought ardently to convince the trustees that he was exactly the wrong man for this responsibility. The expense involved and his physical weakness were obstacles, and he had a "contemptibleness of speech, presence, and demeanor; with a disagreeable dullness and stiffness, much unfitting me for conversation, but more especially for the government of a college." He also brought up academic inadequacies such as "lack of mathematical sophistication, and knowledge of the classical Greek writings." Perhaps more importantly, he held tightly to a sense of duty, stewardship, and delight in his study, his writing, and the number of important theological projects he had conceived.[47] Appealing to the trustees to understand his perception of future usefulness, he added, "So far as I myself am able to judge of what talents I have for benefiting

---

[45] Edwards, *Works* (Banner of Truth), 1:122.

[46] Edwards, *Works* (Banner of Truth), 1:119.

[47] Jonathan Edwards, *The Works of Jonathan Edwards, Volume 16: Letters and Personal Writings*, ed. George S. Claghorn (New Haven: Yale University Press, 1957–2009), 726.

my fellow creatures by word, I think I can write better than I can speak."[48] They persisted, and he consented.

One of his duties would consist of teaching seniors in a class to give some degree of advanced maturity in their ability to frame, discuss, and answer theological questions. He proposed ninety of them, including these:

> "How does it appear that something has existed for eternity?"
>
> "Did God decree the existence of sin?"
>
> "How is the doctrine of universal absolute decrees consistent with the free agency of men?"
>
> "Are the torments of hell eternal?"
>
> "What is the covenant of redemption?"
>
> "Did Christ redeem all men alike, elect and non-elect?"
>
> "What is the foundation for the duty of prayer, since God is omniscient and immutable?"
>
> "In what does the happiness of heaven consistent?"[49]

He had one opportunity to engage seniors in this exercise, which resulted in "entertainment and profit," so that afterward they "spoke of it with the greatest satisfaction and wonder."[50]

After arriving at Princeton, he heard of the death of his father, Timothy Edwards, on January 27, 1758, at eighty-nine years of age. As soon as possible, Jonathan was settled in the office of president by the "corporation," that is the trustees. Entering with cheerfulness and satisfaction, he not only had some time in instruction of the seniors, but he also preached in the college hall on Sundays.

---

[48] Edwards, *Works*, Volume 16 (Yale University Press).

[49] Edwards, *Works* (Banner of Truth), 1:690–691.

[50] Edwards, *Works* (Banner of Truth), 1:clxxvii

On February 13, 1758, Edwards was inoculated against smallpox. Soon pustules developed in his throat so that he could not swallow, which prohibited medicines and water. The disease advanced and prevailed, ending his life on March 22, 1758. The attending physician wrote Sarah about his death and observed, "Never did any mortal man more fully and clearly evidence the sincerity of all his professions, by one continued, universal, calm, cheerful resignation and patient submission to the Divine will, through every stage of his disease, than he."[51] Sarah responded in a letter to her daughter Esther Burr, who also had lost her husband,

> What shall I say? A holy and good God has covered us with a dark cloud. O that we may kiss the rod, and lay our hands on our mouths! The Lord has done it. He has made me adore his goodness, that we had him so long. But my God lives; and he has my heart. O what a legacy my husband, and your father has left us! We are all given to God; and there I am, and love to be.[52]

EDWARDS'S SPIRITUAL LIFE

In May or June 1721, Edwards recorded "that change by which I was brought to those new dispositions, and that new sense of things." He described an "inward, sweet delight in God and divine things that I have lived much in since." This came while he was reading 1 Timothy 1:17: "Now unto the King eternal, immortal, invisible, the only wise God, be honour and glory for ever and ever, Amen" (KJV). He testified that the words diffused through his soul a "sense of the glory of the Divine Being; a new sense, quite different from any thing I ever experienced before." He saw the divine excellency and desired to "enjoy that God, and be rapt up in him in heaven, and be as it were swallowed up in him for ever!" His heart went out to this excellent being in prayer and

---

[51] Edwards, *Works* (Banner of Truth), 1:clxxviii.
[52] Edwards, *Works* (Banner of Truth), 1: clxxix.

joy "with a new sort of affection." Only in later reflection did he discern the saving nature of this experience.[53]

His life of meditation on Scripture increased in intensity and depth of feeling from that time forward. Sometimes this new sense of things would "often of a sudden kindle up, as it were, a sweet burning in my heart; an ardor of soul, that I know not how to express." These impressions stayed clearly with Edwards all his ministry and, through study, intensified and formed the basis of his life's work. His works on religious affections, the will, original sin, analysis of revival, the true virtue, and the end for which God created the world all focused on the point of divine/human encounter: the excellence of the divine being and the "new sense of things" the human must grasp and the resultant relish for the holy beauty of God. In the very first section of his "Observations on the facts and evidences of Christianity, and the objections of infidels," he said, "It is easily proved that the highest end and happiness of man is to view God's excellency, to love him, and receive expressions of his love. This love, including all those other affections which depend upon, and are necessarily connected with it, are expressed in worship."[54]

What did Edwards mean when he spoke of a "new sense of things"? You will meet this concept of "sensibility" at every turn in Edwards. Showing some influence from John Locke's empiricism, Edwards gave new intensity to the Puritan invocation of sense as fundamental to saving faith. His constant references to one's being "sensible" of a biblical truth denoted a state in which both the mind and the affections are convinced of and approve a biblical idea, as if the senses themselves had recorded it on the consciousness as an invincible and indelible fact. True faith has tasted that the Lord is gracious (1 Peter 2:3); true faith means a true hearing of the word of God—"He who knows God hears us" (1 John 4:6); true faith comes when God's light shines "in our hearts to give the light of

---

[53] Edwards, *A Jonathan Edwards Reader*, 284.
[54] Edwards, *Works* (Banner of Truth), 2:460.

the knowledge of the glory of God in the face of Jesus Christ" (2 Cor. 4:6). Edwards expressed this as he examined the ground of his assurance, fearing that "I do not feel the Christian graces sensibly enough, particularly faith." He went on to explain that he feared they were "only such hypocritical outside affections which wicked men feel as well as others." Then he continued his ruminations by focusing on the positive substance of sensibility. He called such perceptions "inward, full, sincere, entire, and hearty." They should be "substantial" and "wrought into my very nature."[55]

This idea of "sensibility" does not promote emotional attachment apart from objective revealed truth. In section IV of *Religious Affections*, Edwards wrote, "Holy affections are not heat without light; but evermore arise from some information of the understanding, some spiritual instruction that the mind receives, some light or actual knowledge." Any affection not arising from "light in the understanding" most certainly is not spiritual. This light, however, is not mere information, nor only a notional understanding of true doctrine. Spiritual understanding of Scripture involves having "the eyes of the mind opened to behold the wonderful, spiritual excellency of the glorious things contained in the true meaning of it."[56]

Edwards's spirituality, in summary, consisted of three components. One, every biblical proposition was to be believed as revealed truth. Biblical truths go far beyond any truth derived from philosophical reasoning or empirical investigation and lead to a knowledge of the attributes and decrees of the three-personed divine being. Edwards spent long hours and intense mental energy in seeking to grasp the meaning of these biblical doctrines and their internal unity.

Two, Edwards continually subjected his biblically derived worldview and large armory of biblical propositions to rational demonstration. Affirming them as true in themselves and sensing

---

[55] Edwards, *Works* (Banner of Truth), 1:xxiv.
[56] Edwards, *Works* (Banner of Truth), 1:285.

their eternal glory was fundamental and sufficient for saving faith. Gaining an understanding of the superiority of these truths to all other intellectual, religious, and philosophical attempts to speak to the same issues helped demonstrate the absoluteness and exclusivity of the Christian revelation that culminated and found summation in the person and work of Christ.

Three, Edwards meditated on the glory, excellence, and transformative purpose of these truths. Scripture passages and analogies from nature, along with meditations on holiness, on the person of Christ, on divine sovereignty, on heaven, on repentance, on an abandoned dependence on God, on union with Christ, on the mystery of the singular essence of three distinct persons in the Trinity, and on the "bottomless, infinite depths of wickedness, pride, hypocrisy and deceit left in my heart," all converged to form an inexhaustible body for rich spiritual contemplation. These workings of the soul were felt "very sensibly" and were described in such terms as "exceedingly amiable, . . . ravishingly lovely, . . . in a calm rapture, . . . sweet and refreshing, . . . sweet and glorious doctrines, . . . affecting and delightful, . . . ineffably excellent," and other expressions of spiritual delight.

In one of his descriptions of spiritual engagement with the doctrines of Scripture, Edwards focused on the content of the gospel:

> I have loved the doctrines of the gospel; they have been to my soul like green pastures. The gospel has seemed to me to be the richest treasure; the treasure that I most desired, and longed that it might dwell richly in me. The way of salvation by Christ, has appeared in a general way, glorious and excellent, and most pleasant and beautiful. It has often seemed to me, that it would in a great measure spoil heaven, to receive it in any other way. That text has often been affecting and delightful to me, Is. 32:2, "A man shall be an hiding place from the wind, and a covert from the tempest; as rivers of water

in a dry place, as the shadow of a great rock in a weary land."[57]

EDWARDS'S ANALYSIS OF REVIVAL

After the first movement of spiritual awakening in Northampton, Edwards recorded the phenomenon and its spiritual outworkings in a volume entitled *A Faithful Narrative of the Surprising Work of God* (1737).[58] It had four parts: a historical narrative, a section entitled "Manner of conversion various yet bearing a great analogy," illustrations of the breadth of the movement by citing two instances of conversions in the four-year-old Phoebe Bartlett and the mature woman Abigail Hutchinson, and warnings of Satan's opposition. This was manifested by ministerial opposition, on the one hand, and some distressing results of melancholia on the other, including suicide. As he began to see evidence of a withdrawing of the Spirit of God, Edwards sought to conserve the results of the Awakening by preaching on the distinction between true and false faith.

In the winter of 1737, he preached "True and False Christians," based on the parable of the wise and foolish virgins (Matt. 25:1–13). In this sermon, Edwards emphasized that saving faith embodies love for Christ that is initiated in the effectual operation of love from the groom to the bride. Because the church is espoused to Jesus, statements of love between Christ and the church focus on bridging a gap of deep separation. The gap is bridged because Christ is first in pursuing it. In response, the church freely consents to this relationship and in great delight "gives up herself to him" in an act of true rejoicing. This union with Christ involves "a deep, real, living conviction of the truth

---

[57] Edwards, *A Jonathan Edwards Reader*, 291.

[58] Jonathan Edwards, *The Works of Jonathan Edwards, Volume 4: The Great Awakening*, ed. C. C. Goen (New Haven: Yale University Press, 1957–2009), 144–211.

and excellency of divine things,"[59] particularly as these things are embodied in Christ Himself. In fact, even in view of all the spiritual advantages involved in following Christ, "he that don't follow Christ for his own sake, won't follow him long."[60] Justifying faith unites us with Christ to make us one with Him. Faith is the "very act by which we close with him. And thus it is that faith justifies and gives an interest in Christ's satisfaction and merit, not any goodness or worthiness in the act of faith."[61] Justification is not given as the reward of faith, as if righteousness resided in the act, but from the nature of faith to unite to the Mediator in whom the perfect righteousness of active and passive obedience resides. The oil needed by those who were to attend the wedding is the necessity of the anointing of the Spirit (according to 1 John 2), by which alone true faith comes.

In 1741, Edwards preached "Sinners in the Hands of an Angry God" at Enfield, Connecticut, and also wrote *The Distinguishing Marks of a Work of the Spirit of God.* In that work he gave a more formal analysis of the true marks of revival. He based the positive description of divine operation in bestowing true spiritual life on 1 John 4. Because so many other phenomena were connected with the dominant progress of spiritual awakening, Edwards isolated nine by which a work can be judged neither negatively nor positively concerning its origin as a work of God.[62] That the work is carried on, in part, outside the parameters normally experienced through the use of means in ongoing church life neither negates nor affirms its origin from the Spirit of God. That the movement produces extraordinary effects on the bodies of some people provides no determining evidence of its origin. Also, effects on

---

[59] Jonathan Edwards, *Sermons by Jonathan Edwards on the Matthean Parables: True and False Christians* (Eugene, Oregon: Cascade Books, 2012), 152.

[60] Edwards, *Matthean Parables*, 154.

[61] Edwards, *Matthean Parables*, 49.

[62] Edwards, *Works, Volume 4* (Yale University Press), 228–248.

the mind creating a great stir and ado and noise about the things of religion would naturally happen in a time of true spiritual stirring but do not constitute its spirituality nor serve as evidence of mere emotionalism. So it would be with effects on the mind making great impressions on the imagination. That the example of others is greatly used in promoting it would be a natural side effect, for "'tis agreeable to Scripture that persons should be influenced by another's good example, thus is also reasonable." At the same time, while many of its subjects are guilty of imprudence and irregularities, such do not necessitate a negative view of the awakening. So it is with errors in judgment and some delusions of Satan mixed with the work. When some supposedly "wrought upon" fall into gross errors or scandalous practices, these may indicate an energetic opposition of Satan to a genuine work of kingdom expansion on the part of God's Spirit. Finally, some complained that the apparent energy of supposed spirituality was promoted by ministers insisting on the terrors of God's holy law, and that with a great deal of pathos and earnestness. Edwards observed wryly, "If I am in danger of going to hell, I should be glad to know as much as possibly I can of the dreadfulness of it." If such an eternity is real, "he does me the best kindness, that does most to represent to me the truth of the case, that sets forth my misery and danger in the liveliest manner."[63]

The second part of *The Distinguishing Marks* contained five positive evidences that a movement is of divine origin.[64] First, Edwards found in 1 John 4:2–3 the principle that genuine spirituality would raise esteem in the minds of its subjects of that Jesus who was born of the virgin and crucified without the gates of Jerusalem. This is that Christ who came in the flesh, and worked and taught in the flesh, and died in the flesh, and was buried in the flesh, and rose in the flesh—not a mystical Christ, or an inner Christ only, or a Gnostic Christ.

---

[63] Edwards, *Works, Volume 4* (Yale University Press), 247.

[64] Edwards, *Works, Volume 4* (Yale University Press), 248–288.

Second, a true work of the Spirit operates against the interests of Satan's kingdom (1 John 4:4–5). Edwards compared this operation to 1 John 2:15–16 and noted that such a work takes the minds of people off the corruptible things of this age; removes our affections from the accumulation of worldly profit, pleasure, and prestige; and engages us to a contemplation of the future and eternal happiness of that invisible world. The Holy Spirit moves us earnestly to seek the kingdom of God and His righteousness and to desire the new heaven and the new earth wherein dwelleth righteousness.

Third, such a powerful movement of God's Spirit gives a greater regard to Holy Scripture (1 John 4:6). The Spirit effects a submissive regard to the apostles and "all the penmen of Holy Scripture," as well as those who follow in their system of truth and are under their authority. Compare this with Jesus's words: "They have Moses and the prophets; let them hear them" (Luke 16:29). Edwards asked, in light of the obvious incongruity of the opposite, "Would the spirit of error, in order to deceive men, beget in them an high opinion of the infallible rule, and incline them to think much of it, and be very conversant with it?"[65]

This fits perfectly with the fourth sign of the Spirit's distinguishing work: He operates as a Spirit of truth as opposed to a spirit of error. Anything—any movement, any influence—that leads us to deeper discoveries of the truth and disposes our mind to seek it and to love it is of God (see Eph. 5:13).

Fifth, 1 John 4:7 to the end of the chapter shows that a work of the Spirit of God operates as a spirit of love to God and to man.

> There is sufficient said in this passage of St. John that we are upon, of the nature and motive of a truly Christian love, thoroughly to distinguish it from all such counterfeits. It is a love that arises from an apprehension of the wonderful riches of free grace and

---

[65] Edwards, *Works, Volume 4* (Yale University Press), 254.

sovereignty of God's love to us in Christ Jesus; being attended with a sense of our own utter unworthiness, as in ourselves the enemies and haters of God and Christ, and with a renunciation of all our own excellency and righteousness.[66]

After dealing with an objection raised from 2 Corinthians 11:13–14, Edwards made several concluding observations. As for himself, he expressed strong confidence that the current movement was a work of the Spirit of God. He had abundant opportunity to observe every phenomenon of the revival, including all of its supposedly objectionable parts. He reiterated certain observations of the variety of manifestations of conversion and also imprudences and irregularities that had appeared. Next, Edwards warned those who would oppose the work and receive no benefit by it. They could be at the edge of committing the unpardonable sin—blaspheming, speaking ill of, an obvious work of the Holy Spirit. Finally, he instructed the beneficiaries of the Spirit's work as to what to cultivate in the way of biblical and spiritual graces, and what to avoid. They must beware of spiritual pride, resist any expectation of special revelation or restoration of extraordinary spiritual gifts, and avoid a spirit of censoriousness.

The next year, 1742, Edwards produced his third writing devoted peculiarly to the phenomenon of revival: *Some thoughts Concerning the Present Revival of Religion in New England.* Consisting of five parts, this work, again, called the extraordinary attention to spiritual life "a glorious work of God." This first section included Edwards's observations concerning his wife, Sarah, whom he called "the person." She would dwell "for some considerable time together, in such views of the glory of the divine perfections, and Christ's excellencies, that the soul in the meantime has been as it were perfectly overwhelmed, and swallowed up with light and love and a sweet solace, rest and joy of soul, that was altogether

---

[66] Edwards, *Works, Volume 4* (Yale University Press), 257.

unspeakable."[67] On occasion, these contemplations and a sense of unchallenged joy would last for five or six hours. At times it seemed that her soul was perfectly swallowed up in an "infinite ocean of blessedness," which produced "an unavoidable leaping for joy." There were seasons of a deep and almost terrifying sense of the pollution of her own soul left to itself and of the dreadfulness of hell torments alleviated only by "an overwhelming sense of the glory of the work of redemption, and the way of salvation by Jesus Christ."[68] There was a consistent sense of delight "in singing praises to God and Jesus Christ, and longing that this present life may be, as it were, one continued song of praise to God."[69] None of these raptures, however, diminished "this person's" sense of responsibility in daily task consistent with her duty. Indeed, it increased her sense of devotion so that such work was virtually equal to prayer. Along with that was a "very great sense of the importance of moral social duties, and how great a part of religion lay in them."[70] Her sense of encouragement and commendation of others, and her resignation to God's glory and fullness of joy even in times of pain, sickness, and the near approach of death, led to a "constant sweet peace and calm and serenity of soul."[71] Given all this and much more that Edwards described, he concluded, "Now if such things are enthusiasm, and the fruits of a distempered brain, let my brain be evermore possessed of the happy distemper."[72]

Part two pressed the obligations of all different levels of society to "acknowledge, rejoice in, and promote this work." He warned of dangers to the contrary. In part three, Edwards answered ten criticisms that had been brought against the promoters of the work. Several points dealt with the manner and the content

---

[67] Edwards, *Works, Volume 4* (Yale University Press), 352.
[68] Edwards, *Works, Volume 4* (Yale University Press), 336.
[69] Edwards, *Works, Volume 4* (Yale University Press), 337.
[70] Edwards, *Works, Volume 4* (Yale University Press), 335.
[71] Edwards, *Works, Volume 4* (Yale University Press), 340.
[72] Edwards, *Works, Volume 4* (Yale University Press), 341.

and the frequency of sermons. One can detect a defense of his powerful images of hell in preaching "Sinners in the Hands of an Angry God" at Enfield. "I am not afraid to tell sinners," Edwards insisted, "that are most sensible of their misery, that their case is indeed as miserable as they think it to be, and a thousand times more so; for this is the truth."[73] Keenly aware of the necessity of maintaining faithfulness to "the business of their particular callings," and of the possibility that religious meetings could degenerate into a mere show of religion without heart, he defended the frequency of sermons because their main impact came in the immediate impression upon hearing and the accumulation of these impressions led to greater spiritual knowledge and desire for ongoing transformation. Complaints about loss of time and substance with so many meetings prompted this response.

> And besides, if the matter be justly considered and examined I believe it will be found that the country has lost no time from their temporal affairs by the late revival of religion, but have rather gained time; and that more time has been saved from frolicking and tavern-haunting, idleness, unprofitable visits, vain talk, fruitless pastimes, and needless diversions, than has lately been spent in extraordinary religion; and probably five times as much has been saved in person's estates, at the tavern and in their apparel, as has been spent by religious meetings.[74]

Part four dealt with certain tendencies that should be corrected and errors to be avoided in promotion of this work. Edwards dealt with both causes of errors and also particular errors. The first cause of error, and a gross error in itself, is spiritual pride. He described it as "the main door, by which the devil comes into the hearts of those that are zealous for the advancement of religion."[75]

---

[73] Edwards, *Works, Volume 4* (Yale University Press), 392.
[74] Edwards, *Works, Volume 4* (Yale University Press), 396–397.
[75] Edwards, *Works, Volume 4* (Yale University Press), 414.

Second, he discussed wrong principles, the first of which was the expectation of some that they would be guided "by inspiration, or immediate revelation."[76] Rather than impulses, impressions, and misapplication of scriptural directions, Edwards asked, "why can't we be contented with the divine oracles, that holy pure Word of God, that we have in such abundance and such clearness, now since we have the canon of Scripture completed?" Several other erroneous principles concerned the manner in which persons under deep spiritual impressions interpreted the leadership of the Spirit, the appearance of providence as instruction for personal action, and the tendency to approve all that was done by those appeared to be under the blessing of God.

This included a series of warnings at the end concerning things to be corrected and avoided during a time of religious excitement. Though Edwards still considered the late movement in general a work of God, he was now filled with more warnings about abuse. Some behaviors that he had pardoned, or at least minimized, as evidence concerning the genuineness of the revival, he now considered with greater caution. Under the subject of spiritual pride, he spoke of the beauty of boldness in prayer when it is prompted by true fear and dread of God and forgetfulness of men and their power, but

> for private Christians women and others, to instruct, rebuke, and exhort, with a like sort of boldness as becomes a minister when preaching, is not beautiful. Some have been bold in things that have really been errors; and have gloried in their boldness in practising them, though odd and irregular. And those who have gone the greatest lengths in these things, have been by some most highly esteemed as appearing bold for the Lord Jesus Christ, and fully on his side; while others who have professed to be godly, and who have condemned

---

[76] Edwards, *Works, Volume 4* (Yale University Press), 434.

such things, have been spoken of as enemies of the cross of Christ, or at least very cold and dead.[77]

His fourth treatment of the revival, *A Treatise Concerning Religious Affections*, consisted of a more extended doctrinal discussion of the character of a converting work of grace on the sinner. He began that work, which was published in 1746, by stating, "There is no question of greater importance to mankind, and that it more concerns every individual person to be well resolved in, than this: *What are the distinguishing qualifications of those that are in favour with God, and entitled to his eternal rewards?*" He acknowledged that many answers had been put forth in answer to that question, and professing Christians differed from one another even though so much scriptural light existed on the subject. This fact had long engaged him to "attend to this matter with the utmost diligence and care, and exactness of search and inquiry of which I have been capable." Further he said, "It is a subject on which my mind has been peculiarly intent, ever since I first entered on the study of divinity." He knew that he was seeking to walk on the very dangerous razor's edge of truth. "Many will be hurt," he wrote, "to find so much that appertains to religious affection here condemned: and perhaps indignation and contempt will be excited in others, by finding so much justified and approved."[78]

Because "by the mixture of counterfeit religion with true, not discerned and distinguished," the devil "has had his greatest advantage against the cause and kingdom of Christ," Edwards wanted to give concentrated attention to "the nature and signs of the gracious operations of God's Spirit, by which they may be distinguished from all things whatsoever . . . which are not of a

---

[77] Edwards, *Works* (Banner of Truth), 1:402; Edwards, *Works, Volume 4* (Yale University Press), 427.

[78] Jonathan Edwards, *The Works of Jonathan Edwards, Volume 2: Religious Affections*, ed. John E. Smith (New Haven: Yale University Press, 1957–2009), 84.

saving nature."[79] This was necessary in his day because, like the decline of Christianity into a variety of perversions under Roman Catholicism, the decline of Protestantism into formalism and nominalism, and the decline of New England Puritanism from its original joy and fervor, he had seen the same satanic strategies deployed "against the late, great revival of religion in New England, so happy and promising in its beginning." New England religion now lay "on the ground, in such piteous circumstances, . . . with her garments rent, her face disfigured, her nakedness exposed, her limbs broken, and weltering in the blood of her own wounds."[80]

The book is divided into three sections. Section one introduces the text, 1 Peter 1:8: "Whom having not seen, ye love: in whom, though now ye see him not, yet believing, ye rejoice with joy unspeakable, and full of glory" (KJV). The doctrine is stated succinctly: "True religion, in great part, consists in holy affections."[81] Edwards showed that biblical religion is religion that reaches and intensifies the affections with truth in the understanding and love, worship, and joy in the heart. High affection is not proof of true religion; no affection is proof of no religion. All the truths of the gospel are in their nature sufficient to elicit the response of the affections. The love invoked in both tables of the commandments, the condescension of God in His mercy to save sinful man, the humiliation of Christ and His obedience unto the death of the cross, the grandeur and beauty of heaven, and the prospect of seeing Jesus as He is in His glorified state are not only pieces of doctrinal information but also provocations to heightened affects of the most holy sort.

Section two explores the manifestations that "are no certain signs of truly gracious affections."[82] Edwards warned against either negative or positive evaluations of the graciousness of one's

---

[79] Edwards, *Works, Volume 2* (Yale University Press), 89.

[80] Edwards, *Works, Volume 2* (Yale University Press), 87.

[81] Edwards, *Works, Volume 2* (Yale University Press), 95.

[82] Edwards, *Works, Volume 2* (Yale University Press), 127–190.

experience by the greatness of the affection, its effect on the body, or its relation to fluency of religious speech—that they are not self-generated, or that they come with texts of Scripture brought to mind. In addition, "'Tis no evidence that religious affections are saving, or that they are otherwise," if they appeared to be filled with love, or are accompanied by several kinds of affections, or that joy follows conviction in a certain order. "The unmortified corruption of the heart may quench the Spirit of God (after he has been striving) by leading men to presumptuous, and self-exalting hopes and joys, as well as otherwise."[83] Scripture admonishes us to "try ourselves by the *nature* of the fruits of the Spirit; but nowhere by the Spirit's *method* of producing them."[84] Edwards examined four more fallacious signs in order to arm Christians against false evaluations of certain types of phenomena. Neither zealous engagement in the external duties of religion, nor exuberance in public praise of God, nor personal confidence of one's good estate before God are evidences of genuine spiritual affections. Even if one's discussion of these affections pleases and moves the heart of the godly, still this is not a sure sign of the genuineness of the affection.

Section three discusses twelve distinguishing signs of truly gracious affections. These are not intended to give us leverage to judge others, nor do they serve for assurance to those "who are in a very low state of grace."[85] Edwards gave a lengthy discussion of the "spiritual" nature of these affections,[86] emphasizing the transforming power and objectivity of the work of the Holy Spirit in the conversion of the human soul, combining both revealed truth and heaven-wrought love. The other eleven signs treat the character of the transformed soul as it pursues holiness, manifests love to God, has increasing "sensibility" of the sweetness of divine

---

[83] Edwards, *Works, Volume 2* (Yale University Press), 157.

[84] Edwards, *Works, Volume 2* (Yale University Press), 162.

[85] Edwards, *Works, Volume 2* (Yale University Press), 193.

[86] Edwards, *Works, Volume 2* (Yale University Press), 197–239.

things, gains an elevated sense of the truth of divine things, has a humbling sense of the infinite demerit of sin, operates as an altered nature and not a temporary persuasion, and reflects the condescending humility of Christ, tenderness of spirit, and the resistance to and remorse for sinful fleshly impulses as a permanent and growing quality. Edwards condensed these traits by saying, "As he has more holy boldness, so he has less of self-confidence and a forward assuming boldness, and more modesty." Edwards added that as a person has more confidence of deliverance from hell, "so he has more of a sense of the desert of it." Though he has more assurance in his faith, he is more quickly moved with solemn warnings. "He has the firmest comfort, but the softest heart; richer than others, but poorest of all in spirit; the tallest and strongest saints, but the least and tenderest child among them."[87]

Edwards added that all of these transformed and spiritual affections exist together in beautiful proportion, in some manner, as described just above. Though imbalanced or immature at times through a variety of factors, they do not bear that "monstrous disproportion" like the "counterfeit graces of the hypocrites."[88] They are present in private and in the closet and engender solitary delight in God as much as in the society of other Christians. Also, genuine affections are never satisfied with the present state but create hunger for more in number, volume, and intensity. As the hymns express, "More love to Thee, O Christ, . . . More holiness give me, . . . More like the Savior I would ever be, . . . More about Jesus would I know."

If affections are genuine and truly produced by the Spirit of God, they permeate the whole life of the Christian. The work of true religion defines the spiritual person's daily life. Biblical commands become delightful in social relations, in business, in secular callings, in personal thought, and in moral action. Piety not only exists on the Sabbath but extends to all days, in all

---

[87] Edwards, *Works, Volume 2* (Yale University Press), 364.

[88] Edwards, *Works, Volume 2* (Yale University Press), 365.

circumstances, "through all changes, and under all trials, as long as he lives."[89]

When some objected that Edwards made true religion a matter of works rather than faith, or reception before God a matter of perfected holiness rather than imputed righteousness, he responded by noting that in the Scripture "the freeness of grace, and the necessity of holy practice" are frequently joined with each other so that they are "not inconsistent one with another." He added, "Nor does it diminish at all the honor and importance of faith, that the exercises and effects of faith in practice, should be esteemed the chief signs of it; any more than it lessens the importance of life, that action and motion are esteemed the chief signs of that."[90]

In order to seal the unity of pure grace and holy affections, Edwards wrote thus:

> So that in what has been said of the importance of holy practice, as the main sign of sincerity; there is nothing legal, nothing derogatory to the freedom an sovereignty of gospel grace, nothing in the least clashing with the gospel doctrine of justification by faith alone, without the works of the law, nothing is the least tending to lessen the glory of the mediator, and our dependence on his righteousness, nothing infringing on the special prerogatives of faith in the affair of our salvation, nothing in any wise detracting from the glory of God and his mercy, or exalting man, or diminishing his dependence and obligation. . . . 'Tis greatly to the hurt of religion, for persons to make light of, and insist little on, those things which the Scriptures insist most upon, as of the most importance in the evidence of our interest in Christ.[91]

---

[89] Edwards, *Works, Volume 2* (Yale University Press), 384.

[90] Edwards, *Works, Volume 2* (Yale University Press), 458.

[91] Edwards, *Works, Volume 2* (Yale University Press), 458–459.

CONCLUSION

Jonathan Edwards gave a virtually oppressive amount of energetic doctrinal thought and biblical exegesis to the subject of revival. This was in a sense right at the heart of Edwards's whole intellectual project. Revival was a part of the answer he gave to the end for which God created the world. The purpose of creation is that other rational beings may rejoice in the glory of God in such a way that their joy is ever expanding, thus giving corroborative demonstration that the goodness of God—both in grace and in wrath—truly is inexhaustible. Revival consists of God's glorifying Himself by giving moral union with Himself to marred image-bearers for the purpose of restoration of the divine image. Though the manner of conversion is various—as various as the number of persons upon whom divine power is savingly wrought—there is an analogy because of the singularity of fallen nature, the culpability of transgression, the person of the Redeemer, the oneness of the gospel message, and the goal of God's glory through making His chosen people one in Christ.

Revival is the multiplication and intensification of the effectual working of God in bringing sinners from darkness to light, from deadness to life, from children of the devil to children of God. There is a qualitative difference between religion that is worldly and religion that is heavenly. The Scripture defines, describes, and gives examples of both, and it is the duty of men and the particular calling of gospel minsters to discern the difference. Whereas in their fallen state all persons are God-haters, in the converted, or revived, state they delight in God. As God is happy in Himself, so He will bring His chosen ones to find unending happiness in Him and in the vision of His glory eternally, being wrapped up in His intra-trinitarian love. Revival is of the essence of heaven.

CHAPTER 4

GEORGE WHITEFIELD

"[Righteousness] is what all reformed divines, that have clear heads and clean hearts, call an imputed righteousness, or the righteousness of the Lord Jesus Christ to be imputed to poor sinners upon their believing."

—George Whitefield[1]

INTRODUCTION

George Whitefield (1714–1770) died when he was fifty-six years old, in the thirty-fourth year of his ministry. In a 1991 study of his life entitled *The Divine Dramatist*, Harry Stout called him, in addition to being the colonies' most popular eighteenth-century preacher, "Anglo America's first modern celebrity."[2]

---

[1]   George Whitefield, "The Righteousness of Christ an Everlasting Righteousness," in *The Sermons of George Whitefield*, ed. Lee Gattis (Wheaton: Crossway, 2012), 286. All references to Whitefield's sermons come from this edition.

[2]   Harry S. Stout, *The Divine Dramatist* (Grand Rapids: Eerdmans, 1991), 13. Stout's intriguing treatment of Whitefield fully engages the primary sources and the large bulwark of secondary sources, and it recognizes the impact of what he calls the "filiopietistic" biographies of Whitefield, but seeks to set him in the context of emerging modernity in "exploiting the new media and the emerging marketplace mentality." Stout does not present him as insincere or subject to the allurements of money, sex, and popularity that have developed in the fame-culture of some in modern evangelicalism. He presents Whitefield as earnest and intense but as pressing his natural talents to gain a wide hearing and to develop a mass conformity to his personal convictions. "This same Calvinism informed his self-concept and placed even his most shameless self-promotion within a

If so, it was not for any insincerity or purposeful display of histrionics, but from a natural talent for convincing expression and vocal dynamics. Josiah Smith, a South Carolina pastor, wrote a description of Whitefield's doctrine, his manner of preaching, and his character, along with an observation of God's providence in granting such a figure in their day. Part of his discussion of Whitefield's preaching stated,

> How was his tongue like the pen of a ready writer, touched as with a coal from the altar! With what a flow of words—what a ready profusion of language, did he speak to us upon the great concerns of our souls! In what a flaming light did he set our eternity before us! How earnestly he pressed Christ upon us! How did he move our passions with the constraining love of *such* a Redeemer! The awe—the silence—the attention which sat upon the face of the great audience, was an argument how he could reign over all their powers.[3]

Whitefield's contemporary Bolingbroke wrote, "Mr. Whitefield is the most extraordinary man in our times. He has the most commanding eloquence I ever heard in any person."[4] Beyond that, his consuming love for the gospel and for sinners expressed itself *a fortiori* in his intense and unrelenting public ministry. The *pathos* of his voice and expression created a *bathos* of judgment and grace surrounding his auditory. E. C. Dargan introduced his discussion of Whitefield with this evaluation: "His abundant

---

larger understanding of self and society molded by the premodern tenets of total depravity, original sin, and unconditional election. If I have placed less emphasis on theology in this biography," Stout continued in summary, "it is because it was of less importance to his *significance*, not because it was of less importance to *him*" (xxiii).

[3] Cited in Robert Philip, *The Life and Times of George Whitefield* (Edinburgh: The Banner of Truth Trust, 2007 [first published in 1837]) 170, 171.

[4] Cited in Edward Charles Dargan, *A History of Preaching* (Birmingham, AL: Solid Ground Christian Books, 2003) 2: 312–313.

labors were, and in their fruits remain, a benediction to mankind; his preaching, for earnestness, eloquence, and immediate effect, was the admiration of his own age, and is one of the most sacred traditions of the Christian pulpit for all time."[5]

When he was twelve, as Whitefield recalled, he had "a good elocution and memory" and was "remarked for making speeches before the Corporation at their annual visitation."[6] One of his teachers wrote out plays for him to perform, leading him to recall, "The remembrance of this hath often filled me with confusion of face, and I hope will do so, even to the end of my life." This kind of education became substance for repentance as he observed "how this way of training up youth has a natural tendency to debauch the mind, to raise ill passions, and to stuff the memory with things as contrary to the gospel of Jesus Christ, as light to darkness, heaven to hell." Though Stout might be accurate in his observing how others regarded Whitefield, celebrity was the farthest accolade from the mind of Whitefield.

BIOGRAPHICAL SKETCH

George Whitefield was born December 16, 1714, at the Bell Inn on Southgate Street, Bristol, England. As Whitefield surveyed his own family background, his youth, his givenness to "an impudent temper, lying, filthy talking, and foolish jesting," his brutishness, his roguishness, as well as his tendency to steal even from his mother, he could not but feel that his conversion had been a mighty rescue from outside of himself and in accord with a divine determination that would overcome every sinful propensity of his corrupted and degraded affections. "I can see nothing in me but

---

[5] Dargan, *A History of Preaching*, 2:308.

[6] The Committee of the General Assembly of the Free Church of Scotland, *Sketches of the Life and Labours of the Rev. George Whitefield* (London and Edinburgh: John Johnstone, nd), 12. This volume has the *Autobiography of Whitefield* for the first fifty pages, going up to the time of his ordination.

a fitness to be damned," he observed. "Whatever foreseen fitness for salvation others may talk of and glory in, I disclaim any such thing." He could only conclude, especially when seen in the texts of the Bible, "If the Almighty had not prevented [gone before] me by his grace, and wrought most powerfully upon my soul, quickening me by his free Spirit when dead in trespasses and sins, I had now been either sitting in darkness, and in the shadow of death, or condemned, as the due reward of my crimes, to be for ever lifting up my eyes in torments."[7]

In 1733, Whitefield entered Pembroke College, Oxford, as a servitor (the lowest rank of student, servant to the gentlemen commoners). Soon he met Charles and John Wesley and became a part of the "Holy Club," as they were derisively called, or "Enthusiasts" or the "Bible Moths." Well-known is the name given them, "methodists," supposed by Whitefield to come from "their custom of regulating their time, and, planning the business of the day every morning."[8] Charles gave him a copy of Henry Scougal's book, *The Life of God in the Soul of Man*. In reading that, he learned "true religion" and that to be a Christian, he "must be a new creature."[9] He wrote respectfully, appreciatively, and sometimes in a celebratory manner of these Oxford friends, saying, "I walked openly with them, and chose rather to bear contempt with those people of God, than to enjoy the applause of almost-Christians for a season."[10]

In 1735, Whitefield was converted. During his period of conviction, Whitefield engaged in such rigorous self-denial that he became very sick. His austerities, however, failed to gain him righteousness. In addition to severe mental and spiritual exercises and often vain contemplations and ascetic and quietistic isolation, and sensing the bodily and mental oppression of Satan, he began

---

7 *Sketches of the Life and Labours,* 10–11
8 *Sketches of the Life and Labours*, 24.
9 *Sketches of the Life and Labours*, 21–22.
10 *Sketches of the Life and Labours*, 25.

"to leave off eating fruit, . . . chose the worst sort of food, . . . fasted twice a week," and he wore "woolen gloves, a patched gown, and dirty shoes."

> Having thus undergone innumerable buffetings of Satan and many months of inexpressible trials, by night and day, under the spirit of bondage, God was pleased at length to remove the heavy load, to enable me to lay hold on His dear Son by a living faith, and by giving me the spirit of adoption, to seal me as I humbly hope, even to the day of everlasting redemption. I found and felt in myself, that I was delivered from the burden that had so heavily oppressed me. The spirit of mourning was taken from me, and I knew what it was truly to rejoice in God my Saviour.[11]

In 1736, Whitefield began to work among the poor and the prisoners for their salvation. Bishop Benson noticed his zeal and success and sent for him to be ordained. In June of 1736, he was set aside to holy orders as deacon. (His ordination as priest did not occur until January 14, 1739, after returning from his first trip to America.) He soon preached for the first time and, according to some who observed, he "drove fifteen mad the first sermon." In 1737, at the urging of John and Charles Wesley, Whitefield took his first trip to America after a year of fruitful preaching in England. He had raised money with the possibility of establishing an orphanage in Georgia and went there to raise more. On board ship, Whitefield preached, catechized, married couples, distributed books, threw bad books and cards overboard, prayed, admired the power and beauty of the ocean, and "gave several blows" to a four-year-old child because he would not say the Lord's Prayer, and gave him some figs when he did. He recorded this activity for

---

[11] A. S. Billingsley, *Life of George Whitefield, Prince of Pulpit Orators, with Specimens of his Sermons.* (New York John B. Alden, 1889), 33. Billingsley cited part of a narrative that was eventually edited by Whitefield and part of the 1856 edition of Whitefield's *Journal.*

April 3: "At about eleven, went on board the Lightfoot, prayed with a sick man, and preached my sermon on the penitent thief. Afterwards, went on board the Amy, catechised the children, dined on a dolphin, had some useful conversation, preached to the soldiers, returned home about six, read prayers, visited the sick, interceded for friends, and went to bed praising and blessing God."[12]

On May 7, 1738, Whitefield reached his destination, "Savannah Town."[13] By May 16 he had determined to erect an orphan house after surveying the needs in town around Savannah. Whitefield stayed in Georgia until September. He was incessant in his ministerial stewardship, constantly going from house to house reading catechism, "lessons," and preaching. The twenty-three-year-old Whitefield gave a summary account of his Lord's Day activities:

> On Sunday morning, at five o'clock, I publicly expound the Second Lesson for the Morning or Evening Service as I see most suited to the people's edification; at ten I preach and read prayers; at three in the afternoon I do the same; and at seven expound part of the Church Catechism, at which great numbers are usually present. I visit from house to house, read public prayers, and expound twice, and catechise (unless something extraordinary happens), visit the sick every day, and read to as many of my parishioners as will come thrice a week. And blessed be God, my labours have not been altogether vain in the Lord. For He has been pleased to set his seal to my ministry, in a manner I could not, I dared not in America, expect. Not unto me, O Lord, not unto me, but unto thy name be the glory![14]

---

[12] George Whitefield, *George Whitefield's Journals* (Edinburgh: The Banner of Truth Trust, 1978), 97–152. For the April 3 activities, see 147.

[13] Whitefield, *Journals,* 155.

[14] Whitefield, *Journals,* 160–161.

Whitefield often preached in very hot conditions made even hotter by the number of persons crowded into the building. On one occasion he remarked, "During my stay here, the weather was most intensely hot, sometimes burning me almost through my shoes."[15]

In September 1738, he left for England and landed in Ireland in November after a rough voyage with scanty provisions. When he learned that provisions were washed overboard, he wrote in his journal, "Blessed be God, the prospect pleases me. For now I shall learn, I trust, how to want as well as how to abound, and how to endure hardship like a good soldier of Jesus Christ. O Lord, let the strength be magnified in my weakness, and say unto my soul, 'It is I, be not afraid.'"[16]

On his return to England, the churches began to close to him. He continued to preach in small societies and in some churches that were open to him. Bishop Benson also ordained him to the priesthood. He noted after a day of powerful preaching, "Now know I, that I did receive the Holy Ghost at imposition of hands, for I feel it as much as Elisha did when Elijah dropped his mantle." Just two days before, Whitefield had begun to pray and preach extempore. Of February 2, 1739, he wrote, "This is the first time I have preached without notes (for when I preached at Deptford and Gravesend, I only repeated a written sermon); but I find myself now, as it were, constrained to do it."[17]

The Chancellor of Bristol, acting for "the clergy and laity of the city of Bristol," accused him of preaching false doctrine and said, "I am resolved, Sir, if you preach or expound anywhere in this diocese till you have a license, I will first suspend, and then excommunicate you."[18] Whitefield began to preach more and more outdoors and in private residences. He preached to the

---

[15] Billingsley, 81

[16] Whitefield, *Journals,* 168.

[17] Whitefield, *Journals,* 204–206.

[18] Whitefield, *Journals,* 218.

prisoners at Newgate and often to the colliers of Kingswood as they left the mines. On February 17, 1739, he preached to over two hundred to over two hundred at a place called "rose green" on regeneration, from John 3:3. He stated, "I believe I never was more acceptable to my Master than when I was standing to teach those hearers in the open fields. Some may censure me; but if I thus pleased men, I should not be the servant of Christ."[19]

The resistance to Whitefield focused on two major issues. One, the doctrine of the new birth and justification by faith alone were out of fashion in the established church. Two, the specific measures he used went outside the accepted liturgical tradition of the church. He engaged the people in prolonged prayer meetings, expounding and visiting from house to house, preaching and exhorting in private societies, and his extempore prayers caused offense to many churchmen.

He returned to America from August 1739 to February 1741 and regularly delivered up to twenty sermons a week. Immediately upon his departure, John Wesley published a sermon against the doctrine of predestination and particular atonement entitled *Free Grace*, based on Romans 8:32. Whitefield had heard of Wesley's intent by June of 1739 and begged his co-worker not to publish. He did anyway. Whitefield did not answer and as late as March 1740 affirmed to Wesley his intention to preach final perseverance and election, pleading that both he and Wesley should "offer salvation freely to all by the blood of Christ," and that he had no intention to "enter the lists of controversy" with Wesley. In September he wrote, "What a fond conceit is it to cry up *perfection*, and yet cry down the doctrine of *final perseverance*. But this, and many other absurdities, you will run into, because you will not own *election*." Soon Whitefield saw that a refusal to answer was impossible. So in February 1741, he wrote, "I must preach the gospel of Christ, and that I cannot now do, without speaking of *election*."[20] He came to

---

19 Whitefield, *Journals,* 216.
20 Whitefield, *Journals,* 566.

know the Tennents and Jonathan Edwards on this visit to America and saw in firsthand experience that strong emphases on the sovereignty of grace was blessed of God in powerful conversions. Whitefield penned his answer to Wesley in December 1740 but did not publish until early in 1741 upon his return to England.

His open letter to John Wesley questioned the fitness of Wesley's text (Romans 8:32) to support his argument; his assertion that election eliminated the need for the use of means and contradicted the need for a divine revelation of redemptive truth; his extrapolation of doctrinal falsity from observation of personal idiosyncrasies; his denial of the theology of the Thirty-Nine Articles; and his conclusions by inferences from election, particular redemption, and perseverance. Whitefield asked Wesley this question: "Does not dear Mr. Wesley know many dear children of God, who are predestinarians, and yet are meek, lowly, pitiful, courteous, tender-hearted, kind, of a catholic spirit, and hope to see the most vile and profligate of men converted? And why? Because they know God saved them by an act of his electing love, and they know not but he may have elected those who now seem to be the most abandoned."[21] On October 10, 1741, Whitefield wrote to Wesley, "May God remove all obstacles that now prevent our union! Though I hold particular election, yet I offer Jesus freely to every individual soul. You may carry sanctification to what degrees you will, only, I cannot agree that the in-being of sin is to be destroyed in this life." Near the close of the letter Whitefield pledged, "May all disputings cease, and each of us talk of nothing but Jesus, and him crucified! This is my resolution."[22]

The melancholy controversy with Wesley did not discourage Whitefield's zeal for gospel preaching at any venue available and as many times as possible. During the summer of 1742, Whitefield began preaching in Cambuslang, Scotland, where a

---

[21] Whitefield, *Journals*, 577.

[22] Micahel A. G. Haykin, ed., *The Revived Puritan* (Dundas, Ontario: Joshua Press, 2000), 145.

powerful revival had begun. His work bore immense fruit. The joy of effectuality in preaching, however, did not diminish the challenges of misrepresentation, caricature, and hostility that came from Scotland, England, and America. Whitefield went forward without bitterness or a vengeful spirit and found great joy in the eternal benefits of God's effectual power, making the disdain of worldly detractors mere flea-bitings in comparison.[23]

In November 1741, Whitefield married Elizabeth James. She was a widow. Whitefield felt spiritually secure in seeking a wife, for he had experienced the power of Sarah Edwards's spirituality and witnessed the unflinching support she provided to Edwards's ministry. Together George and Elizabeth had one son whom Whitefield anticipated would be an itinerating evangelist. He died at four months of age. Subsequently, Elizabeth had four miscarriages. She was as committed to Whitefield's incessant preaching and other labors as he was and on occasions bolstered his courage to face the dangers often confronted in his open-air preaching. She died August 9, 1768. Whitefield lost his "Sarah" just over two years before his own death.[24]

Whitefield made his third trip to America in 1744 and in 1748 traveled to Bermuda, where he was used greatly among the black population. He made trips to America in 1751, 1754, 1763, and 1769, each time having a profitable and encouraging time of preaching. On his last visit, he landed in Charleston, South Carolina, where he preached for ten successive days. Then he went to Georgia to view his orphanages in Bethesda. Being very encouraged there, and visiting also in Savannah, he went to Philadelphia, where he preached five or six times a week for

---

[23] For a description of this revival and the joy and challenges it brought to Whitefield, see Arnold Dallimore, *George Whitefield* (Edinburgh: Banner of Truth, 1970) 2:121–137.

[24] See Doreen Moore, *Good Christians, Good Husbands?* (Ross-Shire, Scotland: Christian Focus Publications, 2004), 61–94. Moore examines the marriages of John Wesley, George Whitefield, and Jonathan Edwards.

six weeks. He remarked, "Pulpits, hearts and affections seem to be as open towards me as ever. . . . People of all ranks flock as much as ever." He went on a 150-mile circuit, preaching every day. In June, he went to New York, where "congregations are rather larger than ever." From there he went on a five-hundred-mile circuit, preaching and traveling through the heat every day. Much of this was new work. From New York, he went to Boston, preaching from September 17 through 20. He preached his last sermon on a Saturday morning, September 29, at Exeter, fifteen miles from Portsmouth. The text of the message was 2 Corinthians 13:5. Dallimore records that during this two-hour sermon, his chest heavings were oppressive and made the sermon a difficult experience. His desire to preach overcame what seemed an impossible task, making some hearers say that this last one was "the greatest sermon they ever heard from him."[25]

Afterward, he journeyed to the home of Jonathan Parsons, pastor of the Old South Presbyterian Church in Newburyport, Massachusetts. After eating an early meal, as he went upstairs, he saw that another group of people had gathered to hear him preach. He preached on the stairway until the candle he held burned itself out. He died the next morning, September 30, 1770, after a struggle with asthma that suffocated him. He was attended by friends until it was clear that breath and life were gone and could not return.[26]

GEORGE WHITEFIELD'S CALVINISM

Whitefield believed that true spiritual life came in conjunction with the word of truth. The sovereign efficacious operations of the Holy Spirit coursed through Spirit-revealed doctrine of man's spiritual deadness, helplessness, and unpunctuated rebellion. So alien to proper regard for God is fallen man that only invincible

---

[25] Dallimore, *George Whitefield*, 2:504.

[26] Dallimore, *George Whitefield*, 2:504–506.

mercy can bring him to a saving embrace of Christ as set forth in the gospel. Whitefield's preaching was a continual demonstration of conscientious commitment to these truths as well as the converting power of the doctrines of sovereign grace, combined with the urgency of the sinner's responsibility to turn from sin and place faith in Christ.

Partly in reflection on his own experience of salvation, Whitefield loved to point to biblical narratives that involved the salvation of unlikely candidates for the exalted status of children of God. These demonstrated that sovereign grace can reach and overcome the "worst of people, in the very worst of places."[27] At Jericho, a city under a curse since the time of Joshua, Jesus found Zacchaeus and blind Bartimaeus, proving that the curse does not eliminate the prospect that "some chosen vessels may be therein." The prayer of Bartimaeus—"Jesus, Son of David, have mercy on me!" (Mark 10:47)—was full of the sentiments depicting the "natural language of a soul brought to lie at the feet of a sovereign God." He laid no claim to cure by merit but looked to Christ alone as able and willing to save. Bartimaeus served as an example of one whose inability was absolute, but nevertheless, at the call of Christ, he did what he could not do, that is to rise and make his way to Him. He offered no objection from his inability to see Christ, but at the command of Christ began his walk. Whitefield applied this idea:

> What if we do call you to come and to believe on the Lord Jesus Christ that you may be saved? Does this imply that you have a power in yourselves to do so? No, in no wise, no more than Jesus' saying unto Lazarus's dead and stinking carcass, "Come forth," implied, that Lazarus had a power to raise himself from the grave. We call to you, being commanded to preach the gospel to every creature, hoping and praying, that Christ's power

---

[27] Lee Gattis, ed., *The Sermons of George Whitefield* (Wheaton: Crossway, 2012), 1:454.

may accompany the word and make it effectual to the quickening and raising of your dead souls.[28]

He wanted his hearers, with no promise of an effectual saving work of God, to use their natural and rational powers to do good and to seek to know spiritual truth, and "while you are attempting to stretch out your withered arm," perhaps "Jesus may work faith in you by his almighty power." Whitefield had no hesitance to tell his audience that they were inflicted with original sin from their father Adam, and, as Bartimaeus was blind in body, so were each of them "a blind child of a blind father, even of the father Adam who lost his sight when he lost his innocence and entailed his blindness, justly inflicted, upon thee and me and his whole posterity."[29] As he invited his hearers to play the part of Bartimaeus, Whitefield told them to "lay yourselves at the feet of sovereign grace."[30]

The story of Paul's conversion was another instance of the most unlikely having been "chosen from all eternity by God and hereafter called in time, to edify and build up the church of Christ."[31] As he contrasted what Paul heard with what his travel companions heard on that fateful road to Damascus, Whitefield gloried in the sovereignty of God who will have mercy on whom He will have mercy. Paul understood, while the others only heard a sound, showing the sovereign appointment of God to take one and leave the others to "perish in their sins." Even so, some still hear unto salvation, while many hear but do not understand. Whitefield could only exclaim, "O the depth of the sovereignty of God! It is past finding out. Lord, I desire to adore what I cannot comprehend. 'Even so, Father, for so it seemeth good in thy sight!"[32] Paul's salvation and calling is a clear example of

---

[28] Gattis, *The Sermons of George Whitefield*, 1:460.

[29] Gattis, *The Sermons of George Whitefield*, 1:463.

[30] Gattis, *The Sermons of George Whitefield*, 1:464.

[31] Gattis, *The Sermons of George Whitefield*, 2:170.

[32] Gattis, *The Sermons of George Whitefield*, 2:175.

"that precious but too much exploded and sadly misrepresented, doctrine of God's electing love." While some remain senseless, that others believed is explained in the phrase used of Paul, "they are chosen vessels" and are thus struck down and converted by "the almighty power of efficacious grace."[33]

In a sermon on "The Seed of the Woman and the Seed of the Serpent," Whitefield located the origin of the doctrines of grace in an eternal covenant first revealed in the protoevangelium in Genesis 3:15. Whitefield believed, "God the Father and God the Son had entered into a covenant concerning the salvation of the elect from all eternity, wherein God the Father promised that if the Son would offer his soul a sacrifice for sin, he should see his seed."[34] Previously in the sermon, he had anticipated this by calling it "an amazing scene of divine love . . . which had been from all eternity hid in the heart of God!" This covenantal framework Whitefield judged to be vital to the entire scheme of orthodox theology. In it the orthodox Christology of the early church councils is implied, as well as the undiluted evangelicalism of justification by faith. "They can now do nothing of or for themselves and should therefore come to God, beseeching him to give them faith, by which they shall be enabled to lay hold on the righteousness of Christ." This faith, a gift of the covenant, then results in works of holiness. "Without holding this," Whitefield summarized the importance of this scheme, "we must run into one of those two bad extremes, I mean Antinomianism on the one hand, or Arminianism on the other. From both of which may the good Lord deliver us!"[35]

Whitefield contended that all people are by nature papists or Arminians and that "Arminian principles being antichristian principles, always did and always will lead to antichristian practices." Again, certain perverse things "will infidelity and Arminianism

---

[33] Gattis, *The Sermons of George Whitefield*, 2:184.

[34] Gattis, *The Sermons of George Whitefield*, 1:57.

[35] Gattis, *The Sermons of George Whitefield*, 1:58.

make men speak."[36] Here he had in mind distinctive Arminian doctrine that, in his opinion, led to a spirit of self-justification and the priority of the human will over divine will and grace.

Whitefield argued that if the covenant were seen more clearly by some, then such harsh words against the doctrines of grace would be more difficult to utter. "Would to God," he contemplated, "this point of doctrine was considered more and people were more studious of the covenant of redemption between the Father and the Son!" If this would occur, "we should not then have so much disputing against the doctrine of election, or hear it condemned (even by good men [like Wesley?]) as a doctrine of devils." For Whitefield, the covenant was precious and served as the just and merciful fountain of grace proceeding from the triune God and the guarantee of all the blessings of grace that ever a sinner will enjoy. It is in Christ that these blessings are "made over to the elect."[37]

A sermon on "Walking with God" began with the premise of "the prevailing power of the enmity of a person's heart" against God. This prevailing enmity, received from the infection of sin in the fall of Adam, must be overcome in the initial work of regeneration bringing the sinner to faith. Remaining enmity of the flesh is then gradually removed by taking advantage of all the means of grace given us as revealed in Scripture. Among the treasures of this sermon is a section of instruction including seven directives as to how to walk with God so as to experience continuing sanctification in this life in preparation for the complete freedom from indwelling sin in the next. These seven directives are the revealed means that constitute Whitefield's definition of walking with God: "Walking with God consists especially in the fixed habitual bent of the will for God, in an habitual dependence upon his power and promise, in an habitual voluntary dedication of our all to his glory, in an habitual eyeing of his precept in all

---

[36] Gattis, *The Sermons of George Whitefield*, 1: 262–267.

[37] Gattis, *The Sermons of George Whitefield*, 2:215.

we do and in an habitual complacence in his pleasure in all we suffer."[38] Though his analysis of this subject and his exhortation to it may benefit and be pleasing to true Christians across a spectrum of doctrinal systems, Whitefield soaked the whole narrative in Calvinism and included a strong caveat against antinomianism. One cannot read any of it without breathing in the fragrance of the entire system, from original bondage to sin to a final gracious gift of perfect freedom in Christ and an unclouded vision of His glory.

In a moving message on the offering up of Isaac, Whitefield reached the climax of the provision God made of a substitute for Isaac, and in the denouement pictured a scene of Abraham's celebration of the event with Sarah, and, even those millennia later, saw him "now exulting in the paradise of God and adoring rich, free, distinguishing, electing, everlasting love, which alone made him to differ from the rest of mankind and rendered him worthy of that title which he will have so long as the sun and the moon endure, 'The Father of the faithful.'"[39]

In a sermon to a society of young women, Whitefield preached on "Christ the Best Husband." Both art and careful doctrine co-inhered to give the sermon that rich combination of earnest solicitation and free offer with clear presentation of sovereign grace. In his discussion of mutual choice, he gave a clear manifesto of the initiatory rights of Christ in establishing the relationship. "The Lord Jesus Christ, my dear sisters, doth choose you merely by his free grace. It is freely of his own mercy, that he brings you into the marriage covenant. . . . And you are drawn to make your choice of the Lord Jesus Christ because he first chose you."[40] Asserting in no unclear terms that "Christ doth invite all of you to be his spouse," he also reminded these young women that, with the use of all the means designated by Christ to bring this proposal,

38 Gattis, *The Sermons of George Whitefield*, 1:69.
39 Gattis, *The Sermons of George Whitefield*, 1:91.
40 Gattis, *The Sermons of George Whitefield*, 1:110.

finally, "you will be brought to him by his Spirit. You will then lay hold on him by faith, his Spirit will draw you unto himself. He will make you to be willing in the day of his power. He will give you faith in him." Whitefield reiterated that, even given the utter dependence on the divine eternal choice and the effectual present operation of the Spirit, they should "not be contented till you have received the Lord Jesus Christ."[41]

This same reliance on the effectual work of the Spirit Whitefield emphasized in a sermon on "The Potter and the Clay." These "depraved natures must necessarily undergo an universal moral change." He would rather go to the graveyard to preach to rotten carcasses, and expect them to obey his command to rise, than to preach to depraved souls without "some superior power to make the word effectual to the designed end." Such a change cannot be "wrought by the power of our own free-will. This is an idol everywhere set up but we dare not fall down and worship it." The sermon focused on the Spirit, described by Whitefield as "the third person in the most adorable Trinity, co-essential with the Father and the Son." The Spirit's part in the eternal covenant stretched from the first actions of creation to the point when we are made "more and more meet for and at last" translated to "a full, perfect, endless and uninterrupted enjoyment of glory hereafter." If sinners can be so fitted, it will only be by the power of the Spirit working in us all the graces through which "instead of being vessels in a potter's oven, you will be made vessels of honour and be presented at the great day by Jesus, to his heavenly Father and be translated to live with him as monuments of rich, free, distinguishing and sovereign grace, for ever and ever."[42]

Exactly this transformation occurred with Zaccheus, who, for Whitefield, is a picture of "the doctrine of free grace." At the place in the narrative where Zaccheus has climbed the tree to gain advantage to see Jesus, Whitefield broke into an exuberant

---

[41] Gattis, *The Sermons of George Whitefield*, 1:114.
[42] Gattis, *The Sermons of George Whitefield*, 1:260.

apostrophe: "But sing, O heavens and rejoice, O earth! Praise, magnify and adore sovereign, electing, free, preventing love. Jesus the everlasting God, the Prince of Peace, who saw Nathanael under the fig tree and Zaccheus from eternity, now sees him in the sycamore-tree and calls him in time." Here Jesus called the name on earth of one whose "name was written in the book of life. He was one of those whom the Father had given him from all eternity, therefore he must abide at his house that day. 'For whom he did predestinate, them he also called.'"[43] Thus, with this outward call from the lips of the Son of God, "there went an efficacious power from God, which sweetly over-ruled his natural will." Even as Jesus came to Jericho to call Zaccheus, so He came from heaven to this earth to seek and to save the lost. In a flurry of lengthy and passion-ridden appeals—e.g., "Do not, therefore, put me off with frivolous excuses. There's no excuse can be given for your not coming to Christ"—Whitefield salted such appeals with a clear sense of dependence on sovereign grace—"For I know my calling will not do, unless he, by his efficacious grace, compel you to come in."[44]

With great clarity and confidence in the power of truth to convict, Whitefield preached a robust Calvinism, which was firmly attached to the doctrine of Christ's imputed righteousness, as the central theme of his evangelism. Within those doctrines he found the most profound reason for evangelism, the clearest remedy for present human perdition, and the most satisfying confidence in the sure success of the evangelist's calling. This undergirded and prompted the revival known as the First Great Awakening.

---

[43] Gattis, *The Sermons of George Whitefield*, 2:79.
[44] Gattis, *The Sermons of George Whitefield*, 2:79.

CHAPTER 5

SECOND GREAT AWAKENING

"That heavenly calling, which the inhabitants of Vermont received will never be forgotten—the illustrations of vengeance and mercy that have been given there, the clear shining of justice, the amazing majesty of grace displayed in the redemption of souls, will be among the themes and the acclamations of eternity."

—Joshua Bradley[1]

Sydney Ahlstrom concluded that in the first half of the nineteenth century, beginning with the Second Great Awakening, "evangelical Protestant churches with their message and methods tuned to the patriotic aspirations of a young nation, reached their high point of cultural influence."[2]

POLITICAL AND INTELLECTUAL CLIMATE

The political atmosphere was energized by the new Constitution and the intellectual interchange that had produced it. The *Federalist Papers* at the end of the eighteenth century (1787–1788) had discussed the question, "Are societies capable of establishing good government from reflection and choice? Or are nations forever destined to depend on accident and force for their political constitutions?" The election of Jefferson in 1800 saw a policy of

---

[1] Joshua Bradley, *Accounts of Religious Revivals in Many parts of the United States from 1815 to 1818* (Wheaton: Richard Owen Roberts, Publishers, 1980), 148.

[2] Sydney E. Ahlstrom, *A Religious History of the American People* (New Haven: Yale University Press, 1972), 387.

agrarian utopianism seek to oust the federalism of Hamilton. The country was divided in its opinion about the French Revolution, but most saw it as confirmation of the American Revolution being a trailblazer for democratic liberties. The change from the Articles of Confederation to the Constitution gave confidence in the stability of the new nation.

Samuel Stanhope Smith (1751–1819) celebrated the political wisdom involved in that switch. When the Constitutional Convention seemed at an impasse, "they were ready to abandon their work in despair, when, suddenly, a luminous wisdom disembroiled their embarrassment, a spirit of conciliation compromised all interests and opinions." Could this remarkable resumption of progress be ascribed to any factor other than "to the mercy and direction of heaven? For, although the philosopher and politician may be able to develop the causes that conspired to produce the event, yet, are not the springs of all causes in God? Does not he hold in his hand their eternal chain and guide, by an invisible energy and wisdom, their infinite relations and results?"[3]

Another important element of the energy that inhabited the spirit of revival was the national institution of religious liberty. The General Committee of Baptists in Virginia worked against oppressive measures such as a "general assessment." They argued that legislative acts enforcing regulations for religion were "repugnant to the spirit of the Gospel." Human laws cannot effect genuine religion and, thus, "every person ought to be left entirely free in respect to matters of religion." They asserted with confidence that "the holy Author of our religion needs no such compulsive measures for the promotion of His cause; that the Gospel wants not the feeble arm of man for its support." Their work culminated in the Act for Establishing Religious Liberty, sponsored by Thomas

---

[3]   Samuel Stanhope Smith, *The Divine Goodness to the United States of America.* A discourse, on the subjects of national gratitude, delivered in the Third Presbyterian Church in Philadelphia, on Thursday the 19th of February, 1795, https://catalogue.nla.gov.au/catalog/4847557.

Jefferson. An important sentiment expressed in this act stated, "Nor shall he otherwise suffer on account of his religious opinions or belief; but that all men shall be free to profess, and by argument to maintain their opinion in matters of religion, and that the same shall in no wise diminish enlarge or affect their civil capacities."[4]

In *The Rights of Conscience*, the Baptist John Leland argued for freedom of speech as necessarily involving freedom of religion. Every man must speak freely without fear, "maintain the principles that he believes, worship according to his own faith." He must meet "no personal abuse or loss of property for his religious opinions." Rather, each person must be encouraged to "bring forth his arguments and maintain his points with all boldness; then if his doctrine is false it will be confuted, and if it is true (though ever so novel) let others credit it." This right of freedom to preach in accord with one's true convictions was secured in the First Amendment of the Constitution: "Congress shall make no law respecting an establishment of religion, or prohibiting the free exercise thereof; or abridging the freedom of speech, or of the press; or the right of the people peaceably to assemble, and to petition the Government for a redress of grievances."[5]

Baptists were particularly happy with this dear cluster of freedoms. Each functioned as elements of a whole: Quakers would not be hanged, Baptists would not be whipped or jailed, but all would be free to assemble, to write and publish, to preach and debate, and to form churches. The Second Great Awakening rode the wave of these freedoms as perfectly concordant with the means of seeking and promoting revival.

Other ideas were also given the power of propagation. The nineteenth century witnessed the rise of Unitarianism and provided a foe, an enemy to the faith, that prompted surges of devotion and earnest zeal to the proclamation of the gospel in its orthodox

---

[4]   Robert A. Baker, *A Baptist Sourcebook* (Nashville: Broadman Press, 1966), 38.

[5]   Baker, *A Baptist Sourcebook*, 41–42.

form. Liberalism in general also began to press the boundaries of confessional evangelicalism and orthodoxy. The phenomenon that was America energized economic and patriotic optimism. A new world was being forged, filled with self-sufficient, independent, free-thinking, and optimistic opportunists. The American was the new Adam, blessed with restored innocence, loosed from the sins of former captivity, now given a second chance to remain in Eden.

This fomented receptivity to specific doctrinal shifts. Man migrated from helplessness to confident ability. His need no longer resided in conversion and radical spiritual confrontation; no, the new way highlighted gradual progressivism and continuity. No longer would society be divided into the converted and unconverted. The sentiment behind the Halfway Covenant gained the victory without the covenantal purpose of conversion. Obsolete was any doctrine of eternal f; now there would be future probation. Charles Chauncy had begun an exposition of this doctrine in 1750, but it was not finally published until 1784, and then anonymously, in London. Libertarian notions replaced confessional unity in the churches.

The moderate Calvinists David Tappan (1752–1803) and Joseph Willard (1738–1804) died. Tappan had been the Hollis Professor of Divinity since 1792 and was replaced by the Unitarian Henry Ware. Ware served in that position 1805 to 1840, leading to Unitarian dominance at Harvard. Jedidiah Morse opposed these changes and founded the *Panoplist*, a periodical committed to presenting orthodox viewpoints. Andover Seminary was founded in 1808 in Massachusetts and was committed to the moderate Calvinism of the New Divinity and combatting Unitarianism and Arminianism. It served the cause of missions on the frontier and led in promoting foreign missions.

The drive toward Unitarianism featured an open-letter debate between William Ellery Channing (1780–1842) and Samuel Worcester (1770–1821). Worcester's engagement included three letters from 1815 entitled *Letters to the Rev. Dr. William Ellery Channing*. Channing was minister of the Federal Street Church in Boston. In one letter, Channing minimized the distinction between Unitarians and the orthodox by claiming that a bare belief that "the Father sent the Son, and gives, to those that ask, the Holy Spirit" should be sufficient as a biblical affirmation. In that sense, "We are all Trinitarians." But the orthodox wanted more. "The Trinitarian believes that the one God is *three distinct persons,* called Father, Son and Holy Ghost; and he believes that each is the only true God, and yet that the three are only one God. This is Trinitarianism." On the other hand, without all the contorted metaphysical nuances, "the Unitarian believes that there is but one person possessing supreme Divinity, even the Father." He believed that many who called themselves Trinitarians would fit more easily into that category of thought. "In fact," he summarized, "as the word Trinity is sometimes used, we all believe it. Christians ought not to be separated by a sound."[6] Channing removed all doubt about the difference in 1819 in his ordination sermon of Jared Sparks, in which he issued a manifesto for "Unitarian Christianity." Harvard University became fully and self-consciously Unitarian throughout the nineteenth century. Longfellow, Lowell, and Holmes all taught there during those years and were Unitarian, as was William Emerson, the father of Ralph Waldo Emerson.

Second Great Awakening in the East

The Awakening in the East was characterized by doctrinal preaching and a challenge to the growing popularity of various forms of infidelity in both college and church.[7] With increasing tenacity, university life among students was dominated by infatuation with revolutionary philosophers such as Voltaire and Tom Paine, and thus tinged with deism and skepticism. Both Paine's *Age of Reason* and Ethan Allen's *Reason, the Only Oracle of Man* attacked

---

[6] Ahlstrom, *A Religious History,* 395.

[7] "Infidelity" is a general term denoting a variety of philosophical opinions that deny the need for a special revelation for religious truth. Each version, therefore, rejects central orthodox doctrines of the Christian faith.

orthodox Christianity as dependent on miracle and revelation, thus rendering void the sufficiency of divine wisdom as manifest in creation and the full potential of human reason. Students called each other by the names of their favorite philosopher, Voltaire and Rousseau being among the most used.

In a 1795 Thanksgiving Day sermon entitled "The Divine Goodness to the Unites States of America," Samuel Stanhope Smith, vice president and professor of moral philosophy and divinity at the College of New Jersey (Princeton), issued a challenge to the burgeoning impact of this intellectual trendiness. "Lately," he said, "there has sprung up a sect of political emperies who pretend to deny the necessity or utility of religion, and who would willingly discard it from the state, as they have eradicated it from their hearts." The "apostles of atheism" are "more fanatical than the disciples of Omar." They assault wisdom as seen in the Creator who by wisdom founded the world and all of reality and have substituted an "admiration of their own wisdom." This they have canonized. "Blessed Savior!" he cried. "Are these the substitutes which infidelity invents for the purity and glory of thy holy religion? Are these the works of those strong and superior minds who affect to despise thy humble birth; thy innocent and instructive life! The condescension of thy mercy! The sacrifice of thy cross! The hopes of immortality which thou hast revealed, and which thou hast verified by thy resurrection!" The puerilities and arid hopelessness of these products of so-called reason are among "the strongest proofs of the truth and excellence of thy gospel!— Ever, may we cherish it as the dearest, the most sacred treasure that heaven has conferred on mortals!"[8]

Timothy Dwight (1752–1817) confronted this worship of reason and bold infidelity with the straightforward preaching of historic orthodoxy in the university chapels. Dwight was born in Northampton, Massachusetts, on May 14, 1752, to Timothy

---

[8] Smith, *The Divine Goodness.*

and Mary Dwight, who was a daughter of Jonathan Edwards.[9] Dwight was educated at Yale College, beginning when he was thirteen. He showed great talent in art and music but devoted himself to an arduous regiment of study. He graduated at seventeen and at nineteen was chosen tutor. He became part of a group known as the "Connecticut Wits." In 1772, at twenty years of age, he received a master of arts degree and delivered a commencement address entitled "A Dissertation on the History, Eloquence and Poetry of the Bible." A true polymath, Dwight also pressed himself in writing poetry and mastering the "higher branches of Mathematics." The unreasonable demands he made on himself for study, his lack of exercise, a mild bout with smallpox, and his contrived diet led to severe physical difficulties. At age twenty-three, he developed an eye problem that reduced his reading capacity to about fifteen minutes in a twenty-four-hour period. In March of 1777, he married Mary Woolsey, with whom he had eight sons.

In October 1777, he became a military chaplain in the Revolutionary army to General Parson's brigade. He produced some of his best poetic work during this time (including *The Conquest of Canaan*) and wrote several songs for the soldiers that were popular and inspiring and kindled enthusiasm for the "cause of freedom," one of which was entitled "Columbia." His biographer said, "The troops who composed the brigade were principally, Connecticut farmers; men who had been soberly educated, and who were willing to listen to the truths of the Gospel, even in a camp. On the Sabbath, they heard him with profound attention. During the

---

[9]   Timothy Dwight, *Theology: Explained and Defended in a Series of Sermons*, (New Haven: S. Converse, 1825), 1:3. The four volumes contain 178 sermons of Dwight arranged in systematic form. They begin with "The Existence of God" and end with nine sermons on "Death," "The Immediate Consequences of Death," and "The Remoter Consequences of Death." The biographical data are taken mainly from Dwight's memoir in 1:1–61.

week, they beheld him exerting himself, as far as lay in his power, to instruct them in morals and religion."[10]

Late in 1777 his father died in Natchez, Mississippi, the news of which the family did not receive for twelve months. Dwight then left his position with the army and moved to Northampton to care for his mother and siblings. He worked the farm on weekdays and preached on Sabbaths. He also started a coed school at Northampton and immediately had to employ two assistants because of the number of pupils who came. After the Revolution he studied with his uncle, Jonathan Edwards Jr., interacting more directly with the developing New Divinity theology. In 1783, he became pastor of the Congregational church in Greenfield, Connecticut, where he continued his theological and poetic writing with *Theology, Explained and Defended* and the poems "Greenfield Hills" and "The Triumph of Infidelity." Having declined a unanimous call to serve as pastor of the Dutch church in Albany, in 1795 he accepted an invitation to become president of Yale College and remained until his death in 1817.

AWAKENING AT YALE

Virtually without hesitation, Dwight began an intellectual confrontation with the forces of infidelity. His sermons against the French Enlightenment sparked a series of small revivals on the campus. Though some have pointed to this as the first movement of the Second Great Awakening, others point to evidence that the campus revival was only one phase of a more general awakening among the churches that was occurring in Connecticut at this time. Students, easily impressed and by natural propensity inclined, had rejected what they deemed "the shackles of habit and superstition." So far had they gone that many had assumed the names of leading English and French infidels and were more familiarly known by those names than by their own. "Under

---

[10] Dwight, *Theology*, 1:13.

circumstances like these he entered upon the duties of his office as President of Yale College."[11]

Dwight took the instruction of the senior class upon himself. He involved them in recitations of various sorts, mainly concerning the questions of the day as they related to philosophical and theological issues. Because of the impact of infidelity, many of the students believed that Christianity was supported by authority and not by argument. It was therefore surprising to them when Dwight suggested a debate on the topic "Are the Scriptures of the Old and New Testament the Word of God?" Most of the students came forward on the negative side of the question. According to his biographer, in the introduction to Dwight's *Theology: Explained and Defended*, Dwight responded with nerve and aggressiveness.

> When they had finished the discussion, he first examined the ground they had taken; triumphantly refuted their arguments; proved to them that their statement of facts was mistaken or irrelevant; and to their astonishment, convinced them that their acquaintance with the subject was wholly superficial. After this, he entered into a direct defence of the divine origin of Christianity, in a strain of powerful argument and animated eloquence which nothing could resist. The effect upon the students was electrical. From that moment, Infidelity was not only without a strong hold, but without a lurking place. To espouse her cause was now as unpopular as before it had been to profess a belief in Christianity. Unable to endure the exposure of argument, she fled from the retreats of learning ashamed and disgraced.[12]

Dwight's combination of logic, rhetoric, and conviction drove his points home with power. After arguing for the existence of God through the relation of cause and effect, in which he challenged the views of David Hume, he issued his final defense

---

[11] Dwight, *Theology,* 1:20.

[12] Dwight, *Theology,* 1:23.

by reflecting on how speech and argument both require an *a priori* commitment to cause and effect. He asserted, "No absurdity can be greater than to argue with a man who denies this connection." Then he demonstrated this.

> He himself, *in speaking*, exhibits himself as the cause of all the words uttered by him, and the opinions communicated; and, in the *act of arguing*, admits you to be a similar cause. If his body be not a cause, and your eyes another, you cannot see him. If his voice, and your ear, be not causes, you cannot understand him. In a word, without admitting the connexion between cause and effect, you can never know that *he* is arguing with *you*, or *you* with *him*.[13]

Another sermon dealt with man's inability to obey the law of God. "This disinclination to obedience is still so obstinate and enduring, that it is never relinquished by man, except when under the renewing influence of the Spirit of God."[14] Then, after several Scripture proofs, Dwight reiterated, "Thus it is completely evident from the Scriptures, that the natural disinclination of man to obey the Divine Law is so obstinate, that it will not be overcome, or removed, by itself."[15] Having argued from revelation, Dwight turned to the universal testimony of experience. There he found a unanimous consciousness of personal failure in escaping guilt and danger or of turning to comply with the requirements of repentance and faith. Beginning with the stated experience of the apostles and continuing through the history of the church in each succeeding age, Dwight showed how all ascribed praise to the Creator for His agency in effectuating their moral and spiritual change and attributed such alteration of disposition "to the efficacious grace of God."[16] Were such consistent testimonies of experience the

---

13 Dwight, *Theology,* 1:78–79.

14 Dwight, *Theology,* 4:21.

15 Dwight, *Theology,* 4:22.

16 Dwight, *Theology,* 4:25.

products of delusion or actually in service of a falsehood? Such a conclusion drawn from the universal experience of those who testify to the truly saving mercy of God could not be wrong.

Like his grandfather before him, however, Dwight insisted that such absolute dependence did not arise from any natural incapability to understand and obey the requirements of the gospel. The "cannot" is a "will not." "Every one who is willing, has the full permission of Christ to come to him, and partake of his blessings. Indisposition to come to Christ is, therefore, the true and the only difficulty which lies in or way."[17]

Three remarks show the practical implications of how the sinner is to be confronted for this moral indisposition. One, our disobedience is our own fault; two, our "inability to obey the Divine Law does in no case lessen our guilt"; three, it is appropriate and urgent to direct "sinners to immediate repentance."[18] Later in the century, Charles Finney would adopt with full energy and conviction that final remark but reject the concept of invincible moral indisposition, telling the sinner not only that he must change his heart, but that he can.

Dwight is generally classified as one of the New Divinity, or New England, Theologians, who took particular ideas of Jonathan Edwards and molded them in a systematic way. Dwight shared the New Divinity theology of original sin and disinterested benevolence, but he was more suspicious of the powers of "rational consistency" in theological construction and more intent on the priority of special revelation than his contemporary New Divinity men were. All of them were strongly Trinitarian and opponents of Unitarianism. They accepted the covenant of redemption as eternal and set forth Christ as Prophet, Priest, and King. Dwight argued for the divinity of Christ from the names given to Him, from the attributes and actions ascribed to Him, from His relationship to the Father and the Spirit, and from the worship that was required

---

[17] Dwight, *Theology,* 4:25.

[18] Dwight, *Theology,* 4:25–26.

and rendered to Him. That Christ is God in the flesh is the only ground of His being the light of the world, the Savior of the world, and the propitiation for sin. Dwight defined propitiation as Christ having done something for the sinner so that the sinner may be forgiven and restored. If this was not done, the sinner "must be punished according to the sentence of the Law, by which he is condemned."[19] Everything to be accomplished in the redemption of sinners can only be completed by one of infinite worth and moral excellence. No mere man can perform the work needed for the salvation of a host of sinners. If Christ is not God, He has not done the work that Scripture declares He has done.

Given this strong argument for the necessity of Christ's deity, it seems incongruous that Dwight viewed Christ's propitiatory death in terms of a moral government theory of atonement. God's government manifests itself in both rules and motives. It consists of laws, rewards, and punishments. If these are not enforced, or are seen to be merely arbitrary and unrelated to true righteousness, they become weak and inefficacious. A violated law unvindicated loses its authority. A moral governor absent condign punishment will cease to be regarded with veneration. Motives for obedience, in terms of both intrinsic righteousness and punishment, are essential for the dignity of one who is a moral governor. Thus, motives to obedience must be continued in the view of the subjects in full force. An atonement for sin that is a complete atonement must leave these motives unimpaired. Any scheme of forgiveness, therefore, must maintain the inviolable character of its moral requirements and leave it no less venerable than before the pronouncement of forgiveness. "To pardon sinners, therefore, without a propitiation, would have been inconsistent with divine justice, and of course impossible."[20]

Mere repentance is not enough. If death was threatened but left unexecuted upon the exhibition of sorrow for sin, the execution

---

[19] Dwight, *Theology,* 1:567.

[20] Dwight, *Theology,* 2:206.

of the threat is removed and its true seriousness deflated. A means must be introduced by which the eternal and immutable rule of the law of God is established. "If Christ made an Atonement for the sins of mankind; all the magnificent expressions concerning his mission, and character; the declarations, that he is the only Saviour of mankind; and that there is Salvation in no other; are easily understood; if not, I am unable to see how they can be explained."[21]

An atonement must accomplish four things, according to Dwight in the development of his theory. First, it must make sufficient amends for fault so that both the law and government of God are maintained in honor. Second, forgiveness must come in a way that motives to obedience are not diminished. Third, the character of God, when pardoning sinners, "must appear perfectly consistent with itself and exactly expressed by the Law." Fourth, "God must be seen to be no less opposed to sin, and no less delighted with holiness, that when the law was formed."[22]

None can doubt that such an atonement could only be accomplished by Christ and that He has provided just such an avenue for forgiveness through the ransom He gave in His propitiatory death. Equally necessary and demonstrably present in this work of Christ is active obedience as "essentially concerned in his atonement."[23] An examination of scriptural assertions on this point led Dwight to affirm that "Christ stood in the place of mankind, bore their sins, and healed them by the stripes which he suffered; that our iniquities were laid on him, that he washed our sins away, became a curse for us, was wounded for our transgressions, made reconciliation for iniquity, and was cut off, not for himself, but for mankind."[24]

---

[21] Dwight, *Theology,* 2:204.

[22] Dwight, *Theology,* 2:206.

[23] Dwight, *Theology,* 2:215

[24] Dwight, *Theology,* 2:209.

Concerning the extent of the atonement, Dwight clearly rejected the idea of any limitation of its potential efficacy. Christ died in such a way that all mankind are equally concerned in it and all may partake of forgiveness through the provision He made. It was in the most pure way "sufficient in its extent to open the door for the pardon of all human sinners."[25] The "infinite dignity and excellence of the Redeemer rendered" His atonement "infinitely meritorious." He further reasoned that if Jesus "has not made a sufficient Atonement for others beside the Elect; then his Salvation is not offered to them at all; and they are not guilty for not receiving it." In addition, if it be not for all people, then the gospel is not addressed to all people. If a minister is to preach the duty of faith for all, but Christ has not died for all, then some have no object for their faith, and cannot obey the command to believe. The atonement makes the way even and open to all; "he who does not accept" the invitations of proffers of salvation through Christ "ought to remember, that nothing stands in his way, but his own impenitence and unbelief."[26]

Dwight was able to make propitiation and universality work in his view of the atonement through his understanding of imputation—or rather his rejection of it. For Dwight, justification included forgiveness, freedom from future punishment, and the surety of heaven. He excluded the imputation of Christ's righteousness. It is difficult to see exactly what Dwight was driving at when he insistently argued for the necessity of substitutionary atonement, but not in the form of a satisfaction and payment of debt. Dwight wrote:

> The supposition, incautiously admitted by some divines, that Christ satisfied the demands of the law by his active and passive obedience, in the same manner as the payment of a debt satisfies the demands of a creditor, has, if I mistake not, been heretofore proved

---

[25] Dwight, *Theology*, 2:217.
[26] Dwight, *Theology*, 2:217–218.

to be unfounded in the Scriptures. We owed God our obedience, and not our property; and obedience in its own nature is due from the subject himself, and can never be rendered by another. In refusing to render it, we are criminal; and for this criminality merit punishment. The guilt, thus incurred, is inherent in the criminal himself, and cannot in the nature of things be transferred to another. All that, in this case, can be done by a substitute, of whatever character, is to render it not improper for the Lawgiver to pardon the transgressor. No substitute can, by any possible effort, make him cease to be guilty, or to deserve punishment. . . . This it is evident, that the sinner, when he comes before God, comes in the character of a sinner only; and must, if strict justice be done, be therefore condemned. If he escape condemnation, then he can derive these blessings from mercy only, and in no degree from justice. In other words, every blessing which he receives, is a free gift.

Dwight emphasized the pure mercy of God as the foundation of justification, resisting all works righteousness but also leaving no place for the imputation of the righteousness of Christ.

The Impact of Dwight's Theology

Dwight's example of preaching and intellectual interaction with the students became a model in many cases. Basil Manly Sr. implemented this way of intellectual and apologetic interaction at the University of Alabama. Yale led the Eastern colleges in sending forth spiritually awakened graduates to found and preside over Christian colleges in the American South and West, becoming known as the "mother of colleges." From 1800 to 1860, the number of colleges in America increased from twenty to 180, and the college population grew four times faster than the general population.

As Harvard adopted Unitarianism, Yale and Princeton became promoters of revival and expansionist Christianity. Yale Divinity

School began as a department of theology in 1822. Nathan W. Taylor, the first professor at the divinity school, was a potent force in shaping the "New Haven Theology," which gave theological justification to the revivalism of Finney.

An Awakening in the Churches

The *Connecticut Evangelical Magazine* began publishing in 1800. Its purpose was to carry reports of revivals that had been occurring in the churches since 1797. It also included reports of missionary endeavors, historical articles, theological articles, biblical exegesis, polemical discussions, and sobering reminders of the preciousness of time in light of the coming of eternity. As the year 1804 began, the magazine declared, "Another year is gone. Yes, irrevocably gone. Millions are gone with it to the grave, and to judgment. All the living, solemn thought! have been wafted one year nearer to eternity and their final doom." The author then entered a discussion of the necessity of redeeming the time: "Redeeming time, implies recovering it from impenitence, unbelief, ungodliness and a state of sin." The issue of time was peculiarly pressing on those in the United States—for the great blessings endemic to the land itself and even more for the blessings of freedom, industry, and distance from the conflicts of Europe. Particularly important in redeeming the time was the great opportunity afforded by the state of revival. "To some churches in the United States," the writer said, "the last year has been a year of refreshing. The happy effects of the late revivals in others are abundantly manifest, in the increase of their numbers, zeal, spiritual life, peace, order and beauty." Several reports from churches indicated the "they have not, for many years, been in a more flourishing condition."[27]

Testimonies of conversion in many different circumstances composed a large percentage of the magazine. We find pithy statements of converting power. "The vile invectives of Thomas

---

[27] *Connecticut Evangelical Magazine*, January 1804, 241–250.

Paine were believed and read, by the head of the family, to the utter exclusion of God's revealed word. But, in the course of the preceding season, Jehovah was so gracious as to send his Spirit, which banished infidelity from their dwelling, and hopefully renewed the hearts of both the parents, as well as their child."[28]

The report of a sacramental meeting in a Presbyterian church showed the impression of divine power often present in such assemblies. Thomas Robbins, a visiting missionary from Connecticut, called it "the most solemn scene I ever witnessed." After describing the event in terms of "the solemnity, the impression, the evidence of the divine presence, were such as not to be told," he added, "But you will remember that the present is not an ordinary but a very extraordinary time." He then turned to make observations about the "extraordinary work of divine grace in these western countries." He reported on the nature of the work that he observed in Pennsylvania. He believed that in many respects it resembled "the great revival of religion in New England in 1740, '41, '42." Though the sparser population meant that not as many subjects of revival could be reported as in Connecticut, "I trust there is a good number delivered from the reign of sin, who will adore the riches of sovereign grace forever." These movements received the "same ridicule and reproach" as the work of "sixty years ago," though not with the same "external violence." The preaching was much the same as formerly, "Calvinistic in sentiment, serious, earnest and pathetic." Also, the "general attention and commotion which is produced among all classes of people" matched that of the former New England awakening.[29]

The writer then described scenes of pressing physical responses to the presentation of divine truth and the presence of the convicting power of the Spirit. Some people would fall, others would sit, some needed to be held. "But it must be remembered, that the degrees of bodily affection are indefinitely various. From

---

[28] *Connecticut Evangelical Magazine*, January 1804, 272.

[29] *Connecticut Evangelical Magazine*, February 1804, 314–319.

the least nervous agitation, every grade to the most violent you can conceive; or to a death-like weakness and inaction." After giving more details of these physical phenomena and the possible skeptical responses, Robbins wrote, "Persons of all ages are subjects of this works. Old middle-aged, youth and children. Some children quite young. So are all characters. Infidels, philosophers, physicians, many remarkable instances, lifeless professors, the stupid, the thoughtless and the gay. But as in other revivals, young persons and those who have had religious education, constitute the greater proportion." In giving some detailed analysis of this puzzling response, the writer surmised that the force of truth as it related to a variety of circumstances was the provoking cause.

> Christians, when they are led to a feeling sense of the goodness and mercy of God, of his long suffering and patience, of their extreme ingratitude, their great abuse of privileges, the danger of their being deceived in their hope, the solemn account which they must render to an omniscient Judge, and their just exposure to eternal death, they find themselves unable to sustain the pressure of truth, but must yield to its weight.[30]

On other occasions the writer observed manifestations of an inability to speak, a temporary detachment from consciousness of their surroundings, and a "view of the glories of the divine character, the wonders of sovereign grace, the riches of the Savior's love, and the glorious work of man's redemption." These vivid impressions of revealed redemptive truth "opened to them with such clearness, that they can no more bear it than Moses could a sight of God's glory." Observation of similar phenomena among hardened sinners evoked this description and judgment. "Sometimes a consideration of the danger of sinners, their infinite hardness and stupidity, and the certainty of their being brought into judgment, is more than their natures can bear." When they fall, they do not

---

[30] *Connecticut Evangelical Magazine*, February 1804, 314–319.

lose their sense but are more alert and receptive of instruction than formerly. Their minds are uncommonly riveted on the "interests of eternity." If they speak, it is in broken sentences and words, "begging for mercy, deprecating wrath, groaning under sin, calling upon perishing sinners, or giving glory to God." Though this observation of weeks of such events was radically distinct from his observations of awakening in Connecticut, Robbins concluded, "I firmly believe this to be a conspicuous and glorious work of divine grace; and that thousands of immortal souls, the subjects of it will adore the riches of divine mercy, thro' eternity. May the Lord of all grace carry on his work gloriously, to the honor of his great name and the enlargement of Zion!"[31]

In his account of the revival that occurred in New England from the mid-1790s through 1815, Bennet Tyler painted a picture of a different type of response. Seeking to avoid the criticism of the earlier Awakening, Tyler said that the ministers were "aware of the fanaticism and delusion which succeeded the 'Great Awakening' in the days of Whitefield and Edwards, and of their disastrous influence upon the churches." They took note of "the disorders which prevailed in those days and the human devices resorted to by misguided zealots which excited the disgust of intelligent, unsanctified men, and strengthened their prejudices against all experimental religion." These kinds of exaggerations they avoided and "adopted no measures, suited only to produce excitement; for they believed that all religious excitement is injurious, which is not the result of clear apprehensions of Divine truth." They used only biblically ordained means such as "the plain and earnest preaching of the gospel, and the faithful discharge of all the duties of the pastoral office."[32]

---

[31] *Connecticut Evangelical Magazine*, February 1804, 314–319.

[32] Bennet Tyler, *New England Revivals as they existed at the Close of the Eighteenth, and the Beginning of te Nineteenth Centuries* (Wheaton: Richard Owen Roberts Publishers, 1980; first published in 1846), vii–ix.

Tyler emphasized that their content of preaching was the "doctrines of grace" and that they had no fears that the preaching of these doctrines would hinder the progress of revival." In fact, the opposite was true. Though sinners have an insuperable disaffection for God, His holiness, His law, His glory, and His requirements of repentance and faith, nevertheless they "set before them their obligation to obey every Divine command—demolished all their vain excuses, and pressed upon them with great plainness, the duty of immediate repentance." This manner of proceeding brought great conviction and sober reflection on the true evidences of evangelical repentance and saving faith. Then "they were established in the faith and not easily carried about by every wind of doctrine."[33]

Samuel Hopkins (1721–1803) was one of the "New Divinity" theologians, influenced in part by Jonathan Edwards, whose ethical idea of disinterested benevolence led them to assert that true faith began with a willingness to be damned to the glory of God.[34] In the thirty-five accounts of revival from 1797–1814, hundreds of testimonies were presented. One in Durham, Connecticut, was representative of the doctrine and the demeanor of those who professed conversion. "Here new feelings occupied my breast. I thought I felt wholly resigned to the will of God, and that I could praise him, even were he to send men to hell." That sentiment reflected the Hopkinsian test of true affections, a willingness to be damned to the glory of God. The testimony continued, "Since that evening, my feelings have been very different from what they ever were before. Every thing appears new. My Bible is quite a new book, and the doctrines of grace I cordially approve." The testifier stated with confidence that "it was on the evening above mentioned, if ever, that God made me willing to accept salvation, and embrace the Saviour on the terms of the gospel." He then

---

[33] Tyler, *New England Revivals*, ix–x.

[34] See Joseph A. Conforti, *Samuel Hopkins and the New Divinity Movement* (Grand Rapids: Christian University Press/Eerdmans, 1981), 7–8.

gave an earnest statement of gratitude to the "boundless mercy and free grace of God, that he has been pleased to bring my soul out of the horrible pit and miry clay, and cause it to rest as I humbly hope, on the rock Christ Jesus."[35] At the climax of another testimony, we read, "I endeavored to pursue my secular business, but it was with great indifference, for my soul was full of anguish, till by sovereign grace it was brought home to God."[36] Similarly a testimony indicated great rigors of mind in doubt and resistance and an attempt "to dwell no longer on so gloomy a subject." His conscience, however, would not allow so easily a dismissal nor let him rest while the "fear of atheism aggravatedly oppressed me." At that point, "it pleased the Most High, in a sovereign manner graciously to enable me, as I hope, to stay my soul on Jesus Christ." He was enabled to say, "Though he slay me, yet will I trust in him."[37] Another testimony indicated the strong principle of self-distrust in the matter of accurate perception of spiritual status. After describing a torturous, reclusive, and suicidal period of conviction, a testimony speaks of deliverance from despair and a particular distress endured with "hope that the enmity of my heart was subdued." He did not fix on a particular time this change occurred and expressed little confidence "respecting myself." "I know," he continued, "the heart is deceitful above all things, and desperately wicked." In spite of that, "I entertain a hope, grounded upon the submission and peace which, if I am not deceived, I sometimes find in contemplating the character of God, and the Saviour, and the truths and precious promises of his Word, and in a desire to be conformed to his holy will."[38]

Following a report of revival and conversions over a three-year period, Josiah Andrews of Killingsworth, Connecticut, summarized his careful observation:

---

[35] Tyler, *New England Revivals*, 302.
[36] Tyler, *New England Revivals*, 296.
[37] Tyler, *New England Revivals*, 288.
[38] Tyler, *New England Revivals*, 178.

The persons mentioned in this narrative have all of them been hopefully in the school of Christ more than three years, and some of them much longer; which must have been some trial of their faith, and affords a comfortable hope that the things which they have experienced are not the result of a heated imagination, or the wild effusions of a disordered brain, but the genuine effects of God's Holy Spirit. There has as yet been no instance of any one professing godliness that has turned back, or dishonored his professions. But God only knoweth what may be in the future; and to us it belongeth to bow with reverence before him, giving thanks at the remembrance of his holiness.[39]

In 1819, Joshua Bradley published an account of revivals that had occurred for the two previous years around the United States. He mentioned all evangelical denominations with brief narratives from forty-seven ministers. In these reports, sometimes only by the mention of a name, 416 churches and associations were reported as having observable and extraordinary movements of the Spirit. A summary of the movement in Troy, New York, is typical of a large majority of these narratives:

By this time, almost every part of the city became more or less the theatre of illustrious displays of divine power and grace. Publick assemblies on the Lord's Day were crowded: private meetings, which were now held every evening in the week, were solemn, and silent as the grave. The hearts of their ministers were fired. The prayers of the churches were fervent; and the publick mind seemed awed down before the majesty of divine grace, which laid the proudest sinner low. Infidelity was abashed—stood astonished—and shut her mouth. Scarcely a whisper was heard against a work in which the divine hand was so manifest. It was the almighty Redeemer riding forth

---

[39] Tyler, *New England Revivals*, 299–300.

in the midst of them in the triumphant chariot of his gospel, conquering and to conquer.

As in all the works of God, and in all revivals of religion, there is a great variety; so there was here in the mode of divine operation. Convictions, generally, were pungent and short; and transitions from guilt and horror, often sudden and rapturous. While some were aroused by the terrours of the law, others were allured by the grace of the gospel; while one was called with a still small voice, another trembled under the thunder of Jehovah.[40]

The Philadelphia Association reported a great movement of the Spirit of God in Baptist churches in 1812: "Communications were made by our brother Rogers relative to a glorious work of the Lord that has lately taken place in Bristol in the state of Rhode Island, and which has also been felt in Providence, Harwich and other towns in the New England states." Rogers also communicated the events that led to "the addition of 1000 persons and upwards within a short period to the Green River Association, Kentucky; and of more than 3000 to the churches in Virginia, in Essex and King William's county, in the course of about 18 months." Beyond that, new associations were being formed in New England, Nova Scotia, the Tennessee country, and in almost "every part of America." Henry Holcombe reported to the association about "revivals he had lately heard of, in the Southern states." William Staughton "supplied us with some acceptable communications on the state and prosperity of the churches in England." Rejoicing in the enlargement of the Mediator's kingdom, the Association offered their heartfelt and vocal praises "to his adorable name."[41]

In 1814 they again heard a "heart-animating narration" of the "rise and flourishing condition of a blessed revival of religion in

---

[40] Joshua Bradley, *Accounts of Religious Revivals in Many parts of the United States from 1815–1818* (Wheaton: Richard Owen Roberts, Publishers, 1980), 174–175.

[41] *Minutes of the Philadelphia Baptist Association, 1812.*

Wilmington, in Delaware." Others "cheered our bosoms with an account of an astonishing work of God in Coventry and Warwick, Rhode Island, particularly in our own denomination." Many, if not most, of those affected were young persons in whom "the spirit of prayer and the powers of holy exhortation have delighted and surprised great numbers of pious spectators." The Association expressed gratitude for such evidence of the work of God and "offered up a song of praise."[42]

The news of revival brought a letter of correspondence from the Philadelphia Association to other associations celebrating this manifestation of grace and power. They expressed joy in the reports "relative to the prosperity of a Redeemer's kingdom, and feel an aspiring sense of gratitude to the great Head of the church for those indications of supreme love continued towards his Zion, amid the reiterated confusions of sin so lamentably perpetuated in the world." Worldly powers contend for worldly treasures, while "the Sovereign of the universe is giving incontestable evidence that his kingdom shall stand until all the purchase of a Redeemer's blood converted by his grace shall rally round the standard of the cross." Evidence of this was seen when

> the good hand of God is most marvelously displayed in converting some of his most virulent enemies of every age and character, corresponding with that gracious prophecy of our God, that the wolf shall lie down with the lamb, the leopard with the kid, the young calf, the fatling and the lion together, and nothing shall hurt or destroy in all his holy mountain because the knowledge of his salvation shall cover the earth as waters cover the sea.[43]

These reports—coming from sober-minded, experienced, observant witnesses to powerful changes in a variety of people in

---

42 *Minutes of the Philadelphia Baptist Association, 1814.*
43 *Minutes of the Philadelphia Baptist Association, 1814.*

their views of sin, the gospel, the world, the cross, the work of the Holy Spirit, and the purpose of God—are too consistent to be either an invention or the product of minds prone to hallucination or exaggeration. An extensive awakening of minds and hearts to gospel truth was underway in the new nation.

REVIVAL ON THE WESTERN FRONTIER

A description of New Salem, Illinois, during the days when Abraham Lincoln when clerked at Offut's store on the Sangamon, included this unspiritual information: "Everybody came on Saturdays to trade, gossip, wrestle, raffle, pitch horseshoes, run races, get drunk, maul one another with the fists, and indulge generally in frontier happiness, as a relief from the week's monotonous drudgery on the raw and difficult farms."[44] This account gives a brief glance at the problems that a gospel preacher would confront on the frontier.

One difficulty that clearly created both civil and familial tension was the problem of drink. In 1804, a leader of the Cumberland Presbytery, Ephraim McLean, "came forward and confessed to the Presbytery that he had been guilty of intoxication, hoping to be restored upon his confession as he had voluntarily ceased from his public ministration since the crime was committed."[45] James McGready (1763–1817), in a sermon on "The Dangerous and Destructive Consequences Attending the Use of Spiritous liquors," wrote, "I would pray you, in the name of the Lord Jesus, to pause, to reflect, and consider the wounds, the reproaches and deadly stabs that the church of Christ has received just by the use of spiritous liquors." What a great blessing and obvious advantage it would be for the church and the progress of the gospel "if Christ's professed followers would just disarm the Devil of one of his heaviest weapons against the cause of God, and deprive

---

[44] Albert J. Beveridge, *Abraham Lincoln* (New York, 1929) 1:110, 497.

[45] William Warren Sweet, *Religion on the American Frontier* (Grand Rapids: Baker, 1975), 2:295.

him of one of his principal sources of temptation, by which he destroys the souls of men, and disgraces the religion of the blessed Jesus." This can be done by "refraining, and forever avoiding the use of ardent spirits." The simple fact is, that if a person never tastes or touches alcohol "in any place, in any company, or upon any occasion whatsoever, you will never be intoxicated." That temptation will never ensnare the person of such a resolution. He exhorted his hearers to "avoid going into taverns and still-houses, and tippling shops, as you would avoid the road to hell."

William Warren Sweet informs us that "the principal cause of discipline among the members of frontier Presbyterian churches was intoxication." Every cabin welcomed its guests by the offer of a swig from a bottle or jug. Refusal of this mark of hospitality was an "unpardonable incivility."[46]

A second issue that had to be confronted on the frontier was deism. Sweet characterized the post-revolutionary intellectual atmosphere in general this way:

> The general decadence in religion and morals was due to a combination of causes, among them being the influences flowing from the French Revolution and the general political, social and intellectual upheavals which attended it. In America also Deism of the Tom Paine type was widely accepted, especially by the rising generation, causing orthodox views of religion to lose their appeal.[47]

McGready's sermon on "The Bible, a Revelation from Heaven" was presented to counteract the misrepresentations of deism. He interacted with the deistical idea that "reason and the light of nature, unassisted by a divine revelation, are a sure guide to happiness." This is because these two sources of truth "teach us that there is a God—one true and Eternal God, a being of all

---

[46] Sweet, *Religion on the American Frontier*, 2:65.

[47] Sweet, *Religion on the American Frontier*, 2:54

possible goodness and perfection." McGready agreed that reason and nature "teach us that there must be a god or First Cause of all things," but "whether there be one or twenty Gods, reason cannot tell." The deist must smuggle his idea of one God as the source of all things from the Bible. In fact, he "is indebted to the Bible for this and every genuine truth, which his system contains."[48]

A third difficulty in the work of those who sought to bring the gospel to the frontier was the distance between houses and settlements. Again, we look at James McGready. He was born in Pennsylvania a Presbyterian of Scotch-Irish parentage. He studied theology under John McMillan and was licensed to preach by the Redstone Presbytery in 1788. On his way to North Carolina to preach, he stopped for a while at Hampden-Sydney College, which was experiencing a great revival. He became convinced of the necessity of evangelical preaching. His preaching in North Carolina led to a sweeping religious awakening in which he was accused of "running people distracted." He painted horrifying, and true, word pictures of the final and then eternal perceptions of the lost person who has had gospel advantages. "The remembrance of misimproved sermons and sacramental occasions flashed like streams of forked lightning through his tortured soul." As the lost soul descended deeper and deeper into hell, even as "Indians, Pagans, and Mahometans stood amazed," he was confronted with the knowledge that "he had slighted the mercy and blood of the Son of God." Dragged further down by a company of devils "sinking into the liquid, boiling waves of hell," his awareness of rejected opportunities "like a never-dying worm stings him and forever gnaws his soul; and the slighted blood of the Son of God communicates ten thousand hells in one." Further torment came when he caught a view of "that heaven he has lost."[49]

---

[48] James McGready, *The Posthumous Works of the Reverend and Pious James McGready* (Nashville: Printed and Published at J. Smith's Steam Press, 1837), 471.

[49] Jerald C. Brauer, *Protestantism in America*, (Philadelphia: The Westminster Press, 1965), 107.

Among McGready's converts were ten or twelve men who went into the ministry, including Barton W. Stone. McGready soon settled into a pastorate in Orange County. Because of his fierce denunciation of sin, the congregation in North Carolina was divided into strong supporters of McGready and violent opposers. His pulpit was torn out of his church and burned, while a threatening letter was written to him in blood.

McGready decided to move west in 1796, where he pastored three Presbyterian churches in Logan County, Kentucky. As he preached at Red River, Gasper River, and Muddy River, religious interest peaked from 1797 to 1799. Many conversions at the time of the taking of the sacrament were recorded. These revivals he described as "a few scattering drops before a mighty rain" compared with the "overwhelming floods of salvation" that "poured out like a mighty river" in the following year.[50]

He sent out notices of a communion service to be held in the Gasper River church. Pioneers came from as far as a hundred miles away and stayed for days, expecting to see a work of God. This was probably the first camp meeting in American history. Contemporary reports gave a picture of excited animation.

> The woods and paths seemed alive with people and the number reported as attending is almost incredible. The laborer quitted his task; Age snatched his crutch; youth forgot his pastime; the plow was left in the furrow; the deer enjoyed a respite upon the mountains; business of all kinds was suspended; dwelling houses were deserted; whole neighborhoods were emptied; bold hunters and sober matrons, young women and maidens, and little children, flocked to the common center of attraction; every difficulty was surmounted, every risk ventured, to be present at the camp-meeting.[51]

---

[50] Sweet, *Religion on the American Frontier: The Presbyterians*, 2:85.

[51] Robert Davidson, *History of the Presbyterian Church in the State of Kentucky* (New York: Robert Carter, 1847) 136–137.

The camp meeting generated much opposition from within Presbyterianism, particularly from the Old School Calvinists who became stigmatized as the *anti-revival* men. McGready responded with *Vindication of the Exercises in the Revival of 1800*, based on Matthew 11:4–6. In this work, he gave a brief statement on the "present work of God: e.g. At muddy River, on the first Sabbath in September." That was a service in which the sacrament of the Lord's Supper was administered. He wrote that "divine power seemed to attend the preaching of the word, and a general solemnity was visible. About this period, the work spread through all the congregations. Deep concern appeared in almost every company, and every family. A great number progessed to experience a sweet sense of pardoned sin."[52] He recorded the number that "professed to obtain religion at each service. At Gaspar, 45 persons, at Muddy River, 50, at the Ridge, 45, and at Shiloh, 70."

He not only shared the number of professions, but the effects, "which prove it to be a work of divine power." Professions arose from "a deep rational and scriptural conviction." Persons near the end of themselves in despair, lying on the very brink of destruction, were "delivered by a view of the glory, sufficiency, and willingness of Christ to save." They were possessed of a "loving benevolent disposition." At the moment of their own transformation from the despair of the certainty of a deserved hell, and as they discovered "the glory of the Redeemer, and feel his love shed abroad in their souls, their hearts bleed with pity for poor sinners." Beyond the settledness of mind upon such release from anticipated doom, the convert showed a clear "knowledge of Christ and divine things, of which the person, before, was ignorant." The moral change was also remarkable. "To see him who frolicked and danced, become the humble, praying christian; to see the drunkard, the swearer, and the gambler, leaping and praising God and telling what the Lord has done for their souls; to see the profane scoffer at God and religion, praying in secret"—all these things taken together,

---

[52] McGready, *The Posthumous Works*, 471.

do they not portray spiritually "the blind receiving their sight, the deaf hearing, the lame walking, the cleansing of the lepers, and the raising the dead to life"?[53]

When detractors claimed the strange events of these camp meetings as indicative of their falsity, McGready borrowed from the analysis that Edwards had given in *The Distinguishing Marks of a Work of the Spirit of God.* When observers reported falling down, boisterous noise and confusion, deep distress about sinners in their dreadful state, leaping and skipping about, strange agitations of body, smiling and laughing, conduct unbecoming the exercises of religion, McGready pointed to the positive aspects of these experiences and the spiritual change present in those who professed conversion. He did not seek to defend every idiosyncrasy of personal response and joined in criticizing some as manifesting carnal exuberance. Overall, however, he defended the services and the professed conversions as genuine manifestations of a work of the Spirit of God.

The activities of the revival leaders eventually led to the excision of the Cumberland Presbytery from the Presbyterian Synod of Kentucky. There were four issues: their use of revivals, laxness on ministerial education, lack of precision and confessional adherence in doctrine, and irregularities with the requirements of the constitution. According to the information gathered by those who brought charges, in October 1805 the Cumberland Presbytery had licensed "about 27 persons to preach and exhort and but few of them, according to the information we had, believe the doctrines of our confession." Permitting such irregularity was calculated to "diffuse enthusiasm and error through the world."[54]

Peter Cartwright (1785–1872) was a Methodist frontier preacher. According to his testimony, he lived a wicked life loving horse racing, dancing, card playing, and swearing. He received religious instruction from his mother that led to a camp meeting

---

[53] McGready, *The Posthumous Works,* 473

[54] Sweet, *Religion on the American Frontier,* 2:365–369

conversion in 1801. He described the Cane Ridge Camp Meeting this way:

> The mighty power of God was displayed in a very extraordinary manner; many were moved to tears, and bitter and loud crying for mercy. The meeting was protracted for weeks. Ministers of almost all denominations flocked in from far and near. The meeting was kept up by night and day. Thousands heard of the mighty work, and came on foot, on horseback, in carriages and wagons. It was supposed that there were in attendance at times during the meeting from twelve to twenty-five thousand people. Hundreds fell prostrate under the mighty power of God, as men slain in battle. Stands were erected in the woods from which preachers of different Churches proclaimed repentance toward God and faith in our Lord.[55]

Soon after the Cane Ridge meeting, Cartwright attended a meeting planned by McGready. There he reported a breakthrough of converting power after weeks of deep conviction. "To this meeting I repaired, a guilty, wretched sinner. On the Saturday evening of said meeting, I went, with weeping multitudes, and bowed before the stand, and earnestly prayed for mercy." As he struggled solemnly in soul, he had a deep impression "as though a voice said to me, 'Thy sins are all forgiven thee.' Divine light flashed all round me, unspeakable joy sprung up in my soul." He rose to his feet and opened his eyes, and "it really seemed as if I was in heaven; the trees, the leaves on them, and everything seemed, and I really thought were, praising God." His mother who had taught him, who had prayed and advised during his turmoil of spiritual conviction, "raised the shout, my Christian friends crowded around me and joined me in praising God." Since that time, though not always faithful, he "never, for one moment,

---

[55] Peter Cartwright, *Autobiography,* Northern Illinois Digital Library, https://digital.lib.niu.edu/islandora/object/niu-lincoln%3A37050, 30.

doubted that the Lord did, then and there, forgive my sins and give me religion."[56]

Cartwright's experience was so profound that he was licensed as an exhorter in the Methodist Episcopal Church in spring 1802 by the Red River circuit of the Western conference. He entered Browns Academy in Lewiston County in the fall of 1802. He was persecuted by both the rowdy students and by the teacher . Eventually he could no longer endure it and left, "regretting that I was thereby deprived of the privilege of finishing my education."[57]

In October 1803, at just over eighteen years of age, Cartwright was assigned a circuit in Logan County. At his first preaching opportunity he prayed for the conversion of one soul "as evidence that I was called to this work." He preached on Isaiah 26:4 and an unbeliever was present. "The word reached his heart by the eternal Spirit. He was powerfully convicted, and, as I believe, soundly converted that night."[58] This is just one example of the intuitive reliance on divine sovereignty that peppers Cartwright's recollections of ministry.

The circuit was very large, reaching from the north of Green River to the Cumberland River, and into Tennessee. It was a vast field with a large number of talented Baptist preachers. "In the four weeks that it took us to go around the circuit, we had but two days rest, and often we preached every day and every night." He was only in his nineteenth year, beardless, and still cutting teeth. He was called "the boy preacher," and that novelty caused many come to hear him. "A revival broke out in many neighborhoods, and scores of souls were converted to God and joined the Methodist Episcopal church; but there was also considerable persecution."[59] From his experience at many of these camp meetings, Cartwright summarized,

---

[56] Cartwright, *Autobiography*, 37–38.

[57] Cartwright, *Autobiography*, 61–62.

[58] Cartwright, *Autobiography*, 63.

[59] Cartwright, *Autobiography*, 64.

I have known these camp-meetings to last three or four weeks, and great good resulted from them. I have seen more than a hundred sinners fall like dead men under one powerful sermon, and I have seen and heard more than five hundred Christians all shouting aloud the high praises of God at once; and I will venture to assert that many happy thousands were awakened and converted to God at these camp-meetings.[60]

This exuberance was perplexing and opposed by "some of the old dry professors," while "some of the old starched Presbyterian preachers preached against these exercises." In spite of doubt and ministerial opposition, "still the work went on and spread almost in every direction, gathering additional force, until our country seemed all coming home to God."[61]

In reflecting on these difficult days of the early circuit riding, Cartwright looked at the "insurmountable disadvantages and difficulties that the early pioneer Methodist preachers labored under in spreading the Gospel in these Western wilds in the great valley of the Mississippi." He contrasted "the disabilities which surrounded them on every hand, with the glorious human advantages that are enjoyed by their present successors." Looking at the relation between advantages and results, he observed with elements of lamentation that "it is confoundingly miraculous to me that our modern preachers cannot preach better, and do more good than they do." Would they condescend to endure the life of the itinerant, as they had to "camp out, without fire or food for man or beast"? They had no access to the learned books of the academy but, Cartwright gloried, only "our pocket Bible, Hymn Book, and Discipline constituted our library. It is true."[62]

---

[60] Cartwright, *Autobiography*, 45–46.

[61] Cartwright, *Autobiography*, 46.

[62] Cartwright, *Autobiography*, 6.

Cartwright revealed no shyness in speaking of conflicts with ministers and members of other denominations, especially the Baptists. As a young preacher, he had to learn of the "proselyting tricks of those that held to exclusive immersion as the mode, and the only mode, of baptism."[63] He relished to narrate a story about the conversion of Betsy, a Baptist preacher's daughter, in one of his meetings. He also had severe judgments for Mormons, Shakers, Millerites, Presbyterians, Calvinists of all types, and the New Light movement. He expressed forcefully his doubts about the value of formal education for a preacher. When he was around those educated preachers in their attempts to preach to common people, they "forcibly reminded me of lettuce growing under the shade of a peach-tree, or like a gosling that had got the straddles by wading in the dew."[64] He assaulted infidelity and deism and opposed slavery and radical abolitionism.[65] He was fearless in his preaching and tireless in his labors.

Cartwright gave one of the most graphic presentations of the phenomenon of "the jerks" that we have from the contemporary literature. He observed that such movement "was overwhelming in its effects upon the bodies and minds of the people. No matter whether they were saints or sinners, they would be taken under a warm song or sermon, and seized with a convulsive jerking all over, which they could not by any possibility avoid, and the more they resisted the more they jerked." Usually, Cartwright observed, good earnest prayer and not striving against it would bring abatement. "I have seen," he testified, "more than five hundred persons jerking at one time in my large congregations. Most usually persons taken with the jerks, to obtain relief, as they said, would rise up and dance. Some would run, but could not get away. Some would resist; on such the jerks were generally very severe." When proud young gentlemen and finely dressed young ladies would "take the

---

[63] Cartwright, *Autobiography*, 65.

[64] Cartwright, *Autobiography*, 80.

[65] Cartwright, *Autobiography*, 415–430.

jerks," it would bring laughter to him. "The first jerk or so, you would see their fine bonnets, caps, and combs, fly; and so sudden would be the jerking of the head that their long loose hair would crack almost as loud as a wagoner's whip." Cartwright developed a definite view of this exercise as it related to God's purpose. "I always looked upon the jerks as a judgment sent from God, first, to bring sinners to repentance; and, secondly, to show professors that God could work with or without means, and that he could work over and above means, and do whatsoever seemeth him good, to the glory of his grace and the salvation of the world."[66] Even the great Methodist frontier revivalist could not shove aside God's sovereign prerogative in executing His purpose of salvation.

Barton Stone (1772–1844) spent his youth in the domestic turmoil endemic to the Revolutionary War. Upon victory and the return of the men of the army, he witnessed a precipitous decline in morals and escalation of vice. Concerning the returning soldiers, he lamented, "Their influence in demoralizing society

---

[66] Cartwright, *Autobiography*, 48–51. Barton Stone, another firsthand observer of this unusual action, gave this narrative: "The jerks cannot be so easily described. Sometimes the subject of the jerks would be affected in some one member of the body, and sometimes in the whole system. When the head alone was affected, it would be jerked backward and forward, or from side to side, so quickly that the features of the face could not be distinguished. When the whole system was affected, I have seen the person stand in one place, and jerk backward and forward in quick succession, their head nearly touching the floor behind and before. All classes, saints and sinners, the strong as well as the weak, were thus affected. I have inquired of those thus affected. They could not account for it; but some have told me that those were among the happiest seasons of their lives. I have seen some wicked persons thus affected, and all the time cursing the jerks, while they were thrown to the earth with violence. Though so awful to behold, I do not remember than any one of the thousands I have seen ever sustained an injury in body. This was as strange as the exercise itself." Barton W. Stone, *A Short History of the Life of Barton W. Stone (1847)* (St. Louis: The Bethany Press, 1954), Abilene Christian University, https://webfiles.acu.edu/departments/Library/HR/restmov_nov11/www.mun.ca/rels/restmov/texts/bstone/barton.html.

was very great. These vices soon became general, and almost honorable. Such are universally the effects of war, than which a greater evil cannot assail and afflict a nation."[67] Tory preachers left and the land was destitute of any gospel witness and vice escalated. Stone recalled that a few Baptist preachers came and preached to the people with impressive effects. "Multitudes attended their ministrations, and many were immersed. Immersion was so novel in those parts, that many from a distance were incited to come in order to see the ordinance administered."[68]

His first contact with education was under "a very tyrant of a teacher," from whom he could learn nothing due to fear. Stone remained with him but a few days, went to a teacher of a different temper, and received "the first rudiments of an English education, reading, writing, and arithmetic." He registered a strong protest against "tyrannical and ill-disposed teachers" as a curse to their neighborhoods and advised that teachers be "the most patient, self-possessed, and reasonable of men," yet with firmness to achieve legitimate authority.[69] His first contact with the Bible was in his school classroom; though he wanted other books to read, he affirmed the value of consistent Bible reading in school. "Here I wish to leave my testimony in favor of making the Bible a school book. By this means the young mind receives information and impressions, which are not erased through life." He viewed the failure to maintain this practice as "one leading cause" for the "present growth of infidelity and skepticism."[70]

Seeking to ignore religion and find significance through training to be a lawyer, Stone pursued a classical education in a private academy under the instruction of a Presbyterian minister, David Caldwell. He could not escape, however, the genuine piety that he observed in several classmates who had been greatly

---

[67] Stone, *A Short History,* 33.

[68] Stone, *A Short History,* 35.

[69] Stone, *A Short History,* 33.

[70] Stone, *A Short History,* 34.

changed by Christian conversion. One classmate asked Stone to go with him to hear a preacher. Stone consented, and his first contact with James McGready was before him. He described the experience in gripping emotion. McGready "rose and looked around on the assembly. His person was not prepossessing, nor his appearance interesting, except his remarkable gravity, and small piercing eyes." McGready's voice, however, was coarse and tremulous and sounded unearthly. His gestures were original and inimitable, "the perfect reverse of elegance." Nothing seemed present in his mind "but the salvation of souls." Stone could not remain a mere unattached observer. "Such earnestness—such zeal—such powerful persuasion, enforced by the joys of heaven and miseries of hell, I had never witnessed before. My mind was chained by him, and followed him closely in his rounds of heaven, earth and hell, with feelings indescribable." McGready concluded his overwhelming discourse of eternity in the balance by an appeal to the sinner "to flee the wrath to come without delay." Stone had never before in such a manner "felt the force of truth. Such was my excitement, that had I been standing, I should have probably sunk to the floor under the impression."[71] After more than a year of struggle, under spiritual repression concerning divine sovereignty in the time of granting salvation (like an "electric shock to renew the soul and bring it to salvation"), he was converted after hearing William Hodge preach on the text "God is love" (1 John 4:8). Eventually the barriers of sovereignty, as Stone perceived them, were removed, and he felt in his soul that "a poor sinner was as much authorized to believe in Jesus at first, as at last—that now was the accepted time, and day of salvation."[72] He finished his course of study at the academy but now was intent on gospel ministry.

Stone's first experience with theological education depressed him, particularly the study of the Dutch theologian Hermann

---

[71] Stone, *A Short History*, 38.

[72] Stone, *A Short History*, 41.

Witsius and his detailed statements of the orthodox doctrine of the Trinity, Stone moved away from pastoral aspirations and became a teacher, but he was driven by both conscience and affections to move once again toward Christian ministry. During the time of licensure, Stone preached often along the Western frontier, and in 1798 he consented to complete the process of ordination. Knowing that he would be required to consent to the Westminster Confession as an accurate expression of biblical doctrine, he renewed his study. "This was to me almost the beginning of sorrows," he confessed. "I stumbled at the doctrine of the Trinity as taught in the Confession; I labored to believe it, but could not conscientiously subscribe to it." In addition, those doctrines of divine sovereignty and prerogative, such as "election, reprobation, and predestination, as there taught," were alien to his understanding of salvation. He had learned how to divest those doctrines "of their hard, repulsive features, and admitted them as true, yet unfathomable mysteries." He simply had ignored these in his preaching to this point and confined himself to the "practical part of religion, and to subjects within my depth." This reexamination of the confession, however, convinced him that they could not be covered over quite so easily. "Indeed, I saw they were necessary to the system without any covering." On the day of ordination, therefore, he informed two of his questioners of his difficulty. They asked him to what degree he was willing to receive the confession. He replied, "As far as I saw it consistent with the word of God." They consented that this was sufficient. "I went into Presbytery, and when the question was proposed, 'Do you receive and adopt the Confession of Faith, as containing the system of doctrine taught in the Bible?' I answered aloud, so that the whole congregation might hear, 'I do, as far as I see it consistent with the word of God.' No objection being made, I was ordained."[73] On October 2, 1798, Stone was ordained to the Presbyterian ministry without consenting to the system of doctrine implied in that

---

[73] Stone, *A Short History,* 59–60.

ordination. He became pastor of two Presbyterian congregations at Concord and Cane Ridge in Bourbon County.

Stone continued his theological struggle with severe bouts of disgust, distrust, depression, and thoughts that he was on the verge of blasphemy. Finally, after severe mental agony, he rejected with clear conscience and a sense of absolute biblical warrant the entire system of historical Calvinism and summarized his thoughts succinctly:

> Calvinism is among the heaviest clogs on Christianity in the world. It is a dark mountain between heaven and earth, and is amongst the most discouraging hindrances to sinners from seeking the kingdom of God, and engenders bondage and gloominess to the saints. Its influence is felt throughout the Christian world, even where it is least suspected. Its first link is total depravity. Yet are there thousands of precious saints in this system.[74]

No longer was his theological hesitation a matter of seeking to circumvent his doubts; he had reached absolute certainty that Calvinism was an insult to the God of love who desired to save sinners. Indeed, he had concluded, it imposed a formidable barrier between heaven and earth.

He attended the camp meetings in Logan County directed by McGready and became convinced that they were the work of God. Viewed over a course of several days, Stone saw and heard persons falling down, "as men slain in battle, and continued for hours together in an apparently breathless and motionless state—sometimes for a few moments reviving, and exhibiting symptoms of life by a deep groan, or piercing shriek, or by a prayer for mercy most fervently uttered." Some would lie for hours until, with "smiles brightened into joy—they would rise shouting deliverance, and then would address the surrounding multitude in language truly

---

[74] Stone, *A Short History,* 63–64.

eloquent and impressive." He heard men, women, and children declaring "the wonderful works of God, and the glorious mysteries of the gospel." Observing closely these phenomena, he saw them as resurrections from the dead resulting in "humble confession of sins—the fervent prayer, and the ultimate deliverance—then the solemn thanks and praise to God—the affectionate exhortation to companions and to the people around, to repent and come to Jesus." Stone developed the solid conviction that this "was a good work—the work of God; nor has my mind wavered since on the subject." He saw much that he "considered to be fanaticism; but this should not condemn the work." Although the devil counterfeits the work of God in order to deceive, Stone contended that it "cannot be a Satanic work, which brings men to humble confession and forsaking of sin—to solemn prayer—fervent praise and thanksgiving, and to sincere and affectionate exhortations to sinners to repent and go to Jesus the Saviour." Stone commented that he was "always hurt to hear people speak lightly of this work. I always think they speak of what they know nothing about. Should every thing bearing the impress of imperfection be blasphemously rejected, who amongst us at this time could stand?"[75]

Revival broke out under his preaching at Concord.

> The effects of this meeting through the country were like fire in dry stubble driven by a strong wind. All felt its influence more or less. . . . The whole country appeared to be in motion to the place, and multitudes of all denominations attended. All seemed heartily to unite in the work and in Christian love. Party spirit, abased, shrunk away. To give a true description of this meeting cannot be done; it would border on the marvelous. It continued five days and nights without ceasing.[76]

---

[75] Stone, *A Short History,* 64–65.

[76] Stone, *A Short History,* 67.

Stone planned the Cane Ridge sacramental service in August 1801 in Paris, Kentucky. "The roads were literally crowded with wagons, carriages, horsemen, and footmen, moving to the solemn camp." Military men present judged that between twenty and thirty thousand people attended. Four or five preachers would speak at the same time, distributed in strategic places through the crowd. "Methodist and Baptist preachers aided in the work, and all appeared cordially united in it—of one mind and one soul, and the salvation of sinners seemed to be the great object of all." All were united in singing, united in prayer, and spoke with one voice proclaiming a "free salvation urged upon all by faith and repentance." Some events "were so much like miracles, that if they were not, they had the same effects as miracles on infidels and unbelievers; for many of them by these were convinced that Jesus was the Christ, and bowed in submission to him." Peter Cartwright said, "I suppose since the day of Pentecost, there was hardly ever a greater revival of religion than at Cane Ridge." He judged that, along with other similar meetings, "a new Impetus was given to the work of God, and many, very many, will have cause to bless God forever for this revival of religion throughout the length and breadth of our Zion."[77]

Stone's theology and practice eventually separated him from the Presbyterian denomination and he became the founder of the "Christian" movement in the dissolution of the so-called Springfield Presbytery in Spring 1804. A trial of ministers Richard McNemar and John Thompson led to conviction of Arminian tenets considered to be dangerous theologically and a violation of the constitution of the church. Five ministers presented a protest to the Synod of Kentucky in September 1803, claiming to be bound by no authority other than Scripture in doctrinal controversies and formulations. They claimed to remain "inviolably attached to the doctrines of grace which through God have been mighty in every revival of true religion since the Reformation." As a caveat, however,

---

[77] Cartwright, *Autobiography*, 33.

they expressed concern that these doctrines are "darkened by some expression in the confession of Faith which are used as the means of strengthening sinners in their unbelief and subjecting many of the pious to a spirit of bondage." After stating their refusal to be "prosecuted before a judge [i.e., the confession of faith], whose authority to decide we cannot in Conscience acknowledge," they stated, "We bid you adieu until through the providence of God it seem good to your Rev'd body to adopt a more liberal plan respecting human creeds & Confessions."[78] After refusing admonition, the objecting ministers were deposed from their churches.[79]

Cartwright, a close contemporary observer of this denominational/doctrinal transition, made this evaluation of the effects of the separation: "These ministers then rose up and unitedly renounced the jurisdiction of the Presbyterian Church, organized a Church of their own, and dubbed it with the name of Christian." These New Light Christians "renounced the Westminster Confession of Faith, and all Church discipline, and professed to take the New Testament for their Church discipline. They established no standard of doctrine; every one was to take the New Testament, read it, and abide his own construction of it." He called the development a "trash trap." Such an unmooring from discipline and doctrinal responsibility led to massive "diversity of opinion" so that "they got into a Babel confusion." The door was opened for the preaching of "Arian, some Socinian, and some Universalist doctrines." In a relatively short time, "you could not tell what was *harped* or what was *danced*. They adopted the mode of immersion, the water-god of all exclusive errorists; and directly there was a mighty controversy about the way to heaven, whether it was by water or by dry land."[80] Stone recorded the doctrinal

---

[78] Sweet, *Religion on the American Frontier*, 2:318–319

[79] Stone, *A Short History*, 74–84. Chapter 7 gives a full account and includes the "Last Will and Testament of the Springfield Presbytery."

[80] Cartwright, *Autobiography*, 31–32. Stone discusses briefly the concord between the New Lights and the Campbellites on pages 107–108.

leveling process that led him to nondescript views of atonement, sin, the Trinity, anti-confessionalism, and baptismal salvation. Having rejected substitution, propitiation, satisfaction, and any necessary connection of the death of Christ with forgiveness, all Stone could do was quote John 3:16 and say, "The gift of Jesus was before his death, and this, according to the system, must be before the satisfaction. A door against mercy is in our heart, and it is closed; but the Lord is represented as knocking at that door, and pleading for entrance. When we open, the Lord with his fulness enters, and blesses us."[81]

Cartwright summed up Stone's ministry: "B. W. Stone stuck to his New Lightism, and fought many bloodless battles, till he grew old and feeble, and the mighty Alexander Campbell, the *great*, arose and poured such floods of regenerating water about the old man's cranium, that he formed a union with this giant errorist, and finally died, not much lamented out of the circle of a few friends."[82]

RESULTS

Jerald C. Brauer observed this about the Second Great Awakening: "So revivalism came to the Church's rescue. It became one of the distinctive features of American Protestantism. It defeated deism and indifference, it overcame the problem of space and won thousands of members for the voluntary churches. In revivals the Churches found an answer to the question of how to present the judgment and redemption of God, yet in so doing they also limited their message and bound it to emotionalism."[83]

As Brauer indicated, the "voluntary" denominations were strengthened. There was a great increase in the number of Baptists and Methodists. The Awakening prompted the beginning of the

---

[81] Stone, *A Short History,* 88.

[82] Cartwright, *Autobiography*, 31–32

[83] Brauer, *Protestantism in America*, 116,

Cumberland Presbyterian, the Christian Church, and the Church of Christ or Restorationist movement. Cartwright noted,

> In the fall of 1804, when I joined the conference, there were a little over 9,000 members in the Western Conference; in 1811, 30,741. There were then a little over forty traveling preachers, and in 1810 over one hundred; and yet, at this time there are not more than six of us left lingering on the shores of time to look back, look around, and look forward to the future of the Methodist Episcopal Church, for weal or for woe. Lord, save the Church from desiring to have pews, choirs, organs, or instrumental music, and a congregational ministry, like other heathen Churches around them![84]

David Benedict, writing in 1813, summarized the development among Baptists. "It was computed that about ten thousand were baptized and added to the Baptist churches in the course of two or three years. This great work progressed among the Baptists in a much more regular manner than people abroad have generally supposed. They were indeed zealously affected and much engaged."[85]

This Awakening brought about the rise of the missionary organizations. In 1810, Congregationalists sent out missionaries under the sponsorship of the American Board of Commissioners, which included Presbyterians under the Plan of Union of 1801. This group included Adoniram and Ann Judson and Luther Rice, who became Baptists and prompted the founding among Baptists in 1814 of the General Missionary Convention. Preaching about the evangelical necessity and moral dignity of missions, combined with publication of the letters of missionaries and biographies of

---

[84] Cartwright, *Autobiography*, 116–117.

[85] David Benedict, *A General History of the Baptist Denomination of America* (Freeport, NY: Books for Libraries Press, 1971; first published 1813) 2:164–69; 251ff.

missionaries, was a means of propagating interest in missions. The preface to the *Memoir of Mrs Ann H. Judson* stated,

> Information concerning the real condition and wants of the heathen world must be spread among the churches, before they can be excited to a proper state of feeling in regard to missions. Christians, therefore, may serve the cause of the Redeemer, by circulating authentic accounts of the deplorable situation of the heathen nations, and statements of the nature, designs and progress of the benevolent efforts which Christians are now making for the conversion of the world.[86]

In 1815, the year after the founding of the General Missionary Convention, William Staughton composed a circular letter for the Philadelphia Association on the importance of "not living to ourselves." It contains this passage near the end that specifically related the movement in missions to the power of the revivals:

> In proportion as revivals in religion occur in our churches and with individuals believers, the expanding influence of divine grace is realized; loins are girded and lamps are trimmed. The desire to be happy is surmounted by the desire to be useful. The language of the heart is, Lord, what wilt thou have me to do? What for my poor fellow creatures lying in wickedness, what for the glory of thy adorable name. How shall I best testify my love for they character, and the sense I feel of my obligation to thy sovereign, redeeming sanctifying and matchless grace! My soul is thine, my body thine, my possessions thine. O teach me to employ them for thy praise. Faith and hope have a luster inferior to the charity which "seeketh not her own."[87]

---

[86] James D. Knowles, *Memoir of Mrs. Ann H. Judson* (Boston: Lincoln & Edmands, 1829), iv.

[87] *Minutes of the Philadelphia Association,* 1815.

The revival improved the moral atmosphere and the cultural values of the nation. The confrontation with drinking, gambling, prostitution, and profuse Sabbath-breaking on the frontier helped tame the West. Barton Stone recalled, "The soldiers, when they returned home from their war-tour, brought back with them many vices almost unknown to us before; as profane swearing, debauchery, drunkenness, gambling, quarreling and fighting. For having been soldiers, and having fought for liberty, they were respected and caressed by all."[88] Radical transformation of individual moral perceptions and actions resulted from these revival engagements. Virtually all of the accounts of the revival, both in the east and the west, in the halls of learning and the churches, record striking examples of the moral impact of the revival. Putting a stop to life-destroying vices so greatly improved family stability, law and order, and even length of life, that spirituality and holiness became identified with stopping these things.

In many places, both east and west, the revival arrested the influence of Unitarianism, deism, and other forms of infidelity. One letter from Georgia summarized the impact of the awakening there. It read, "The hearts of sinners melt before the word of truth, like wax before the sun. Infidelity is almost ashamed to show its head. Several deists have been constrained under a sense of their lost condition, to cry aloud for mercy. A few, even of those who attributed the effects produced among us to infernal agency, have been reached, and overcome by an influence, which they acknowledge to be divine."[89] Timothy Dwight's aggressive polemical theology had the effect of virtually eliminating philosophical infidelity at Yale. Some commented that the revival had isolated the "Fatherhood of God and the Brotherhood of Man to the neighborhood of Boston."

While schools for training ministers were developed, a large segment of American evangelicals became characterized by anti-

---

[88] Stone, *A Short History*, 32.

[89] Benedict, *A General History*, 2:166.

intellectualism, primitivism, and suspicion toward education. Some of this was built on inadequate concepts of the nature of spiritual giftedness and its enhancement through discreet and relevant training, but some of it came as wise warning. Cartwright warned against preachers who had no itinerant experience or whose education made them unwilling to endure the hardship of living and preaching in frontier situations. Complaints about the rigors and abstruse nature of theological and philosophical study was seen as unfitting of preachers. Complexity and formality of argument, juxtaposed to straightforward confrontation with unbelief, moved the plain observer toward resistance to an educated ministry.

The Awakening gave evangelicals confidence that organization and action could root the moral evil out of society. The number of benevolent societies increased. Jerald Brauer summarized,

> There was hardly an evil that did not have a society organized to combat it. There were religious tract and Bible societies to publish and spread both the Bible and various religious pamphlets and books among the godly and godless. There were groups centering around the express purpose of saving the wayward girls who had succumbed to sin in the big cities. Sailors' rest centers were developed to keep the seamen out of evil saloons and to provide them with a place of worship. The temperance movement attacked the use of alcohol. There were prison reform societies, women's rights groups, world peace movements, and Sabbath observance organizations. All these, in addition to the home and foreign missions and educational agencies of the Churches, were expressions of new life in the Spirit.[90]

Beyond these, the greatest moral crusade enhanced by the Awakening was the abolition movement.

---

[90] Brauer, *Protestantism in America*, 148.

Though it had the temporary effect of union and cooperation between denominations in the great matter of converting the nation and subduing the west, the gravity of the time eventually promulgated an increase of denominations and denominational antagonism. The Christian Church, under Barton Stone, left the Presbyterians and fragmented Baptist churches. Methodist Arminian preachers found creative and confrontive ways to oppose the Calvinism of the Baptists, Presbyterians, Congregationalists, and Reformed Episcopalians. Ridicule and *reductio ad absurdum* became effective tools for the battle. The 1801 Plan of Union dissolved in 1837, prompted not only by misunderstanding between Congregationalists and Presbyterians, but also by agitating the New School/Old School Divisions of the Presbyterians. Alexander Campbell, though a champion of Baptists in debate with a variety of paedobaptists, eventually turned his polemical talents against the Baptists. Robert Semple, a Virginia pastor, queried Campbell in 1825 as to the meaning and probable outcome of his developing views.

> Your opinions on some other points are, I think dangerous, such as casting off the Old Testament, exploding experimental religion in is common acceptation, denying the existence of gifts in the present commonly believed to exist among all spiritual Christians, such as preaching, &c. Some other of your opinions, though true, are pushed to extremes, such as those upon the use of creeds, confessions, &c. your views of ministerial support to ministers, directed against abuses on that head, would be useful, but leveled against all support to ministers (unless by way of alms) is so palpably contrary to scripture and common justice, that I persuade myself that there must be some misunderstanding. In short your views are generally so contrary to those of the Baptists in general, that if a party was to go fully into the practice of your principles

I should say a new sect had sprung up, radically different from the Baptists as they now are.[91]

Five years later, the Appomattox Association in Virginia wrote of the "mischievous influence" Campbell was having on Baptist churches by "stirring up envy and strife, and fomenting divisions among those who had before lived in fellowship and peace." They resolved, therefore, "that it be recommended to the ministers and churches composing this Association, not to invite into their pulpits any minister who holds the sentiments or creed named above."[92]

The Second Great Awakening pressed a variety of evangelical and quasi-evangelical denominations and doctrinal options into America, especially on the rapidly expanding frontier. Edwardsean thought became more formalized as a system of doctrine and held dominance in the eastern expression of the Awakening. The energy generated overall gave impetus toward a commitment to social reform as an element of awakening. At the same time, a body of external expressions of religion began a process of eroding the carefully developed doctrinal engagement with manifestly Spirit-wrought conversion. These amendments to analysis of spiritual experience and theology of conversion would become increasingly prominent in the decades to follow and would produce another source of religious controversy in American Christianity.

---

[91] Robert A Baker, *A Baptist Sourcebook with Particular Reference to Southern Baptists* (Nashville: Broadman Press, 1966), 77–78.

[92] Baker, *A Baptist Sourcebook*, 78.

CHAPTER 6

•———— • ————•

ASAHEL NETTLETON

"We may please our fancies, and gratify our self-righteousness, by adopting loose Pelagian sentiments on this subject; we may remonstrate against such absolute dependence on the grace of God as has now been advocated, but a new heart, and a right spirit will after all be found of such absolute necessity, that without them we must perish forever."

—Asahel Nettleton[1]

In 1848, four years after the death of Asahel Nettleton (1783–1844), Rev. R. S. Smith wrote *Recollections of Nettleton and the Great Revival of 1820*. Smith expressed a high opinion of the evangelist and revivalist, saying, "We look upon Mr. Nettleton as specially raised up by Providence, for conduction of a great and pure Revival of Religion, and that taking him altogether, he was at the time we speak of, the best qualified of any man we have known, for such a service."[2] For about twenty years, Nettleton's careful procedures in preaching, counseling, and encouraging the elements of true Spirit-wrought conversion perpetuated the outstanding traits of the revival theology of Jonathan Edwards. Yet near the end of Smith's account of Nettleton, the writer lamented, "It is well known that about the year 1824 or '25 what

_____

[1] Asahel Nettleton, "Regeneration" in *Asahel Nettleton: Sermons from the Second Great Awakening* (Ames, Iowa: International Outreach, 1995), 149. Portions of the material in this chapter appeared in an introductory essay I wrote for this book (iv–xviii).

[2] R. S. Smith, *Recollections of Nettleton and the Great Revival of 1820* (Albany: E. H. Pease & Co, 1848). 20.

have usually been styled New Measures, began to be adopted for promoting Revivals." Those measures included "protracted meetings, the anxious seat, the more vehement excitements of natural sympathies, and corresponding instructions, as to human ability and the ease of obtaining Religion." Nettleton, Smith noted, did not approve of these measures or the doctrinal views that gave rise to them. They would be the death knell of true revival. But "finding he could not resist them successfully," Nettleton "retired from that time into comparative obscurity."[3] Perhaps obscurity at that point was a gift of providence, for it allowed the revival theorist and practitioner to consolidate and perpetuate his ideas in different venues, though he continued preaching in various places. His practice of revival, his resistance to New Measures, and his careful defense of revival as a legitimate expression of biblical Christianity and Christian hope should encourage Christians to seek and expect revival.

BIOGRAPHICAL SKETCH OF NETTLETON

On April 21, 1783, Asahel Nettleton was born into the home of a Connecticut farmer, the second child and eldest son of six children. He was baptized at six days old under the terms of the Halfway Covenant. His parents, Samuel and Amy, were baptized as infants and formally "owned the covenant" on November 25, 1781, but never publicly professed faith. Asahel was reared in the rural atmosphere of Killingworth, Connecticut.

In his youth, he was catechized in the Westminster Shorter Catechism, giving him a mental apprehension of truths that, when God brought them home to his heart, greatly increased his effectiveness as an evangelist. In the year 1800, Nettleton became convicted that his life was dangerously frivolous; as a result, he sought to change both himself and his friends. Yet an increasing sense of the wickedness of his heart brought about a corresponding

---

[3] Smith, *Recollections of Nettleton*, 114.

attempt to prove the Bible wrong. He disliked the God he found there, for he knew that such a Holy Being must of necessity condemn him. He wished for God's non-existence.

After Nettleton struggled in spiritual distress for ten months, God's Spirit changed his heart and brought him to embrace the Savior. His conversion culminated in the first part of a massive revival in Killingworth in the autumn of 1801. The revival is recounted in the May 1804 edition of *The Connecticut Evangelical Magazine*. Josiah Andrews described the effect of a series of meetings for "religious instruction" initiated at the invitation of young people: "At this time about 60 were found deeply affected with the plague of their own hearts, and the others seriously alarmed." When Andrews had to leave for some time, the people were distressed at being deprived of continued gospel preaching. Andrews wrote, "They had no where to go but unto God, to whom they ought to have repaired before; but depending too much on human aid, they were at last left to feel their absolute dependence upon the great Proprietor of all, and nothing remained for them to do, but to repent and believe." In September through December, thirty-two "hopeful converts" were added to the church.[4]

Nettleton did not at first recognize his change as conversion, but he now found delight in objects that before had "given him so much distress." His views and feelings were the same as those "whom he regarded as the friends of Christ." Now, instead of hoping for God's non-existence, the attributes of the triune deity appeared lovely, and "the Saviour was exceedingly precious." Now, instead of feelings of bitter opposition, he contemplated the doctrines of grace with delight and "had now no doubt of their truth." This astounding change, he knew, was "not the result of any effort of his own, but of the sovereign and distinguishing will of God."[5]

---

[4] *The Connecticut Evangelical Magazine,* Vol. 4, No.11 (May 1804), 421.

[5] Bennet Tyler, *Nettleton and His Labours* (Edinburgh: Banner of Truth, 1975), 29. This volume was first published in 1844 and was repub-

In 1805, despite pressing hardships, Nettleton entered Yale College, then under the presidency of Timothy Dwight. During his years there, Nettleton justly gained the respect of his classmates as having unmixed sincerity in his devotion to Christ and earnestness in his desire for the salvation of his friends. He showed deeper interest in pursuit of Bible study and theology than other liberal arts studies. He also counseled fellow students having spiritual struggles and was particularly effective in this ministry during an 1807 revival at Yale. In the debate between Edwardseans, he adopted Samuel Hopkins's position of the sinfulness of every action of the unregenerate men, even their use of means. They should be encouraged to nothing short of immediate repentance. This was opposed to Dwight's view, which stated that sinners should be exhorted to the diligent use of means. Nettleton did not share some of Hopkins's other peculiarities, such as the willingness to be damned to the glory of God and the rather shocking proposition that God is the author of sin. Nettleton's career at Yale prompted this judgment from Timothy Dwight: "He will make one of the most useful men this country has ever seen."[6]

Nettleton, along with Samuel Mills, envisioned a life of service on the mission field among those who had never heard the gospel. Three factors converged to preclude that possibility for Nettleton. First, a debt incurred while in school needed to be paid, and he felt he must stay until that was done. Second, his preaching in destitute areas of Connecticut was so effective that leaders of the Congregational church urged upon him the duty to stay. Third, his contraction of typhus in 1822 eliminated all remaining hopes he had of work on the mission field.

---

lished in Scotland in 1854 with an introduction and occasional notes by Andrew Bonar, who also "Remodelled in some parts" the work. Special mention will be made of Bonar when it is clear that the text is a part "re-modelled" by him or inserted on the basis of his own knowledge. Note that the original title page has *Nettleton and His Labours* as the title, while the spine has *The Life and Labours of Asahel Nettleton*.

[6] Tyler, *Nettleton and His Labours*, 41.

In 1812, at the invitation of pastors, Nettleton began itinerating. Nettleton had seen the effects, and in fact had interviewed some eyewitnesses, of the inordinate affectations of James Davenport in the Great Awakening. He entered into this ministry with several convictions. One, he must do nothing to win affection from or destroy the influence of the settled pastorate. No lasting good could be done without the support and long-term influence of faithful pastors. Two, he would not seek to stir up interest where it was clear the Spirit of God had not preceded him. If he detected a spirit of "enthusiasm," he would work to root it out. He had no fear at all that his opposition to this type of misguided zeal was "quenching the spirit." Three, he would not stay where there appeared to be any reliance on him. He felt he could be of no use if a church's anticipation fostered hope and excitement because of confidence in the human instrument rather than remorse for sin and desire for the favor of God. Four, he believed that those converted during seasons of revival had a fervor for God purer and more sustained than those who made professions in times without general revival. Nettleton made the following observation in 1829:

> During the leisure occasioned by my late illness, I have been looking over the regions where God has revived his work for the two years past. The thousands who have professed Christ in this time, in general appear to run well. Hitherto, I think they have exhibited more of the Christian temper, and a better example, than the same number who have professed religion when there was no revival. . . . When I look back on revivals which took place ten or fifteen years ago, I have been agreeably surprised to find so many of the subjects of them continuing to adorn their profession. Take the whole number who professed religion as the fruit of these revivals, and take the same number who professed religion when there was no general revival, and I do think that the former have outshined the latter. I have not made a particular estimate, but from what I have

seen, I do believe that the number of excommunications from the latter is more than double in proportion to the former.[7]

For eleven years, Nettleton immersed himself, virtually without respite, into the cause of revivals. This involved preaching three times on Sabbaths and usually twice, maybe thrice, during the week, along with personal interviews and visits to homes where small but spiritually interested groups would be gathered. This schedule came to a halt in October 1822 when, after visiting a sick person, Nettleton contracted typhus fever. For more than two years he was unable to engage in any revival activity but took advantage of the time to compile his *Village Hymns for Social Worship*. After that, he could engage in far less strenuous activity, was more selective in engagements, and took longer periods of rest between revival efforts. Though the impression of his person was less powerful than before, accounts of his visits to churches still abound with testimonies of the effectual working of the Spirit of God. He traveled not only in New England during these years but also into the south as far as Virginia and South Carolina.

He went to the United Kingdom in 1831, ostensibly to rest, but he preached frequently. In addition, he regularly had opportunity, as well as necessity, to distinguish between revivals in America and the more recent impact of the New Measures excitements. One report of the American revivals concentrated on methods, events, and results characteristic of the New Measures fervor. Nettleton responded, "I am exhausted in my attempts to vindicate our revivals. I can only tell the good ministers here, that I do not, and never did, approve of the practice mentioned in the above letter."[8]

---

[7] From a Letter of Nettleton quoted in "A brief sketch of an Argument respecting the nature of Scriptural, and the importance and necessity of numerous, rapid, frequent, and extensive Revivals of Religion," in *Biblical Repertory & Theological Review*, January 1834, 124.

[8] Tyler, *Nettleton and His Labours*, 289.

That practice Nettleton had opposed with increasing conviction since 1826, when he had been drawn into a controversy with Charles Finney. The controversy was never really about methods, although that issue prompted the initial meetings between Nettleton and Finney. Though Finney declared, "He could have led me almost or quite at his discretion," there is no evidence in any of Finney's relationships with older, more experienced, and wiser people that he had any penchant for being led.[9]

The conflict climaxed at New Lebanon, New York, in July 1827. Nettleton had written publicly opposing the methods employed in Finney's meetings.[10] Finney responded with a sermon, "How can two walk together except they be agreed?" The conference was arranged by Nathan Beman, a Finney supporter, and Lyman Beecher.[11] Amidst wrangling, charges and counter charges, and some histrionic posturing on the part of Lyman Beecher, Nettleton felt strongly the futility of such discussion. Near the close of the meeting, Nettleton read a letter outlining the disturbing practices, and the conference approved resolutions rejecting the use of such practices. Finney and his followers, while

---

[9] Garth M. Rosell and Richard A. G. Dupuis, eds., *The Memoirs of Charles G. Finney: The Complete Restored Text*, ed. (Grand Rapids: Zondervan Publishing House, 1989), 204. One also should consult John F. Thornbury, *God Sent Revival* (Welwyn, UK, and Grand Rapids: Evangelical Press, 1977), 164–179.

[10] This was eventually published in 1828 along with other letters in a volume entitled *Letters of the Rev. Dr. Beecher and Rev. Mr Nettleton on The New Measures in Conducting Revivals of Religion* (New York: G. & C. Carwill, 1828).

[11] Beecher's autobiography records that Beecher said, "Finney, I know your plan, and you know that I do; you mean to come into Connecticut and carry a streak of fire to Boston. But if you attempt it, as the Lord liveth, I'll meet you at the State line, and call out all the artillery men, and fight every inch of the way to Boston, and then I'll fight you there." Charles Beecher, ed., *Autobiography of Lyman Beecher* (New York, 1864), 2:101. Beecher eventually signed a truce with the party of Finney and invited him to preach at his Boston church in August 1831.

clearly advocating some of the measures that gave rise to those complaints, denied that their measures consisted of such abuses as outlined in the letter.[12] Perhaps, Finney proposed, a resolution against lukewarmness should also be adopted.

Several factors conspired against any satisfactory resolution to this conflict, especially in the dynamics of the New Lebanon Conference. One, the issue continued to be reduced to one of methods, and the underlying theological distinctions garnered only brief attention. The orthodox participants, in fact, seemed unaware at this time that distinction in methods arose from radically different theological assumptions. Only in the next few years was the reason for this impasse understood more fully.

Two, one of Nettleton's chief protagonists, Lyman Beecher, agreed with Finney's anthropology and would soon be visibly aligned with the theological shift voiced in 1828 by Nathan W. Taylor. In his famous address *Concio ad Clerum*, Taylor rejected the Westminster Confession's doctrine of original sin. Sinfulness is not innate, according to Taylor, and neither guilt nor necessary predisposition toward sin are innately connected with the human

---

[12] Rosell and Dupuis, *The Memoirs of Charles G. Finney*, 222. Finney's version of the conference and all its connections is recorded on pages 216–231 as well as in valuable footnotes by the volume's editors. These footnotes contain references to related source material. Finney continued to defend the profitableness of his measures with an unusual sense of their virtual divinity. "I have always & everywhere used all the measures I used in these revivals, & have often added other measures such as the anxious seat whenever I have deemed it expedient. I have never seen the necessity of reformation in this respect. Were I to live my life over again, I think that with the experience of more than forty years in revival labors I should under the same circumstance use substantially the same measures that I did then. And let me not be understood to take credit to myself. No indeed. It was no wisdom of my own that directed me. I was made to feel my ignorance & dependence & led to look to God continually for His guidance. I had no doubt then nor have I ever had that God led me by his Spirit to take the course I did. So clearly did he lead me from day to day that I never did nor could doubt that I was Divinely directed," 227.

heart. Sin is always a deliberate moral choice and has no pre-existence to the choice. One always has the power of contrary choice. This theology blended perfectly with the revival techniques of Finney. Nettleton and Taylor were close friends all of their lives, but Nettleton ardently opposed Taylor's "New Haven Theology."[13]

Three, others who complained against Finney's methods were actually susceptible to many of Finney's theological caveats concerning human responsibility. They were followers of the "consistent Calvinists" Samuel Hopkins and Nathanael Emmons.[14]

Four, Finney and his co-adjutants went to the conference fully convinced that the charges against them were false or, where correct, merely reflected a theological or methodological insight superior to those of their accusers. Finney claimed the same after

---

[13] See Nathan William Taylor, "Advice to the Clergy (1828)" in *Issues in American Protestantism,* ed. Robert L. Ferm (Gloucester, MA: Peter Smith, 1976), 138–148. Taylor's emphasis that the power of contrary choice should be prominent in preaching clearly had impact on Finney and subsequently D. L. Moody. "We see the importance of this view of man's depravity, compared with any other, in its bearing on the preaching of the gospel. . . . And it is only by delivering such a message, that we, Brethren, can be 'workers together with God'" (146–147).

[14] Again, Finney's representation of their ideas was extravagant, but the floodgate of his radical opposition to Edwards certainly arose from their alterations in Edwards's theology in diminishing the direct connection between original sin and the sinner's sinning. They made it appear that each individual's sin arose from the decree and overruling providence of God. For example, Taylor presented confessional Calvinists, such as Edwards, in this manner: "If so, preach it out—preach it consistently,—preach nothing to contradict it,—dwell on our message, that God creates men sinners and damns them for being so.—Tell them such is *their* nature and such the mode of his interposition, that there is no more hope from acting on the part of the sinner than from not acting; tell them they may as well sleep on, and sleep away these hours of mercy, as attempt anything in the work of their salvation; that all is as hopeless with effort as without it." Ferm, *Issues in American Protestantism,* 147.

the conference opposition to his revival efforts decreased.[15] He said that the opposition of Beecher and Nettleton was "impertinent & assuming, uncalled for & injurious to themselves, & the cause of God." Besides that, in spite of their efforts, Finney could say, "Their opposition never made me ashamed, never convinced me that I was wrong in doctrine or practice, & I never made the slightest change in conducting revivals as a consequence of their opposition. I thought I was right."[16]

In 1832, after his return from England, Nettleton joined efforts to conserve the orthodox theology of the past from the destructive force of Taylorism and the dispiriting effects of Finneyism. A vital part of this effort consisted of the founding of the Theological Institute of Connecticut. Nettleton, refusing an invitation to become a regular faculty member, was retained as an occasional instructor. He spent his last years lecturing on evangelism, counseling students, writing letters to friends making observations on the condition of religion in New England and America, and preaching as strength allowed. In May 1844, he died after a lengthy season of suffering and in a great deal of pain. His comforts in Christ, however, outstripped the rigors of his calamitous sickness, and to the end he affirmed that it was "sweet to trust in the Lord."[17]

---

[15] Interpretations of the New Lebanon conference from distinctly different perspectives may be seen in Keith J. Hardman, *Charles Grandison Finney 1792–1875* (Grand Rapids: Baker Book House, 1990), 133–149; and Iain Murray, *Revival and Revivalism* (Edinburgh: Banner of Truth, 1994), 225–252. That the theological tendencies of Finney were not clear at this time probably contributed to the focus of the discussion on method more than doctrine and also explains some of the support he received from settled pastors who believed the Westminster Confession. Hardman's discussion of Beecher's zeal for the "social order" explains both his initial opposition to Finney and eventual friendship (148–149).

[16] Rosell and Dupuis, *The Memoirs of Charles G. Finney*, 239–240.

[17] For an account of his sickness see Thornbury, *God Sent Revival*, 220–225. Thornbury's book gives a sensitive and engaging portrayal of Nettleton's entire life.

NETTLETON'S PREACHING

Lyman Beecher described Nettleton's preaching as "highly intellectual" and "discriminatingly doctrinal." Calvinistic doctrines were "explained, defined, proved, and applied," and objections were stated fairly and given clear answers. These traits he opposed to mere declamation or "oratorical, pathetic appeals to imagination or the emotions." Though avoiding a direct appeal to the emotions, his sermons, nevertheless, were "deeply experimental in the graphic development of the experience of saint and sinner."[18]

Examples of this applicatory manner abound in Nettleton's sermons. His careful, relentless, and "graphic" pursuit to expose every refuge of the unconverted and illuminate the dark corners of their irrational resistance controlled his application of the parable of the virgins to unready sinners.

> Another is under deep conviction, and has labored long, and so he thinks he has done much; for a while he feels resolved that nothing shall divest his attention from this great subject. If there is any thing in religion he is determined to find it, but growing faint and discouraged, he concludes that there is no such thing; and so they that were foolish took their lamps and took no oil in them.
>
> Another equally anxious and distressed for his soul, and casting about to find some relief, catches at every appearance and persuades himself that there is grace in his heart. And not being careful to examine, he settles down on a false hope and sleeps on secure. And so they that were foolish took their lamps and took no oil with them.
>
> Sometimes the sinner, having long been anxious, and finding no relief, is persuaded and prevailed on to

---

[18] Charles Beecher, ed., *Autobiography of Lyman Beecher* (New York, 1864), 2:363–365. Cited in Iain Murray, *Revival and Revivalism*, 199.

believe that the most probable method to find relief is to profess religion. At length he is resolved to profess religion in hope that grace may thus be given. But the experiment has been followed sometimes with sad disappointment, no love to God, no renewing of the Holy Spirit has followed. Sometimes it has ended in still greater security; and in this manner they that were foolish took their lamps and took no oil with them.[19]

As Beecher indicated, doctrinal explanations also abounded in Nettleton's preaching. And, as in the sermons of Jonathan Edwards, the explanations are couched within searching and sometimes frightening application. It is such a fright as is designed not to evoke immediate "decision," but an increased sense of utter dependence on the grace of God for salvation. If the preacher gives the sinner any hope other than sovereign mercy, he destroys him and causes him to stop short of that sense of abandonment to both the justice and mercy of God so essential for true spiritual conversion. Rev. Cobb of Taunton, Massachusetts, described the effect of Nettleton's doctrinal preaching in his parish in 1825, soon after Nettleton's debilitating sickness:

> He brought from his treasure the doctrines of total depravity, personal election, reprobation, the sovereignty of divine grace, and the universal government of God in working all things after the counsel of His own will. And these great doctrines did not paralyze, but greatly promoted the good work. Never had brother Nettleton such power over my congregation, as when he poured forth in torrents these awful truths. And at no time were converts multiplied so rapidly, and convictions and distress so deep, as when these doctrines were pressed home to the conscience.[20]

---

[19] Nettleton, *Sermons from the Second Great Awakening*, 101.

[20] Tyler, *Nettleton and His Labours*, 245.

156

His sermon "Regeneration," based on John 1:12–13, is the consummate example of giving explanation, definition, proof, and application of a doctrine. The doctrine itself determined the type of application that is to be given. In this case, the application consisted of a profoundly stark ending of the sermon with a sober assertion of the just verdict of God in the absence of His sovereign choice to display mercy.[21]

No matter how many unregenerate strivings, preparations, and moral actions there may be, or how much knowledge may exist, "after all there must be a new creation." The same power that raised Christ from the dead must be exerted on behalf of the sinner or he will remain dead in trespasses and sins. Nothing can be hoped for to give life other than "the omnipotence of the divine Spirit." Our understanding is darkened, our wills are perverse and rebellious, our merits gain nothing but "utter rejection," and we are without strength. Neither power nor desire for spiritual mindedness exists. Ministers of God, no matter how skilled or spiritual or persuasive, will not change our minds in this matter. "Paul may plant and Apollos water, but God gives the increase." Schemes of religious effort may be devised "by the ingenuity of man . . . to wrest the glory of this work from the hands of the divine Spirit," but when all is done, it is seen that nothing but "the free sovereign grace and Almighty power of God" can effect this change. "The work is all his; and the glory must and will forever belong exclusively to him."[22]

The necessity of such a work implies the whole system of the doctrines of grace. Divine sovereignty in election and redemption only by Christ, as well as human depravity and other doctrines

---

[21] Nettleton, *Sermons from the Second Great Awakening,* 143–149. Nettleton's simplicity, clarity, and uncompromising exposition of the doctrine received strength from the fact that a sermon on the doctrine of regeneration was part of his experience in pointing out his danger by setting in motion a pattern of resistance to the divine sovereignty and attempts at self-righteous justification.

[22] Nettleton, *Sermons from the Second Great Awakening,* 148.

connected with these, all flow from it. "There is one grand, harmonious, and perfect system: and God is the sum—the substance and the glory of all."[23]

Nettleton acknowledged full awareness of the "difficulties incident to the doctrines here laid down." The natural heart, as he knew, strained "both to oppose and misconstrue them." It is enough that "the Bible supports them," and, therefore, "our carnal reason must bow. Here our proud hearts must submit." The resister may charge them with "mystery— with inconsistency— with unprofitableness," but in doing so he assails "not man, but God." It stands "written in characters of light" in Holy Scripture, "which were born not of blood, nor of the will of the flesh, nor of the will of man, but of God."[24]

Nettleton identified any scheme that did not affirm this absolute necessity of the new birth based on the pure sovereign mercy of God as, at bottom, Pelagian. "The fact is," he preached, "that almost the whole system of vague and inadequate notions on this great subject is only the heresy of Pelagius . . . which has now been newly dressed up, after the modern fashion, to secure a better reception." A few paragraphs later, Nettleton reiterated, "To remove this subject of prejudice, Pelagius and multitudes ever since, have maintained that all men receive gifts alike, and are alike furnished to work out their salvation." He listed four assertions that affirm a universal operation of the Spirit: universal provision, universal consonance of human reason with gospel offer, universal capability, and universal reward that he labeled as fundamental principles "of the Pelagian and Arminian scheme." He closed the sermon with a theological summary that implied the urgency of a humble reception of this truth.

> This is the only birth which can fit us for heaven, "Except a man be born again," etc. We may please our fancies,

---

[23] Nettleton, *Sermons from the Second Great Awakening,* 149.

[24] Nettleton, *Sermons from the Second Great Awakening,* 149.

and gratify our self-righteousness, by adopting loose Pelagian sentiments on this subject; we may remonstrate against such absolute dependence on the grace of God as has now been advocated, but a new heart, and a right spirit will after all be found of such absolute necessity, that without them we must perish forever.[25]

And there ends the sermon. Intercession with God was not yet done, however, for Nettleton ended his messages with prayer, supplicating God for mercies in light of the truths discussed and applied in the sermon. Princeton professor Samuel Miller noted that the closing prayers of Nettleton "were, perhaps, never exceeded for appropriate simplicity, and adaptedness to seal the impressions of the preceding sermon."[26]

A sermon on "Indecision in Religion" confronted the unbeliever with the full force of his natural capacities to "choose" for God. "It is not for want of power to alter your disposition or make you willing to repent. You have all the faculties that Christians have. The true penitent has no more natural power than the impenitent. The natural power of the Christian before, and after repentance is precisely the same." God does not condemn the impenitent for

---

[25] Nettleton, *Sermons from the Second Great Awakening*, 149. The references to Pelagianism are on pages 145–146, Nettleton preached plainly and simply on this issue and did not want to confuse or appear to compromise his emphasis on the inability of the sinner to make a new heart and the incontrovertible necessity of a divine creative power to bring about the new birth. On this issue, however, he was clearly Edwardsean and distinguished between natural faculties and moral faculties. He would agree with Edwards that the fall brought about a destruction of the "moral" image of God but not the "natural" image. For example, another paragraph of the sermon on regeneration states that regeneration involved a physical work in that "there is an actual new creation." God's creative power operates so that "a new spiritual taste or discernment, and principle is implanted by a sovereign creative operation, and not simply a new direction given to the old faculties" (148–149).

[26] Samuel Miller, *Thoughts on Public Prayer* (Harrisonburg: Sprinkle Publications, 1985; originally published 1849), 246.

being unable, but unwilling, to repent. That which he lacks is not natural faculty, or power, but desire, "inclination, or disposition to obey his commands."[27]

Regeneration, therefore, is a sovereign creative operation in that new motives, holy dispositions, relish for godliness, and eyes to see and a heart to pursue the excellent beauty and desirability of holiness as seen in the person and work of Christ are generated where they did not exist; that which did exist, in fact, was the opposite of all these new things (Eph. 2:2–3).

Just as impressively as Nettleton placarded the monolithic foundation of God's sovereign pleasure and unilateral efficacy of His regenerative power, so he urged the immediate and unalterable obligation of all sinners to turn from sin, embrace the cross, and run toward heaven. A consistent energy in Nettleton's sermons pressed relentlessly on this infinitely important duty incumbent on creatures made in God's image. "Rejoice, Young Man," "The Destruction of Hardened Sinners," "Indecision in Religion," and "The Contemplation of Death" gave not a moment's rest to the hearer.[28] Nettleton indulged in no word of levity and never let slip a hint of possible respite from the certainty of judgment. He could only strain himself at every point to prove that at judgment we will clearly see that every moment was invested with eternal importance. "But heaven with all its glories, is now brought near at the critical moment, when the world is presenting its charms. Here then is no standing still. A choice must and shall be made. Man is a moral agent," Nettleton reminded his hearers, "destined to act for eternity. He shall walk either in the straight and narrow way to life, or in the broad road to death." He pressed the truth unwaveringly that "all the invitations, commands, threatenings, and warnings in the Bible are so many admonitions to sinners." No thought or action is without a moral element, and thus eternal

---

[27] Nettleton, *Sermons from the Second Great Awakening*, 17–25.

[28] Nettleton, *Sermons from the Second Great Awakening,* 40–52, 30–39; 17–25, 9–16.

significance for "every act of ours will have some influence on us through interminable ages." And Nettleton preached, "All things are now ripening for the day when God shall bring every work to judgment, with every secret revealed." No cultural tolerance of age characteristics will impress God at that day. Instead, "without pity, or allowance for the levity of youth, he will condemn and punish for every failure of perfect obedience." Nothing will be considered innocent that has failed to prepare the soul to appear unblemished before God. "All amusements which prepare the soul for the duties of religion are right, and every Christian is bound to engage in them, and those which do not, will be condemned at the bar of God."[29]

Every moment exploded with urgency, but, particularly, seasons of grace (when the gospel was being preached) were auspicious times. Nettleton consistently placed before the congregation that every moment had a choice embedded within it—either to go on in the way of sin and carelessness about life and eternity, or to choose repentance and Christ and eternal fellowship with God, the source of all joy and true pleasure. Preaching, therefore, must employ unyielding images of the necessity of finding a repentant heart. A sermon to the young, based on Ecclesiastes 11:9, ended this way:

> Young man, I leave you in the hands of your final Judge. Life and death are now before you and God is witness to your choice. If a bleeding Saviour has no charms for you—if the thunder of his vengeance does not strike terror through your guilty soul; then go on. March on your way rejoicing—trample under foot the Son of God— Sport with eternal vengeance and deny the thunder of his power. Your fair morning will soon be turned into darkness, your course run—your bodies fall in the grave, and your souls into the hands of the living God.[30]

---

[29] Nettleton, *Sermons from the Second Great Awakening,* 13, 31, 41, 52.

[30] Nettleton, *Sermons from the Second Great Awakening,* 52. This closing is virtually the same as that from the sermon "Indecision in

Andrew Bonar felt that this was the great strength of Nettleton, to "deal very extensively, and very perseveringly, in full doctrinal statements opened up and pressed home on the conscience." The combination of preaching and personal work—pulpit, lecture room, and private conversation—gave both power and purity to the revivals under Nettleton. Though sometimes "in a high degree eloquent," his eloquence was not overpowering, as was that of Whitefield. Rather, Bonar called it "solemn and impressive, . . . more instructive, and addressed more to the conscience."[31]

THE REPROACH OF CHRIST

This strength of Nettleton, however, was also his weakness, according to the *Biblical Repertory and Theological Review*. In an 1844 review of Tyler's *Memoir of the Life and Character of the Rev. Asahel Nettleton*, the periodical called Nettleton "one of the wisest and best men we have ever known" and expressed sincere admiration for the "extraordinary wisdom with which he discharged the difficult duties of an evangelist, gratitude for the "wonderful success with which God crowned his labours," and an acknowledgment of indebtedness for the "fidelity and skill with which he opposed 'new measures' and 'new Divinity.'" In short, the reviewer had "the highest admiration for his character." All this being said, the reviewer maintained that Nettleton exhibited a lack of proportion in his ministry and his personal spirituality. As a "New England Calvinist," he gave a preponderance of attention to the "psychological doctrines of the Bible, those doctrines which have more immediate relation to the nature and agency of man." The doctrines of depravity, regeneration, divine influence, and particular providence in human affairs, along with the teachings on decrees and election, cut a much wider swath in his preaching

---

Religion." Nettleton at times transported sections from one sermon into another. Jonathan Edwards did the same.

[31]   Andrew A. Bonar, in his introduction to the 1854 edition of Tyler, *Nettleton and His Labours*, viii.

than did the more objective doctrines of the gospel. The reviewer wished for more attention to the doctrines of "justification, of faith, of the mediation and intercession of our Lord." Those doctrines assuredly were not denied, nor were they kept out of view, but they were not "allowed their due prominence and power." On the subjects immediately under his attention, Nettleton preached with "singular adroitness and power," but not "in due proportion."[32]

The peculiarity generated by this so-called lack of proportion tended to produce criticism from potential friend and determined foe. Misunderstandings, such as the one now under discussion, often came from the uniqueness of his style, his conscientious resistance to any element of dependence on his person, and some idiosyncrasies in personality and behavior. Misrepresentations arose from those factors, combined with a lack of sympathy with Nettleton's conscience and his unhypocritical concern that many souls were being deceived and churches polluted by the New Measures. He has been pictured as jealous, furious, threatened, crabby, backward, mentally incompetent, and the "real loser at New Lebanon." Historians sometimes seem to consider it a threat to the objectivity of their craft to give credence to the impact that sincere biblical convictions and theological commitments have on the attitudes and actions of formative personalities. Nettleton's sermons, however, show a preacher driven by a clear vision of the gospel and its exclusive power in the conversion of sinners.

That Nettleton often was misunderstood and his motives and methods misjudged is seen in an interesting reference to him in the diary of Basil Manly Sr. (1798–1868). Manly, an influential Baptist preacher in the deep South, wrote his observations in 1830 during Nettleton's visit to Charleston. Because Manly was at least reticent about the usefulness of the New Measures and one of

---

[32] Review of *Memoir of the Life and Character of the Rev. Asahel Nettleton D.D.* by Bennet Tyler, which appeared in *Biblical Repertory & Theological Review* (October 1844), 595–596.

their most piercing critics in the South, his reactions to Nettleton deserve attention. This is the entire diary entry:

> The Rev. Asahel Nettleton, the respected promoter of revivals in the northern states, has been here for some time attempting to produce a religious excitement in the community. His methods are peculiar: and it is said that tho' he takes a great deal of pains to disclaim the idea of being able to do anything, there seems to be an affectation of singularity for the sake of effect, and an air of self-sufficiency about him. From what I have heard, I believe that an unbiased and discerning mind would not fail to be impressed that those motives & sentiments lurk in his bosom, perhaps unknown in some measure to himself. I was prevented from witnessing his exhibitions for two reasons. As there was a revival in our church when he began and the people were coming to our meetings in great numbers my attention was very much taken up—& Mr. Nettleton's meetings were held of evenings, always I believe, on the same evenings of our meetings. His other meetings I did not choose to attend as they were more private, for this reason— As soon as he came here, I was disposed to welcome him, at Mr. Thomas Fleming's in George St. But he sent word that he was lying down, and declined seeing me. Supposing that he might have, at the moment, some good reason for this, I sent up my name and character—under the idea that if he wished to see me, I should afterward receive from him a visit, or a request to call again. But nothing of this kind occurred—& I concluded that he wished to have no intercourse with me. Yet this gentleman publickly complained . . . that he had received no attention in Charleston—publickly entreated the citizens, again & again, to call on him at his lodgings, if it were only for five minutes. Said that there was no religion in Charleston—intimated strongly that ministers & people were all in fault—and as I have understood from several has now left the city

in disgust—**AMEN** say I. And so may all leave it who behave like him.

I cannot imagine a more regrettable misunderstanding than that entry suggests. Manly's preaching was of the same searching doctrinal character as Nettleton's, and his concerns about the dangers of misguided professions of faith in the climate of "revivalism" were just as profound. Manly described his own preaching as not inclining people "to the acts and exercises which are usual at the close of protracted services. . . . They seem rather disposed to shrink away into retirement; like Peter, to 'go out and weep bitterly.'" R. S. Smith described the impact of Nettleton's preaching as "awfully overwhelming. Men held their breath, and the audience moved slowly away, not to talk of the preacher, but to meditate, to read, and to pray."[33]

Manly warned against periods of "high wrought excitement" and the desire to "make a great show and parade of the converts which we have made." We should do nothing to pollute the church with "unbelievers, unconverted, and graceless persons" who not only will make the church a harlot, but will themselves be hardened beyond the reach of conscience and gospel. Their last estate is truly worse than the first. To the same effect as Manly, Nettleton's meetings displayed solemnity and people were not "merely excited." They were rather "awakened to a sense of their lost condition by nature" and of their "entire dependence for salvation on the sovereign mercy of God." If any felt they were converted by manifested affections that arose merely from self-love, "they were advised to abandon their hopes without delay."[34]

The impact that Manly and Nettleton made on their sympathetic hearers was remarkably similar. Manly was described as a "decided Calvinist" whom none could "preach the gospel more

---

[33] R. S. Smith, *Recollections of Nettleton and the Great Revival of 1820* (Albany: Published by E. H. Pease & Co., 1848), 42.

[34] Tyler, *Nettleton and his Labours*, 324–330.

freely" or "urge sinners more earnestly and successfully to believe in Christ as their Saviour." Those doctrines served to "fire his zeal and stimulate the growth of piety in his own soul." Because the increase was of God, Manly was encouraged to "plant" and "water" the heavenly seed.[35]

Like Manly, Nettleton "preached with great plainness the doctrines of Calvinism." They were seen as the power of God unto salvation and had no tendency "to paralyze" or harden men "into stupidity." On the contrary, "sinners were pricked in the heart and brought to repentance," and saints were "quickened and comforted and incited to fidelity in their Master's service."[36]

One could not concoct a more sympathetic understanding of these infinitely important issues than existed in the theology and practice of Manly and Nettleton. Those who knew Nettleton more thoroughly point out some of the characteristics that were negatively silhouetted in Manly's brief experience. Nettleton indeed took "a great deal of pains to disclaim the idea of being able to do anything." This led him to take measures that some, including Manly, would interpret as an "affectation of singularity." Smith recorded that when Nettleton "discovered that a people or individual were trusting to human instruments," he would seem "to be actually rude in disappointing them." On one occasion he walked away from a place when over a hundred seemingly were under conviction, and one woman exclaimed that he was as bad as Satan for he had come only to torment them and then "leave them to do as they could." The woman was eventually converted. Nettleton's caution in asking any others to participate with him in preaching arose from a high sense of responsibility in the dispensing and application of truth. He would rather appear rude than create any sense of obligation toward a preacher with whom

---

[35] J.P. Boyce, *Life and Death the Christian's Portion* (New York: Sheldon & Co., 1869), 68–69; Samuel Henderson, *Christianity Exemplified* (Atlanta: Franklin Steam Printing House, 1870), 34.

[36] Tyler, *Nettleton and his Labours*, 331–332.

he was not well acquainted.[37] This caution, however, should not be interpreted as pointing to an "air of self-sufficiency."

Sometimes Nettleton's sense of the peculiarity of his call led him to actions that could easily be misjudged. Smith heard him say that he could not labor where there was not already "some religious feeling." Sometimes, however, "on urgent solicitation" he would visit a place to test its readiness. "We remember one such, where he preached, and preached earnestly, for a few times," Smith reported. "They heard him, but that was all, and he left them saying, it was of no use to stay, since it was evident that Christians there could not be brought up to their duty."[38]

If that same scene happened in Charleston, and he indeed "said that there was no religion in Charleston" and put the ministers at fault, his judgment was premature and is to be regretted. At the time, in fact, Manly was experiencing revival in First Baptist Church and, in his diary, recorded some encouraging cases of conviction and conversion. Nettleton's departure led to an inaccurate "disgust" on Manly's part, and sadly precluded what might have been a relationship that could have benefited Southern evangelicals, particularly Baptists, at a time when the New Measures were beginning to take root in their evangelistic practice. Soon to reach the height of his influence on American evangelicalism in the quest for true revival, Charles Finney would substantially alter both the theology and he methodology of the American revival tradition.

---

[37] Smith, *Recollections of Nettleton*, 28, 29.

[38] Smith, *Recollections of Nettleton*, 40.

An Abstract of Nettleton's "Thoughts on Revivals"

Nettleton posed several common objections to revivals and answered them. This is a brief summary of his thoughts.[39]

1. *Revivals are sudden and many profess conversion in a short time.* Answer: The work of the Spirit is like rain. That rain comes suddenly and often in torrents does not make it any less rain.

2. *There is great distress in revivals.* Answer: "Is it surprising that sinners should be distressed when they are brought to realize that they are exposed to eternal destruction? . . . Are Heaven and Hell trifles?"

3. *Persons are terrified by alarming preaching.* Answer: If they have not been terrified before under the same content of preaching, why are they terrified now? And how does such preaching produce first terror and then joy in the same mind? Do not sinners have reason to be terrified? The Bible gives many examples of terrified sinners who embrace the gospel and come "to love what they hated with perfect hatred."

4. *Revival is only the product of sympathy.* Answer: What begins the revival in the first persons who are brought to faith? Cannot deeply felt sympathy also be productive of true feelings of anxiety for the soul that issues in conviction and conversion when explained by biblical truth?

---

[39] Tyler, *Nettleton and his* Labours, 451–454.

5. *It is all enthusiasm.* Answer: "If the distress of sinners is greater than the case demands, then call it enthusiasm." If one's soul is in eternal danger, "not to be distressed is blockish and stupidity. Is it rational . . . to slumber on the "brink of eternal perdition?"

6. *Sudden joy manifest in revival is irrational and cannot be the result of divine influence.* Is the Bible irrational to propose the "peace of God that surpasses all understanding" or "joy unspeakable and full of glory?" Was there joy in Samaria upon Philip's preaching in that place?

7. *Many who are zealous for a season turn back.* Answer: In the time of Christ, "many turned back and walked with him no more." John said, "They went out from us." Were Christ and the apostles void of true conversions? "Because there was a Judas among the apostles, does that prove that Christ had no true disciples?"

CHAPTER 7

A SUMMARY OF THE LIFE AND INFLUENCE OF CHARLES GRANDISON FINNEY

"The death of the sinner may be in itself a very great evil, and yet God sees that, on the whole, taking all results into view, he has the best of reasons to be satisfied with his own plan, and with all that has himself done in its execution."

—Charles Finney[1]

EARLY LIFE AND CONVERSION

Charles Finney was born in Warren, Litchfield County, Connecticut. His family moved to Oneida County, New York, in 1794. He was reared with no gospel privileges, for his parents were not believers. For education, he attended common schools in the area and then went to preparatory school at Warren Academy in Connecticut, preparing to enter Yale. Deciding against attending Yale, he spent two years teaching.

In 1818, Finney returned to Adams, New York, and studied law with Benjamin Wright. He recalled, "Altogether I was, when I went to Adams to study law, almost as ignorant of religion as a heathen. I had been very much brought up in the woods, I had paid very little regard to the Sabbath, and had no definite knowledge of religious truth whatever." Gaining acquaintance

---

[1]   Chares Finney, "God has No Pleasure in the Sinner's Death," in *The Way of Salvation*, 273.

with the Bible through his law books, he began to attend church in Adams and, for the first time, sat under an educated ministry. He considered the pastor, Rev. George W. Gale, to be of the Old School type, thoroughly Calvinistic. Finney testified that he "was rather perplexed than edified by his preaching."[2]

According to Finney's testimony, he was converted remarkably on October 10, 1821. Having heard of conversion, presumably under the preaching of Gale, he made up his mind that he would settle the question of his soul's salvation at once and make his peace with God. He discovered an inordinate pride in his heart that made him afraid of others knowing that he was seeking salvation. As he described the experience, he discovered that salvation was something to be "accepted" as a "finished work." He wrote, "I had to submit myself to the righteousness of God through Jesus Christ. All that was necessary on my part," as he perceived it, "was to get my own consent to give up my sins, and give myself to Christ." In order to effect this, he went to a grove of woods (seeking still to retain secrecy from the observation of any man) with the determination, "I will give my heart to God or I will never come down from here." But still his pride surfaced at every rustling of the leaves, and he found that "I cannot pray; my heart is dead to God, and will not pray." He reproached himself for the rash promise that he would now be obliged to break.[3]

He soon saw the incongruity of such a soul-destroying pride, its infinite sinfulness in being ashamed of the Savior before whom he had appeared for salvation. He thought through the implications of Jeremiah 29:12–13, as quoted in Finney's memoirs: "Then shall ye go and pray unto me, and I will answer you. Then shall ye seek me and shall find me, when you search for me with all your heart." He had known intellectually that the Bible was God's Word, but had never considered the meaning of the heart. He concluded that

---

[2] Rosell and Dupuis, *The Memoirs of Charles G. Finney*, 10. Biographical references will be taken from this work unless noted otherwise.

[3] Rosell and Dupuis, *The Memoirs of Charles G. Finney*, 18–19.

this meant a "*voluntary trust* instead of an *intellectual state*." The "when" of his search was at that moment. As he recalled promise after promise of the Old and New Testaments, they all fell not so much into his "intellect as into my heart, to be put within the grasp of the voluntary powers of my mind; and I seized hold of them, appropriating them, and fastened upon them with the grasp of a drowning man."[4]

He lost all sense of guilt and began to think that his aggressive posture toward the Bible had grieved the Spirit, who, consequently, left him. He thought perhaps he had committed the unpardonable sin. "So perfectly quiet was my mind that it seemed as if all nature listened." After dealing with several office matters that afternoon, in the evening he shut himself up alone, in the dark. His heart poured out to God and he seemed to meet the "Lord Jesus Christ face to face." He made confessions and seemingly bathed the feet of Jesus with his tears. Returning to a room where he had built a fire with large pieces of wood, he found that it was nearly gone out. There, he reported receiving "a mighty baptism of the Holy Ghost."

> Without expecting it, without ever having the thought in my mind that there was any such thing for me, without any recollection that I had ever heard the thing mentioned by any person in the world, at a moment entirely unexpected by me, the Holy Spirit descended upon me in a manner that seemed *to go through me*, body and soul. I could feel the impression, like a wave of electricity, going through and through me. Indeed it seemed to come in waves, and waves of liquid love;— for I could not express it in any other way.[5]

After a couple of unusual personal encounters, Finney went to bed and had a mostly fitful night with intermittent doubt

---

[4] Rosell and Dupuis, *The Memoirs of Charles G. Finney*, 20–21.
[5] Rosell and Dupuis, *The Memoirs of Charles G. Finney*, 23.

and periods of sleep from which he would awake because of the warmth of the Spirit still operating within him. The next morning he had another baptism interlaced with the question "Will you doubt?" He answered, "No! I will not doubt; I cannot doubt." God so cleared his mind on the subject that Finney believed "that the Spirit of God had taken possession of my soul."[6]

This experience confirmed the "doctrine of justification by faith" to his soul as a present experience. All sense of condemnation had dropped out of his mind since the experience in the woods. "I felt myself justified by faith; and so far as I could see, I was in a state in which I did not sin. Instead of feeling that I was sinning all the time, my heart was so full of love that it overflowed. My cup ran over with blessing and with love, and I could not feel that I was sinning against God. Nor could I recover the least sense of guilt for my past sins." He added, in explanation, words about "this experience of justification, and so far as I could see, of present sanctification."[7]

The next morning, he informed a man whom he was to represent in court that he could not represent him for he had a "retainer from the Lord Jesus Christ to plead His cause."[8]

ENTRANCE INTO MINISTRY

Immediately Finney began to speak to people about their souls. He narrated several instances of remarkable success, including some where others had failed miserably. Finney said, "My whole mind was taken up with Jesus and his salvation, and the world seemed to me of very little consequence. Nothing, it seemed to me, could be put in competition with the worth of souls." With candor, he recalled encounters in which his reasoning seemed

---

[6] Rosell and Dupuis, *The Memoirs of Charles G. Finney*, 25.

[7] Rosell and Dupuis, *The Memoirs of Charles G. Finney*, 16–26 narrates the events of Finney's conversion.

[8] Rosell and Dupuis, *The Memoirs of Charles G. Finney*, 27.

overpowering to those opposing the gospel. He used such phrases as these: "The young man saw in a moment that I had demolished his argument," and "I cannot remember one whom I spoke with, who was not soon after converted." Concerning the young people whom he had led in a choir, he noted, "They were converted one after another with great rapidity; and the work continued among them until but one of their number was left unconverted." Finney then went to his father's home, along with his younger brother. "We went in and engaged in prayer. My father and mother were greatly moved; and in a very short time thereafter they were both hopefully converted." A great revival followed in that town, Henderson, which had been, in Finney's words, "a moral waste."

Adams, where Finney had received his retainer from the Lord, became a center of revival in the region. Many periodicals reported the conversions and the elevated state of religion in many of the towns around Adams. Even the *Latter Day Luminary* included reports of these revivals in 1822. Concerning the necessity of maintaining personal spiritual intensity, Finney reported, "I used to spend a great deal of time in prayer; sometimes, I thought, literally praying 'without ceasing.' I also found it very profitable, and felt very much inclined to hold frequent days of private fasting."[9]

Having observed the unusual promptness and power of the effects of Finney's preaching, nearby pastors encouraged him to go to Princeton. He declined; he was confident that "they had been wrongly educated; and they were not ministers that met my ideal at all of what a minister of Christ should be." When the presbytery appointed Gale to be his teacher, Finney noted that the studies were "little else than controversy." He wrote, "These doctrines I could not receive. I could not receive his views on the subject

---

[9] Rosell and Dupuis, *The Memoirs of Charles G. Finney*, 27–43 gives Finney's narrative of the fervency of the conversions and prayer meetings that surrounded his evangelistic encounters in these immediate post-conversion weeks.

of atonement, regeneration, faith, repentance, the slavery of the Will or any of their kindred doctrines." He found nothing logical, convincing, or edifying in the theology books possessed by Gale. Later he remarked, "I had sat under Mr. Gale's preaching for years, and could never see any adaptation in his preaching to convert anybody."[10] Finney noted, "I have always believed that had not the Lord led me to see the fallacy of those arguments, and the manner in which the truth was to be established from the Bible, and had He not so revealed Himself to me personally that I could not doubt the truth of the Christian religion, I should have been forced to be an infidel."[11]

The foundation of all the theological issues with Gale, and with the prevailing orthodoxy of the day, was over the doctrine of imputation. "I could not receive the theological fiction of imputation," Finney stated. He rejected the idea of imputation of Adam's sin to his posterity and the associated implications. He rejected the imputation of Christ's righteousness to us as being antagonistic to the moral government of God. On the same ground, he rejected the imputation of our sin and condemnation to Christ in the atonement. Gale "affirmed that Jesus literally paid the debt of the elect, & fully satisfied retributive justice." Finney claimed that "Jesus only satisfied public justice & that that was all that the government of God could require."[12]

---

[10] Rosell and Dupuis, *The Memoirs of Charles G. Finney,* 153.

[11] Rosell and Dupuis, *The Memoirs of Charles G. Finney*, 55. Finney gave the details of these various doctrinal controversies over the Westminster symbols in pages 44–61. In the preface of his *Systematic Theology*, he wrote, "The distinction between original and actual sin, and the utter absence of a distinction between physical [i.e., depravity of human nature] and moral depravity [i.e., the sinfulness of personal acts of volition], embarrassed me. Indeed, I was satisfied either that I must be an infidel, or that these were errors that had no place in the Bible." Charles Finney, *Finney's Systematic Theology* (Minneapolis: Bethany Fellowship, abridged and published 1976), ix.

[12] Rosell and Dupuis, *The Memoirs of Charles G. Finney,* 44.

Not only did he conclude that Gale's education for ministry had been "entirely defective," but he also challenged his practical views. Gale pointed to every one of Finney's proposed methods and said that God would never use them. When Finney was successful, "it completely upset his theological and practical education as a minister." This probably was due, in Finney's estimation, to another defect in Gale's education. Open to the possibility that Gale had never been converted, he was sure that "he had failed to receive that divine anointing of the Holy Ghost which is indispensable to ministerial success."

In demonstration of his doctrinal and experiential superiority, Finney narrated the results of a debate with a Universalist. When Gale's efforts proved fruitless, Finney asked to join the fray, informing Gale that he would argue based on a different theological rubric, for Finney believed Gale's views logically to entail Universalism. "I delivered two lectures upon the Atonement," Finney recalled. "In these I think I fully succeeded in showing that the Atonement did not consist in the literal payment of the debt of sinners, in the sense in which the Universalist maintained." He felt some newness and special insight in his view that the atonement "simply rendered the salvation of all men possible; and did not of itself lay God under any obligation to save anybody." He rejected as false any idea that "Christ suffered just what those for whom he died deserved to suffer," with confidence that "no such thing as that was taught in the Bible; and no such thing was true." Rather, Christ died "simply to remove an insurmountable obstacle out of the way of God's forgiving sinners; so as to render it possible for him to proclaim a universal amnesty, inviting all men to repent, to believe in Christ, and to accept salvation." Instead of holding the reigning view among Finney's Calvinist acquaintances, that Christ's death had "satisfied retributive justice, and borne just what sinners deserve," Finney argued that Christ "had only satisfied public justice, by honoring the law both in his obedience and death; and therefore rendering it safe for God to pardon sin, and to pardon the sins of any man, and of all men, who would repent and believe in Christ." He viewed the atonement as having accomplished "that which was necessary as a condition of the forgiveness of sin; and not that which cancelled sin, in the sense of literally paying the indebtedness of sinners."

At his ordination, he confessed that he had paid little attention to the Westminster Confession of Faith. His strong belief, however, in the Trinity and the deity of Christ, the reality of the operations of the Spirit of God, the necessity of repentance and faith, the certainty of eternal punishment for unbelievers, and the success of his preaching in evoking conversion, convinced his presbytery to ordain him and send him as a missionary to several counties in New York.

MISSIONARY LABORS IN UPSTATE NEW YORK

His work as a missionary resulted in a series of intensive revivals known as the Western Revivals. "Having had no regular training for the ministry I did not expect or desire to labor in large towns or cities, or in cultivated congregations. I intended to go into new settlements & preach in school houses, & barn & groves, as best I could."[13] In the northern part of Jefferson County, when people complimented his preaching but did not give visible manifestation of repentance, as he viewed it, he began to use measures that were designed to get immediate response. He said that he could not spend his time with them if they were not going to receive the gospel. After remonstrating with them about the absolute necessity of taking a stand for what had been demonstrated as the truth to them, he said, "You who now are willing to pledge to me and to Christ that you will immediately make your peace with God, please rise up. On the contrary, you that mean that I should understand that you are committed to remain in your present attitude, not to accept Christ—please, those of you who are of this mind, to sit still." Virtually the entire congregation resisted

---

[13] Rosell and Dupuis, *The Memoirs of Charles G. Finney*, 63.

and turned to leave. When he became silent, they turned to look back and he announced that he would speak to them one more time. Finney and a Baptist deacon fasted and prayed the next day. That evening the church was filled "to its utmost capacity." Finney noted, "I had not taken a thought with regard to what I should preach,—indeed, this was common with me at that time. I was full of the Holy Spirit, and I felt confident that when the time came for action I should know what to preach."[14] Over the next few days, Finney narrated the story of several conversions, including a group of deists, as well as the death of one ardent opponent of the revival.

When other critics arose who lamented his preaching style and his direct addresses to the people, he pointed to the results of his preaching that far outstripped theirs. They complained of the repetitive nature of his preaching. He would embrace a "thought and turn it over and over, and illustrate it in various ways." He assured his detractors that "it was necessary to do so to make myself understood; and that I could not be persuaded to relinquish this practice by any of the arguments." Such a style, they continued to object, would not interest the educated part of the congregation. "But facts soon silenced them on this point," Finney retorted. "They found that under my preaching judges, and lawyers, and educated men were converted by scores; whereas under their methods such a thing seldom occurred."[15]

He continued to believe that little or no preparation was needed for the pulpit concerning the immediate content of the

---

[14] Rosell and Dupuis, *The Memoirs of Charles G. Finney*, 65, 67.

[15] Rosell and Dupuis, *The Memoirs of Charles G. Finney*, 84. This anecdote culminates a series of stories about the alarms that Finney's style of preaching and pulpit vocabulary and demeanor set off. He said on one occasion, "And in respect to the simplicity of my language I defended myself by saying, that my object was not to cultivate a style of oratory that should soar above the heads of the people, but to make myself understood; and that therefore I would use any language that would best make myself understood, and that did not involve vulgarity and obscenity" (82).

sermon, but that the Spirit would give the subject and all of its parts on the spot. He depended on the Holy Spirit to suggest the text on each occasion, and "to open up the whole subject to my mind." As he recollected, he had no "greater success and power than I did when I preached in that way. If I did not preach from inspiration, I don't know how I did preach." When challenged that he boasted of an extraordinary inspiration not promised to ministers of the gospel in our age, he countered,

> I believe that all ministers, called by Christ to preach the Gospel, ought to be, and may be in such a sense inspired, as to "preach the Gospel with the Holy Ghost sent down from heaven." What else did Christ mean when he said, "Go and disciple all nations;—and lo I am with you always, even unto the end of the world?" What did he mean when he said, speaking of the Holy Spirit—"He shall take of mine and show it unto you?" And also "He shall bring all things to your remembrance, whatever I have said unto you?" . . . All ministers may be & ought to be, so filled with the Holy Spirit that all who hear them shall be impressed with the conviction that God is in them of a truth.[16]

His revivals continued in the western and central parts of New York in Antwerp, Evan Mills, Gouverneur, De Kalb, and Western. Finney narrated remarkable events in each of these places. In a summary, he wanted it understood that none of these things could have occurred without the agency of the Holy Spirit. He stressed the reality of the Holy Spirit "underlying, directing, and giving efficiency to the means, without which nothing would

---

[16] Rosell and Dupuis, *The Memoirs of Charles G. Finney*, 94–96. In this chapter, Finney described and defended his style of preaching as superior to those who use a more formal style and always urged the results of his ministry as proof that his method was right. See the discussion of Hambrick-Stowe, *Charles Finney*, 122, 123. He pointed to Finney's eventual practice of making skeleton outlines of his sermon by 1832, a practice that he continued "for the rest of his life."

be accomplished." He then wrote about the spirit of prayer and especially of his sense of "prevailing prayer." In certain instances, he felt he had such a grasp of the promises of Scripture that he would approach God with this attitude: "I hope thou dost not think that I can be denied. I come with the faithful promises in my hand, and I cannot be denied." He went on to comment, "At that time the Spirit of God made such an application of the promises to my mind, and so revealed their real meaning, as to lead me to understand better how to use them, and to what cases they were especially applicable, than I had ever understood before."[17]

THE OPPOSITION ARISES

The unusual character of Finney's methods led to more widespread opposition and the call to meet and attempt reconciliation at New Lebanon in July 1827. The views that defined the character of this conference were later dubbed "hyper orthodoxy" by one of the early converts of Finney, Truman Hastings, a lawyer from Cleveland who had been in Finney's 1826 Troy revival. Finney met with Lyman Beecher, Asahel Nettleton, and several others seeking to come to an understanding of the reports about his methods that had now gained the nomenclature of "New Measures." A group of ministers from the Oneida Association, where these revivals had been occurring, wrote a "Pastoral Letter . . . on the Subject of Revivals of Religion." They listed twenty-nine things that appeared to be evil or dangerous in the methods that Finney had employed in various places in that county and earlier—such as making ostentation and noise, calling men hard names, making too much of favorable appearances, going to places to obtain the Spirit or be converted, not guarding against false conversions, treating young converts injudiciously, trying to make people angry, talking much about opposition, and praying for persons by name in an abusive manner. Nettleton himself presented a letter describing the dangers that he saw in Finney's approach. Finney said it was

---

[17] Rosell and Dupuis, *The Memoirs of Charles G. Finney,* 139.

all built on misrepresentation. To this point, the issues had not been addressed seriously at the level of Finney's theology. Probably such an investigation would have been difficult, for his *Lectures on Revival* were not published until 1835 nor his *Systematic Theology* until 1846. In his memoirs, however, Finney referred frequently to the doctrines that he preached in these places.[18] Beecher vowed that Finney should never come to Boston, and if he tried Beecher would fight him. Eventually, however, Beecher relented and joined with other ministers in inviting Finney.

From 1827 to 1832, Finney gave intense energy to revivals in the cities. His labors were built on the conviction that revival is "not a miracle nor dependent on a miracle, in any sense. It is a purely philosophical result of the right use of the constituted means— as much so as any other effect produced by the application of means." Finney likened revival to growing a crop. God is involved as much in the one as in the other, and in both He has constituted the relation between means and result. "A revival is as naturally a result of the use of the appropriate means as a crop is of the use of its appropriate means. It is true that religion does not properly belong to the category of cause and effect; but although it is not caused by means, yet it has its occasion, and may as naturally and certainly result from its *occasion* as a crop does from its *cause*." In essence, "A revival is nothing else than a new beginning of obedience to God."[19]

After having tried this conviction in these city campaigns, he published it in his *Lectures on Revival of Religion* in 1835, in part a response to an 1832 publication of the same title. He promoted and preached meetings that had quite visible results in New York, Philadelphia, and Rochester. The "Great Revival of Rochester," 1830 to 1831, has been denominated as the most successful of

---

[18] For example, Rosell and Dupuis, *The Memoirs of Charles G. Finney*, 105–106, 131, 154–155, 190, 438–439

[19] Charles Finney, *Lectures on Revival of Religion* (Chicago: Fleming H. Revel, 1868), 12–13.

Finney's career. "The greatness of the work at Rochester at that time," Finney reported in his memoirs, "attracted so much of the attention of ministers and Christians throughout the state of New York, throughout New England, and in many parts of the United States, that the very *fame* of it was an efficient instrument in the hands of the Spirit of God in promoting the greatest revival of religion throughout the land that this country had ever witnessed."[20]

Three decades later, Finney was still able to receive strong testimonials from pastors as to the solid and persevering good done to their churches by Finney's preaching. He went to Boston from September 1831 through April 1832 only after the Congregational ministers united in their invitation. He was originally invited by the laymen of Boston's Union Church, an invitation the clergy sought to block. Beecher wrote what Charles Hambrick-Stowe called a fawning letter praising Finney's intellect and usefulness but stating that it would be better for Finney himself to enter New England in some place other than Boston.[21] Throughout this episode Beecher sought to benefit from Finney's success while seeking to avoid offending the Boston intelligentsia.

Finney was preaching in Providence in August 1831, and the pastor of Third Church of Boston went to Providence to spy out the message and method of Finney. He was thoroughly pleased, found Finney to be engaging, and under his influence the invitation was received. Beecher consented because he believed that Finney had altered significantly since the New Lebanon conference, an impression that was stoutly denied by Finney himself. He wrote, "I may safely appeal to all who heard me in those revivals & who witnessed the measures that I used, & who have heard me & seen my measures in every place, to say whether I have not always & every where employed the measures that I employed in Central

---

[20] Rosell and Dupuis, *The Memoirs of Charles G. Finney*, 325.

[21] Charles E. Hambrick-Stowe, *Charles G. Finney and the Spirit of American Evangelicalism* (Grand Rapids: Eerdmans, 1996), 119.

New York in those great revivals, & in many places I have added other measures as in my judgment they were demanded."[22] Beecher did not overtly oppose Finney while he was there, but he sought to soften some of the demands for radical repentance and discipleship set forth by Finney. In this, Finney was disappointed. But he continued his labors and finally achieved some warming from the congregations to his calls to repentance.

The flurry of meetings that generated conversions connected to Finney's extraordinary means of concentrating attention on the necessity of immediate response led to another note of public opposition. In 1832, W. B. Sprague published his *Lectures on Revival*, which contained nine of his lectures on the subject and twenty appendices consisting of letters about revival from leading evangelical thinkers—"the most distinguished clergymen of our country, and from six different religious denominations." He had hopes of "promoting such revivals as those for which Edwards, and Dwight, and Nettleton, and a host of others both among the living and the dead, have counted it an honor to labor" and aid in giving discernment to avoid spurious excitements and falsely conceived conversions.[23]

Asa Rand, a Congregationalist (and Hopkinsian), launched into a criticism of Finney's theology being virtually humanistic. Rand was ahead of the crowd in theological analysis because he brought his critique after taking notes on Finney's first presentation of "Sinners Bound to Change Their Own Hearts," preached at

---

[22] Rosell and Dupuis, *The Memoirs of Charles G. Finney*, 227.

[23] W. B. Sprague, *Lectures on Revival*, (Edinburgh: Banner of Truth, 1958), xiv. Sprague included a chapter entitled "Evil to be avoided in Connection with Revivals" (215–258). He discussed nine evils to be avoided: cherishing false hopes, having a spirit of self-confidence, being censorious, having inconstancy in religion, being ostentatious, undervaluing divine institutions and divine truth, diminishing the dignity and influence of the ministerial office, setting up false standards of Christian character, and corrupting the purity of the church by spurious religion.

Park Street Church in Boston in the fall of 1831.[24] Finney was defended by Wisner, the pastor who went on the reconnaissance mission to Providence, and others as not rejecting orthodoxy but making advances in the integration of ideas concerning depravity and responsibility, the cross and the moral government of God, and repentance and the work of the Spirit. He recognized that false impressions could follow from some of Finney's language about the will in relation to the work of the Spirit, but that the overall viewpoint was entirely consistent with orthodoxy. A young Charles Hodge investigated the developing controversy and entered the discussion with very negative evaluations of Finney as a crystallization of Nathan W. Taylor's Pelagianism, and he also pointed to the seeming unimportance of Christ and His atonement in Finney's calls for a return to obedience to God.

MATURING HIS STYLE

Finney carried his revival techniques twice to England. In 1849 to 1850, in addition to an itinerate ministry, he preached for a year at Whitefield's Tabernacle under the charge of John Campbell. In 1859 and 1860, he traveled to many places, including Scotland, where he had some success among the Evangelical Union churches. Although they felt at one with him in most theological concepts, Finney resisted identification for he realized that their separatism created a barrier to widespread participation among the general populace; Finney felt smothered.

In England, his most memorable success was in Bolton, but he was disappointed at Manchester. He also experienced an increasing amount of embattlement on theological issues as the details of his *Systematic Theology* became more widely known among those favoring Calvinistic doctrine and views of conversion. In addition, Andrew Bonar had republished Bennett Tyler's 1844 edition of *The Life and Labours of Asahel Nettleton* in 1854 with some added

---

[24] Charles Finney, *Sermons on Important Subjects* (New York: John S. Taylor, 1836), 4–42.

material. That work highlighted the positive effect of Calvinism in revival preaching and also narrated Nettleton's objections to the tone and long-term impact of Finney's revivals. John Campbell, who had been such an ardent supporter during the first visit and welcomed Finney with exuberance on this second soiree into the mother country, had paid more careful attention to the details of his doctrine and began to use the pages of *The British Banner* to criticize him and also referee letters of both opposition and support.

In the cases of cooler reception to his efforts, Finney seemed to feel that denominational loyalties obstructed the necessary spirit of cooperation for an effective revival. From this experience, he developed another principle for the promotion of a revival that became something of revivalistic orthodoxy in America from this time, throughout the remainder of the nineteenth century and into the twentieth century. Whether it will survive through the twenty-first remains to be seen.

> Indeed, I found it to be true in England wherever I tried it, that the best way to promote revivals of religion was to hold independent meetings; that is, meetings in large halls, where they can be obtained, to which all denominations may come. . . . And I am persuaded that the true way to labor for souls there is to have no particular connection with any distinct denomination; but to preach the true gospel, and make a stand in halls, or even in streets when the weather is favorable, where no denominational feelings and peculiarities can straiten the influences of the Spirit of God.[25]

Charles Finney served three churches as pastor during his ministry: Chatham Street Chapel in New York (1832–1836), Broadway Tabernacle in New York (1836–1837), and First Congregational, Oberlin Ohio (1837–1872). As a contributor to

---

[25] Rosell and Dupuis, *The Memoirs of Charles G. Finney*, 613–614.

theological education, he began his tenure as professor of theology at Oberlin College in 1835 and served from 1851 to 1866 as president, succeeding Asa Mahan, who had resigned under duress. During those days he preached regularly to the students, giving further development to the idiosyncrasies of his theology and promoting his technique, while at the same time seeking to moderate, without quenching, the zeal for abolition among the professors and students and their activity in the Underground Railroad.

Upon the urging of many friends who felt indebted to Finney's system of revival, he began writing his memoirs in 1866 and completed them in 1868. His intent was to set the record straight concerning what he felt were misperceptions about his revivals. These misperceptions, which he largely ignored earlier in his life, were now set before the public by the *Autobiography of Lyman Beecher*, published in 1864 and 1865. Finney did not publish his memoirs during his lifetime, but the work came into print in January 1876. It was never intended to be an autobiography but rather a narrative of his revival career, emphasizing the purity and enduring effects of those revivals.

The last occasion of preaching that he recorded was in the First Church at Oberlin on January 12, 1868. In many ways it demonstrated in microcosm both the theology and the method so central to his ministry.

> Yesterday, Sabbath Jan. 12th, we had a very solemn day in the First church. I preached all day upon resisting the Holy Ghost. At the close of the afternoon service first I called upon all professors of religion who were willing to commit themselves against all resistance offered to the teachings of the Holy Spirit, to rise up and unite with us in prayer under the solemnity of this promise. Nearly all the professors of religion, I should think, rose up without hesitation. I then called upon those that were not converted to rise up, and take the same stand. I had been endeavoring to show that they had always

been resisting the Holy Ghost; that they were stiff-necked and uncircumcised in heart and ears, and had always resisted the Holy Ghost. I asked those of them who were willing then and there to pledge themselves to do this no more, and to rise up, and we would make them subjects of prayer. So far as I could see from the pulpit, nearly every person in the house stood up under these calls. We then had a very solemn season of prayer, and dismissed the meetings.[26]

His Final Day

On August 15, 1875, Finney spent a quiet time of Sabbath reflection and family enjoyment. Upon retiring for the evening, he was seized with heart difficulties and died at the dawn of the next day, August 16. He had resigned his pastorate in 1872 but continued his lectures in theology at the college until July 1875, just a few weeks before his death.[27]

The Matter and Manner of Finney

In *The Memoirs of Charles G. Finney*, the aging evangelist presented his theological differences with the confessionalist stream of Congregational and Presbyterian ministers as having begun early. His recollections from 1866 to 1868 imposed on that time forty-five years earlier may have presented his doctrinal system more defined and clearly stated than it actually was. That his spirit of independence in thought and his attachment to a populist kind of rationalism made him resist the system of his would-be tutors cannot be doubted. How quickly he systematized his thought is a matter of speculation. Given his admittedly complete ignorance of theological literature at the time of his conversion and how quickly he began his revival preaching, that it developed over a

---

[26] Rosell and Dupuis, *The Memoirs of Charles G. Finney*, 633.

[27] Rosell and Dupuis, *The Memoirs of Charles G. Finney*, 636.

two-decade period would not be far wrong. When it did grow into a discernible system, however, it is easy to see why the practical outworking of these ideas troubled Asahel Nettleton and those like him. Finney's ideas developed as the fruit of the pelagianizing tendency of Nathan W. Taylor's New Haven theology. In addition, the content of truth often rested on the foundation of apparent success.

Matter

For Finney, consistent with Arminian views on the subject, election is built on foreknowledge—"God must have foreknown who would and who would not have been saved." He rejected Adam Clarke's view of *selective* foreknowledge as absurd and self-contradictory. Finney's understanding of this issue considered God's unchangeableness. "Has he any new light? Has he changed his mind" at the time of judgment? Divine timelessness meant that "the beginning and the end of time . . . are present to his mind," and thus individual selection unto salvation was done just as it is in accordance with moral government. "If any part of mankind is saved, it is because God can wisely save them." In the wisest possible administration of His government, God "can bring sufficient moral influence to bear upon" those particular persons to convert them without violating the voluntary nature of all human decision. "It is a contradiction," Finney argued, "to say that the same amount of moral influence can be brought to bear upon every individual of the human family." That would be to assert "that every individual could be in circumstances in all respects, precisely similar. But this is a natural impossibility." Election, therefore, is God's foresight of who "could be converted under the wisest administration of his government." Such individuals are chosen to eternal life in light of God's foreknowledge. Finney argued, "Foreknowledge and election are not inconsistent with free agency, but are founded upon it." In light of God's exhaustive foreknowledge, Finney surmised, "The elect were chosen to eternal life, because God foresaw that in perfect exercise of their freedom, they could be induced to repent and embrace the Gospel."[28]

In a sermon entitled "The Salvation of Sinners Impossible," Finney explained, "The simple and plain view of it is, that God, foreseeing all the future of your existence as perfectly as if all were in fact present, determined to deal with you according to your voluntary course; determined to offer you the gospel, and, on your refusal of it to give you over to the doom of those who deny the Lord that bought them."[29] It should be obvious to any observer that this pushes the supposed inviolability and independence of the human will into eternity as the determiner of God's intentions. God has an eternal determination to accomplish that which most magnifies His moral government. Irresistible operations to effect human volition are contradictory to moral government, according to Finney.

Thus, Finney viewed sin as purely *voluntary* and theoretically avoidable. "Voluntariness is indispensable to moral character," Finney instructed. "It is the universal and irresistible conviction of men, that an action, to be praise or blame-worthy, must be free."[30] There is no original corruption of nature, therefore, for that would be both deterministic and connected with imputation, a concept Finney also saw as immoral. Disobedience to moral law "cannot consist in the constitution of soul or body. The law does not command us to have a certain constitution, nor forbid us to have the constitution with which we came into being." Sin consists in "the irrational gratification of the appetites and passion." For a person to be saved, one "must be brought back . . . to a state in which God and reason control the free action of the mind, and appetite is held in due subjection." Moral depravity, as Finney defined it, is "a voluntary attitude of the mind" that consists in "the committal of the will to the gratification of the desire, or as the Bible expresses,

---

28 Finney, *Sermons on Important Subjects*. 129–137.

29 Finney, *The Way of Salvation*, 160.

30 Finney, *Sermons on Important Subjects*, 27.

of the lusts of the flesh, as opposed to that which the law of God requires." Departing from God's law "must consist in the choice of self-gratification as an end . . . committing the whole being, to the indulgence of self-love, as the supreme and ultimate end of life." The wicked heart must be seen as the voluntary state of the will "setting up his own interest in opposition to the interest and government of God," or seeking to "promote his own private happiness, in a way that is opposed to the general good." Given the nature of depravity, it is no surprise that regeneration is seen as a voluntary alteration of one's "ultimate intention." It consists of a "change in the attitude of the will, or a change in its ultimate choice, intention, or preference." Finney exhorted that "a lazy man can not get to heaven," for "to get there costs toil and labour. For his will must be sanctified. The entire voluntary department of his being must be renovated."[31] The change of heart that constitutes regeneration means "changing the controlling preference of the mind in regard to the end of pursuit."[32] Finney stated, with full sincerity of its necessity and of its possibility, "Sinner! instead of waiting and praying for God to change your heart, you should at once summon up your powers, put forth the effort, and change the governing preference of your mind."[33]

Finney preached a sermon entitled "How to Change your Heart." He gave a lengthy explanation of the manner in which both the mind and the conscience are informed of what is right. He included discussion on the foolishness and wickedness of sin and the wisdom and rightness of obeying God. He pointed out that sinners engaged in an uninterrupted course of disobedience to God. Such moral realities of life secured the certainty of eternal punishment for those that persist in it, so on that basis he issued urgent calls for repentance and faith. Repentance is to hate and renounce sin; faith is to "believe his word and walk in the path

---

[31] Finney, *The Way of Salvation,* 142.

[32] Finney, *Sermons on Important Subjects,* 7.

[33] Finney, *Sermons on Important Subjects,* 22.

he points out to you." The atonement has opened a way by which God can receive those who repent and walk in obedience without violating His moral government. We make a new heart by an act of informed volition.

> To choose God and his services—to prefer these to your own interest and to every thing else, is to change your heart. Have you done it? Do you still ask, how shall I do it? You might with much more propriety ask, when the meeting is dismissed, how shall I go home? To go home would require two things, first, to be willing; secondly, to put your body in motion. But here, no muscular power is needed. But one thing is requisite, that is a willing mind. Your consent is all that is needed. Be willing to do your duty, and the work is done.[34]

Finney made regeneration analogous to any change of opinion that can be effected in a person by rational argument. Differences between people on any number of matters do not mean that the substance of their minds, bodies, or rationality is different. This variety comes from "the voluntary state of mind in which they are." Even so, "it is just as unphilosophical, absurd, and unnecessary, to suppose that a physical or constitutional change has taken place in him who has the new heart, as to infer, that because a man has changed his politics, therefore, his nature is changed." A new preference in any matter, but especially in the matter of obedience to God, "needs only to become deep and energetic enough in its influence, to stamp the perfection of heaven upon the whole character."[35]

Salvation from sin and from hell only relates to moral agents. This necessarily involves "a moral government over them, and over them *as moral beings*, which is the same thing as to say, that they must have the liberty of free voluntary action." Finney did

---

[34] Finney, *Sermons on Important Subjects*, 38.
[35] Finney, *Sermons on Important Subjects*, 11.

not imply that God "must preclude himself from throwing in moral influences to affect their action." He did insist, however, "that their liberty of moral action must not be abridged." God's "interposing influences must evermore be of a moral, and not of a physical or compulsory nature." It is the nature of the case that "God cannot save men without their concurrence." Even so, "they could not be holy without their own concurrence," nor could they be happy. "Being constituted moral agents, and made subjects of moral government, it must be in every point of view impossible to save them unless they will turn from their sins." Since God governs as a moral agent, "he can do nothing inconsistent with its moral nature. If, then, God works upon the sinner by means of his providence and his spirit, to the utmost extent he wisely can, and all in vain, there remains nothing more which, as a moral governor, he can do to save him."[36]

Finney's constant drumbeat on the issue of the voluntariness or moral action came from his rejection of the idea that intrinsic moral disposition is fully consistent with the reality of moral freedom. He insisted as a matter of rational presupposition that God's holiness is voluntary. Voluntary moral fitness "is sympathy with God and likeness to him;—the state of mind that God has." When we see that "holiness in God is not a part of his nature in such a sense that it is not voluntary in him, but it is a voluntary exercise and state of his mind," then we learn that by "free will" sinners "must voluntarily conform themselves to rectitude."[37]

If moral *disposition* determines moral action, Finney surmised, then ipso facto it cannot be voluntary. Given this viewpoint, it comes as no surprise that he believed that the distinction between natural ability and moral ability constituted an irrationality, an absurdity. Commands, he averred, always imply present ability. The natural ability to perform a command must include the

---

[36] Finney, *The Way of Salvation*, 266.

[37] Finney, *The Way of Salvation,* 332. This is from a sermon entitled "On Being Holy," based on 1 Peter 1:16.

moral ability. There can be no aspect of inability if persons are true moral agents to whom moral commands apply. This explains his understanding that sinners must change their own hearts. In his view, therefore, conversion consists of four confluent causes:

- *Spirit of God*—"The agent who induces him is the Spirit of God." The Spirit can do no more, however, in a qualitative way than the preacher. He is able to probe more deeply and more alarmingly into the conscience, but He effects no change in the moral disposition.

- *Truth*—"The truth is the instrument, or motive, which the Spirit uses to induce the sinner to turn."

- *The preacher*—He is a secondary agent who presents the truth and must seek to show the absolute absurdity and infinite danger of unbelief. He must earn the operations of the mind and employ all his skills to make the sinner "yield upon the spot."

- *The sinner himself*—"The fact is, that the actual turning, or change, is the sinner's own act." While God by the truth works to convince a person to turn, "still it is strictly true that he has turned and has done it himself."[38]

Conversion occurs when, due to the confluence of the first three agents of conversion, the sinner becomes rationally and cordially persuaded to alter his ultimate intention in life from service of self to obedience to God.

Finney's conviction that only moral suasion and providential arrangement are consistent with the free moral agency of men does not explain the praiseworthiness of God's truthfulness alongside the impossibility of God's lying. Nor does it explain how God Himself is a perfect moral agent who is immutable in His holiness

---

[38] Charles Finney, "Sinners Bound to Change Their Own Hearts," in Ferm, *Issues in American Protestantism*, 164–168.

and perfectly wise and holy in His decree. This conundrum drove Finney to assert that holiness is not natural but voluntary in God. How effectual calling is a violation of moral agency Finney does not explain, other than to assert that compulsion is wrong, that a "physical" change (a change in moral nature) is anomalous to the very essence of humanity and of true holiness, and that, consequently, the nature of the influence must be limited to moral suasion. Does *effectual calling* not respect, and indeed operate on the basis of, humanity in its moral agency? Effectual calling establishes, to use Finney's language, the "concurrence" of man's moral nature with the moral perfections as set forth in the gospel. Effectual calling honors man as a moral agent, even if his sinfulness is much more radical than admitted by Finney. Such invincible calling that operates immediately on the moral disposition imposes no loyalty or response of repentance and faith that is not fully concurrent with a heart made holy. As the Baptist Catechism puts it, "Effectual calling is a work of God's Spirit, whereby, convincing us of our sin and misery, enlightening our minds in the knowledge of Christ, and *renewing our wills*, he doth persuade and enable us to embrace Jesus Christ freely offered to us in the gospel."[39] The New Hampshire Confession of Faith defines regeneration as "giving a holy disposition to the mind; and is effected in a manner above our comprehension or calculation, by the power of the Holy Spirit, in connection with divine truth, *so as to secure our voluntary obedience to the gospel*; and that its proper evidence is found in the holy fruit which we bring forth to the glory of God."[40]

Finney saw that fundamental to the Reformed concept of innate moral corruption was the system of imputation. He considered that system, therefore, immoral. In Finney's theology, justification and atonement lost any content of specific substitution. The atonement falls in line with the moral government theory;

---

[39] The answer to question 34 in The Baptist Catechism.

[40] New Hampshire Confession, Article VII, "Of Grace in Regeneration." Emphasis added.

justification is forgiveness and voluntary obedience unto holiness. "Finally, the greatness of the change requisite in passing from sin to real holiness—from Satan's kingdom into full fitness for Christ's, creates no small difficulty in the way of saving even the converted," Finney preached. Concerning Christ's obedience in the context of justification, Finney noted, "Had he obeyed for us, he would not have suffered for us. Were his obedience to be substituted for our obedience, he need not certainly have both fulfilled the law for us, as our substitute, under a covenant of works, and at the same time have suffered as a substitute, in submitting to the penalty of the law." Connecting the atonement in any way to a substitutionary obedience represents God as requiring 1) the obedience of our substitute; 2) His suffering, as if no obedience had been rendered; 3) our repentance, and 4) our return to personal obedience. And then, legal requirements having been fulfilled, salvation is ascribed to grace. "Strange grace this, that requires a debt to be paid several times over, before obligation is discharged!"[41]

Having done away with any imputation, the atonement is general because of its nature. It has no vital and organic connection with the forgiveness of sins but is only expedient on the part of God to bring about repentance on the part of the sinner. In such an atonement, there is no "lack of provision in the atonement to cover all the wants of sinners, and even to make propitiation for the sins of the world." Christ's death has "entire sufficiency . . . to do all that an atonement can do or need do for the salvation of our race." Recalling the confessional position against which he had pushed back so vigorously, he wrote,

> Some have regarded the atonement simply in the light of the payment of a debt; and have represented Christ as purchasing the elect of the Father, and paying down the same amount of suffering in his own person that justice would have exacted of them. To this I answer: It is naturally impossible, as it would require that satisfaction

---

[41] Finney, *Systematic Theology*, 206.

should be made to retributive justice. Strictly speaking, retributive justice can never be satisfied.[42]

Given his understanding of human ability and the nature of justification, it should come as no surprise that Finney taught that faith involved reaching a state of sinlessness. Since the propitiatory work of the cross involves no substitution or imputation, it operates in conjunction with the voluntary energetic efforts to crucify the habit of our rebellion against God's holiness. "The crucifixion of Christ is an emblem of this, and serves, therefore, in a measure, to show what this must be and should be." Finney argued that the crucifixion of Christ works for forgiveness within the same stream and to the same extent that it operates for holiness. "Does any one suppose," Finney asked, "that the whole intent of Christ's crucifixion is to meet the demands of the violated law?" Then he answered, "Not so; but it was also to be an emblem of the work to be wrought upon and within the Christian's soul. Its old selfish habitudes must be broken up and its powerful tendencies to evil be slain."[43] This work of sanctification then leads to the true status of justification: perfect holiness. Finney described the pilgrimage that "constitutes sanctification," identical with justification. "Every act of obedience to God strengthens this preference," he advised, "and renders future obedience more natural." So natural it becomes that it produces "perfect control of this preference over all the moral movements of the mind." This perfect control "brings a man back to where Adam was previous to the fall, and constitutes perfect holiness."[44] Finney asked the question, "Can God, in any sense, justify one who does not yield a present and full obedience to the moral law?" The doctrine that Christians "are justified without present full obedience" is absolutely "a doctrine of devils." Well, so much for Luther and the other Reformers doctrine of *simul justus et peccator*. God has no right to justify a person "while any degree

---

[42] Finney, *Systematic Theology*, 206–207.

[43] Finney, *The Way of Salvation*, 143.

[44] Finney, *Sermons on Important Subjects*, 11.

of sin remains in him." Based on these premises, Finney concluded that "whenever a Christian sins he comes under condemnation, and must repent and do his first works, or be lost."[45]

He developed this idea at Oberlin after 1836, influenced to some degree by Asa Mahan. Mahan spoke of a perfection of will resulting in a life of continuous voluntary obedience to God. Mahan assumed also the "baptism of the Holy Spirit," which empowered and perfected the will. Finney, in order to achieve consistency, contended that "holiness in God is not a part of his nature is such a sense that it is not voluntary in him, but it is a voluntary exercise and state of mind." To be godlike, therefore, the sinner's voluntary regeneration should "become deep and energetic enough in its influence, to stamp the *perfection of heaven* upon the whole character" (emphasis added). In fact, Finney asserted, perfect holiness is essential to salvation. "The command to be holy implies the practicability of becoming so." Those who do not believe it possible in this life are not true believers. "They do not believe God's word of promise. They have no faith that men can become holy in this life, yet they say they believe in Christ." If Christ saves His people from their sins and God will sanctify us wholly, how can one be a believer and reject the idea of perfect holiness in this life? Finney became struck with the idea of salvation from sinning in this life and "found it everywhere as I read the New Testament, and indeed in the Old Testament also. Oh, how strange that the church should be fighting the ideas of becoming holy through Jesus Christ! How strange that they should insist that he will do no such thing!"[46]

---

[45] Finney, *Systematic Theology*, 53–60.

[46] Finney, *The Way of Salvation*, 337–339.

MANNER

Given this theology, certain distinctions arose in his revival method "to persuade sinners to choose right." In redefining the work of the Spirit as limited to a moral power, he looked at it as "that kind of power by which an advocate moves and bows the heart of a jury." In arguing his case before a congregation, therefore, Finney claimed to "cooperate with the Spirit of God; for this is the very thing the Spirit of God is endeavoring to secure," their "present action in accordance with the claims of God." [47]

More earnest effort should be given, therefore, to immediate conversion under "the voice of the living preacher." When other preachers of his acquaintance dealt with souls in distress, they recommended the use of means and isolated retirement to discover one's calling. "The Lord convinced me," he wrote, "that this was no way to deal with souls," God showed him "clearly that moral depravity must be *voluntary*," Finney argued, "that the divine agency in regeneration must consist in reaching the soul, in argument, in persuasion, entreaty." He continued insisting that "the thing to be done was to set the sinner's duty clearly before him, and depend on the Spirit's teaching to urge him to do it; to set Christ before him, and expect the Holy Spirit to take of the things of Jesus and show them to the sinner; to set his sins before him, and expect the Holy Spirit to show him his awful wickedness, and lead him voluntarily to renounce his sins." In other words, cooperation with the Spirit as an intelligent agent meant that "I must present the truth to be believed, the duties to be done, and the reasons for those duties. This is the very thing that the Spirit is doing, to make the sinner see and understand the force of the reasons urged by the minister, the truth of the facts stated and to give the sinner realizing sense of those truths which the minister presents to him, to induce him to act." To divert the sinner's attention to his dependence on the Spirit "was

---

[47] Rosell and Dupuis, *The Memoirs of Charles G. Finney*, 323.

necessarily to hinder rather than to help forward the work of the Spirit." By such teaching of dependence, "sinners were constantly stumbled, and almost never converted under the voice of the living preacher."[48]

With this view of the kind of attention that the preacher must help the sinner give to the subject, and "just at the point where the sinner is thoroughly instructed, and while under the voice of the living preacher with the strong pressure of truth set home by the Holy Ghost upon him, something was needed to induce him to act then and there upon his convictions."[49] When all the arguments had been presented in their full strength for the irrational and absurd wickedness of resisting the Holy Spirit and rejecting Christ, and done in such a way as had a tendency "to convert him to Christ; and that when this was faithfully and prayerfully done, we had a right to expect the Holy Spirit to co-operate with us."[50]

Finney also claimed, somewhat in the spirit of James Davenport in the First Great Awakening, divine leadership and approval for the development of his methods. As cited above, Finney developed his manner of dealing with souls on the confidence that "the Lord convinced me that this was no way to deal with souls."[51]

The reason for this confidence lay in his sense that the Spirit had given him insight. However minimally Finney observed the work of the Spirit in regeneration, he knew no bounds of the Spirit's work in his own work, both in method and in preaching. "Let no man think," Finney insisted, "that those sermons which have been called so powerful were production of my own brain, or of my own heart, unassisted by the Holy Ghost. They were not mine, but from the Holy Spirit in me." Nor was this gift of inspiration for himself only, but it should be pursued with confidence by

---

[48] Rosell and Dupuis, *The Memoirs of Charles G. Finney*, 321–323.

[49] Rosell and Dupuis, *The Memoirs of Charles G. Finney*, 323.

[50] Rosell and Dupuis, *The Memoirs of Charles G. Finney*, 152.

[51] Rosell and Dupuis, *The Memoirs of Charles G. Finney*, 239–240.

every gospel minister. His was not a "higher inspiration than is promised to ministers, or than ministers have a right to expect." In fact, when the promise was given to the apostle that the Spirit would "take of mine and show it to you," this promise was to all preachers of the gospel. "All ministers may and ought to be," Finney concluded, "so filled with the Holy Spirit that all who hear them shall be impressed with the conviction that 'God is in them of a truth.'"[52] Even in the moment of preaching, the evangelist must make sure that he has not substituted his own preparation for the Spirit's revelation, for, as Finney explained, "I held that the Holy Spirit operates in the preacher clearly revealing these truths in their proper order to him, and enabling him to set them before the people in such proportion and in such order as was calculated to convert them."[53]

As in his unprepared sermons, so was divine revelation at work in his methods. When he earlier insisted on the perpetuity of his methods, he affirmed, "Were I to live my life over again, . . . I should under the same circumstances use substantially the same measures that I did then." This certainty arose from his perception of divine revelation in the methods employed. "It was no wisdom of my own," he explained, "that directed me." No, it was the wisdom from above. "I had no doubt then nor have I ever had that God led me by his Spirit to take the course I did. So clearly did he lead me from day to day that I never did nor could doubt that I was Divinely directed."[54]

All that was needed, therefore, were ways in which the attention of the hearer could be arrested and given opportunity for undistracted concentration on his condition. "It appeared to me then, as it ever has since, that the great failure of the ministry and of the church in promoting religion consisted, in great measure, in the want of a suitable adaptation of means to that end." Finney described the

---

[52] Rosell and Dupuis, *The Memoirs of Charles G. Finney*, 95–96.

[53] Rosell and Dupuis, *The Memoirs of Charles G. Finney*, 153.

[54] Rosell and Dupuis, *The Memoirs of Charles G. Finney*, 227.

"anxious seat" as "a means of promoting revival" because, from his "own experience and observation," he felt "the necessity of some measure that would bring sinners to a stand." Something needed to make the impressions "that they were expected then and there to give up their hearts." At Rochester he first began to employ the anxious seat, for he needed something that would make them act as publicly before the world as they had in their pursuit of sin, "something that would commit them publicly to the service of Christ." Those whom he called to these seats, vacated for this specific purpose, were "so ripe that they were willing then and there to renounce their sins and give themselves to God."[55]

SUMMARY AND EVALUATION

The methods used by Finney in his revival efforts were the immediate result of his theology. He summarized the connection is this way:

> The doctrine upon which I insisted, that the command to obey God implied the power to do so, created in some places considerable opposition at first. Denying also the *moral* depravity was *physical,* or the depravity of nature, and maintaining, as I did, that it is altogether voluntary, and therefore that the Spirit's influences were those of teaching, persuading, convicting, and of course, a moral influence—these doctrines were to a great extent new to many. . . . It was said that I taught self-conversion, self-regeneration; and not infrequently was I rebuked for addressing the sinner as if the blame of his impenitence all belonged to himself, and for urging him to immediate submission. However, I persisted in this course, and it was seen by ministers and Christians that God owned it as His truth, and blessed it to the salvation of thousands of souls.[56]

---

[55] Rosell and Dupuis, *The Memoirs of Charles G. Finney*, 306–307.

[56] Rosell and Dupuis, *The Memoirs of Charles G.* Finney, 154–155.

Finney's doctrine and practice initiated a radical shift in concepts of both revival and conversion among evangelicals. Wildly varied reactions to Finney's New Measures, as well as the theology supporting them, began to flow forth in the nineteenth century. Asahel Nettleton, upon request from pastors with whom he had worked, went to Finney while he was in Troy and interviewed him. He came to believe "there could be no hope of convincing Mr. Finney of his errors, so long as he was upheld and encouraged by ministers of high respectability." Nettleton wrote a long letter to Dr. S. C. Aikin of Utica, New York. He pointed mainly to a denunciatory spirit, the adoption of measures calamitous to revival, and a seeming incorrigibility. "I have long been wishing to correct some of his peculiarities, that I might invite him into my own field, and introduce him to my friends," Nettleton wrote. In addition to poor health, however, one factor made Nettleton hesitate: "Some of his particular friends are urging him on to the very things which I wish him to drop. I fear that their flattering representations will overcome all that I can say."[57]

Asa Rand and Charles Hodge brought early and highly pertinent theological critiques to Finney. Rand attended a service in which he heard Finney preach his sermon "Sinners Bound to Change their Own Hearts." He took notes rapidly and published a sixteen-page pamphlet entitled *The New Divinity Tried*. He did not mention Finney by name, though he used the sermon to make every point concerning the weaknesses he perceived in the New Divinity. He alleged that Finney did not know Scripture in that he omitted from any discussion the massive number of texts that declare the heart of man to be deceived, deceitful, wicked, captive, hateful, and corrupt, and that all human actions arise from such a heart. He ignored decades and centuries of theological development and carefully constructed vocabulary and concepts, such as were present in the Westminster Confession of Faith. In Rand's observation, there is no true conversion in Finney's

---

[57] Tyler, *New England Revivals*, 353

theology, since it is only an act of the sinner's will with powers, both mental and moral, already present within him. Because of this, Finney's views trivialized the work of the Spirit as presented so fully and deeply in Scripture, reducing Him to an outside agent playing the part of a mere persuader, as if He were only another preacher of moral reform.[58]

Hodge agreed with Rand, but went further in his critique. "We believe that the characteristic tendency of this mode of preaching is to keep the Holy Spirit and his influences out of view, and we fear a still more serious objection is, that Christ and his cross are practically made of none effect." The exhortation to make choice of God as the portion of the soul and change the governing purpose of the life are acts, so Hodge understood Finney, that have no immediate reference to Christ. They are only logically compelling responses to transcendent principles of moral government. The soul comes to God without a mediator. "We maintain," Hodge wrote, "that this is another Gospel. It is practically another system, and a legal system of religion." Hodge continued, "We do not intend that the doctrine of the mediation of Christ is rejected, but that it is neglected; that the sinner is led to God directly; that he is not urged, under the pressure of the sense of guilt, to go to Christ for pardon, and then to God." Hodge believed that this defect has a tendency "fatal to religion and the souls of men."[59]

Hodge was close to the heart of the issue in pointing to Finney's minimizing of the place that Christ's mediation has in his scheme of salvation. In his scheme, however, Christ's atoning work was not merely neglected but rejected, for there was no substitution, no propitiation, no imputation, and thus no real dependence on the work of Christ for forgiveness or righteousness.

---

[58] Asa Rand, *The New Divinity Tried, Being an Examination of a Sermon Delivered by the Rev. C. G. Finney, on Making a New Heart.* Boston: Light and Harris, 1832.

[59] Charles, Hodge, "New Divinity Tried," The Biblical Repertory and Theological Review 4, no. 2 (April 1832): 304.

In its review of Finney's memoirs, *The Southern Presbyterian Review* called the discursive autobiography "a very melancholy record." It savored of *enthusiasm,* that is, "an imaginary direct intercourse with the Deity." Finney's anthropology, they judged, "is the baldest Pelagianism," leading to the remark that "such a miserably shallow anthropology must of course have a correspondingly shallow soteriology." Given Finney's arguments for a sinless state of holiness and his view of the simple voluntary nature of depravity, justification, and sanctification, the reviewer surmised, "He had as little use for Christ in his system as for the Holy Ghost." The review continued, "For ourselves, we should prefer being broken on the wheel or burnt at the stake to being the writer of such pages."[60]

Hodge's review of Finney's *Systematic Theology* involved a long and intricate discussion of Finney's rationalistic epistemology. Hodge observed that Finney deduced from principles of moral government based on moral law the entirety of his theological system. For example, on his first page, Finney wrote,

> Moral law is primarily a rule for the direction of the action of free will, and strictly of free will only. But secondarily, and less strictly, it is the rule for the regulation of all those actions and states of mind and body, that follow the free actions of will by a law of necessity. Thus, moral law controls involuntary mental states and outward action only by securing conformity of the actions of free will to its precept.[61]

Finney's relentless logical connections between moral law and the consequent necessity of free will led Hodge to observe, "The Scriptures are throughout recognized as a mere subordinate authority. They are allowed to come in and bear confirmatory

---

[60] *The Southern Presbyterian Review* (Columbia, SC: Presbyterian Publishing House, April 1876), 394–397.

[61] Finney, *Systematic Theology,* 1.

testimony, but their place is altogether secondary." God Himself rests His will in subordination to the necessities of human intelligence so that "his will can impose no obligation; it only discloses what is obligatory in its own nature and by the law of reason." Finney's system tended to make "God but a name for the moral law or order of the universe, or reason in the abstract." The progress from moral government to doctrines of depravity, ability, regeneration, faith, justification, the atonement, perfection in holiness, and divine sovereignty evoked the surmise that Finney's theological method is "eminently logical, rationalistic, reckless and confident." So that "almost without exception" his doctrines first are "proved, demonstrated as true, as the necessary sequences of admitted or assumed principles, before the Bible is so much as named." Finney consistently begged the question when "he lays it down as an axiom that liberty implies ability to obey moral law, and consequently that responsibility is limited by ability." In a pervasive way, his system could not function apart from this assumption. Hodge consented to call Finney "a most important laborer in the cause of truth" but maintained that those who embrace his theology "must either go forward to Oberlin or back to the common faith of Protestants." Finney was right to argue that "obligation is limited by ability." No less obviously true, however, both in experience and in the biblical worldview, is Finney's statement "that an inability which has its origin in sin, which consists in what is sinful, and relates to moral action, is perfectly consistent with continued obligation." Such is the instinctive judgment of men, such is the testimony of conscience, such is the plain doctrine of the Bible, which no vehemence or frequency of contradiction or denial has ever been able to convince sinful men is not true.[62]

Lectures of Revival by W. B. Sprague, published in 1832, contained nine sermons by Sprague on revival and twenty letters

---

[62] Charles Hodge, *Essays & Reviews* (New York: Robert Carter & Brothers, 1857) 245–284.

by leading theological thinkers. These avoided any straightforward emphasis on Finney himself, but clearly discussed several issues of concern raised by Finney's increasing influence. The negative repercussions, both doctrinally and experientially, arising from Finney's revivalistic onslaught should not dampen either the zeal or the positive theology for revival. Wanting to guard a church from objections that had arisen in the Finney's flurry of revival campaigns, Sprague said,

> I hope what has been said may confirm your conviction that the cause of revivals is emphatically the Savior's cause; and that you may be disposed, each one to labor in it with increased diligence and zeal. And may your labors be characterized by such Christian prudence, and tenderness, and fidelity, that while you shall see a rich blessing resting on them, they may have a tendency to silence the voice of opposition, and increase the number of those who shall co-operate with you in sustaining and advancing this glorious cause.[63]

In his letter, Daniel Dana sought to affirm what Finney emphasized that was imitable but warned against one of the major errors. "We cannot speak to sinners too emphatically of their obligation to immediate repentance; of the guilt and danger of delay; nor of their encouragement to give themselves to religion; nor of the absolute certainty that if they truly seek, they shall obtain blessings. Nor can we employ too much pains to wrest from them their ten thousand excuses for impenitence." Given the necessity of such urgency, however, "we may not suffer them to forget their deep depravity; their insufficiency; their dependence on sovereign mercy; nor the necessity of divine influence to change their hearts."[64]

---

[63] Sprague, *Lectures on Revivals*, 59–60.

[64] Sprague, *Lectures on Revivals*, 19.

Other writings seeking to address various errors of Finney were from John W. Nevin in *The Anxious Bench*, written in 1843, and *Nettleton and His Labors* by Bennet Tyler, in 1844. Tyler wanted to highlight the life and ministry of Asahel Nettleton with a view to recommending his approach to revival, and to point to the distinct difference between Nettleton and Finney, by showing the points at which Nettleton himself criticized Finney. Tyler's own judgment was measured. "A great excitement attended the preaching of Mr. Finney and his coadjutors; and multitudes were reported as the subjects of renewing grace. That very many of the reputed converts were like the stony ground hearers, who endured only for a time, few will at this day be disposed to deny. Yet it is believed that some were truly converted to Christ."[65]

BRIEF STATEMENT OF CONTINUITY

We will close this chapter with a brief reassertion of several distinct points Finney held in common with those promoters of revival who had preceded him.

One, in times of declension, revival is needed. The purposeful revival effort is to re-energize spiritually those who are converted and to seek the salvation of the lost. Some could legitimately argue that increased spiritual growth was not really a part of Finney's theory of revival, but due to his views of the sinless status of true believers, a new experience of salvation would be needed for backsliders.

Two, spiritual life exceeds infinitely in importance every other aspect of life.

Three, sinners must be urged to see that their duty is to repent immediately and turn to Christ for salvation. No kind of inability can justify a refusal to come to the saving work of Christ in repentance and faith.

---

[65] Tyler, *Nettleton and His Labours,* 340.

Four, excitements in themselves for themselves are detrimental to true revival. Despite his new methods and his sense of immediate inspiration, Finney sought to minimize excitements that might bypass the rational faculties. Jonathan Edwards spoke more—and approved more—of sense, emotion, and affection than Finney. In reality, the objection to Finney was not that he was too emotional or that he induced too much excitement, but that he was too rational and seemed to have little place for gracious affections.

Five, revival must be built on theological principles. Hodge gave a deep dive on the peculiar theological principles that energized Finney. Hodge found them wanting, but it cannot be denied that Finney built with consistent application to his theology and believed that true revival would conform to those principles.

Six, Finney called for radical, "non-selfish" repentance. No repentance, no salvation. The alteration of one's "ultimate intention," however, was manageable by the human intellect and fully effected by the human will. No hidden elements of sinful propensity on account of the presence of formerly deeply corrupted affections were present, for all sin was related to the will and the intelligent knowledge of precisely the points of disobedience.

Seven, the business of the preacher is to join the Holy Spirit in using the means He requires, pointing to the truths that He has revealed. In that way the preacher does "co-operate" with the Spirit in seeking sinners for Christ. Unlike those previous seekers of revival, however, Finney believed that the Spirit could do no more than the preacher by way of effecting the change implied in regeneration. He could do more quantitatively because of His attributes of knowledge and truth, but the final hope for revival is that the sinner himself will make himself a new heart.

CHAPTER 8

1858 PRAYER REVIVAL

"So noiseless was this work of grace, that one portion of the community did not know what any other portion were doing in the matter. Instead of devising plans, and executing them, to stir up the community, the whole community, as one man, seemed to be already roused."

—Samuel Prime[1]

In the first account given of the revival of 1858 and the days following, Talbot Chambers made this observation:

> That movement which far more than the opening of China, or the reconquest of India, or the laying of the Atlantic Telegraph Cable, has rendered the present year memorable; which without exaggeration may be emphatically called *the event of the century*; which has been more like a literal reproduction of the scenes of Pentecost than any other which has taken place since the tongues of fire sat upon the heads of the Apostles; that movement can justly be traced to no human or earthly source. Look at it as we will, in its commencement, its progress or its results, the conclusion is still the same. This in the finger of God.[2]

---

[1] Samuel Prime, *The Power of Prayer,* (Edinburgh: Banner of Truth, 1991), 18.

[2] Talbot Chambers, *The New York City Noon Prayer Meeting: A Simple Prayer Gathering that Changed the World* (Colorado Springs: Wagner Publications, 2002), 120. Emphasis added.

The phrase "the event of the century" became the title of a book by J. Edwin Orr on this phenomenon.[3] Orr showed, through massive accumulation of contemporary sources, the national spread of the revival and its temporal expansion beyond the year of 1857–1858. To those twentieth-century historians who sought to debunk the spirituality, the broad extent, and the church-strengthening and culture-shaping influence of this awakening, Orr countered, "This research has established its scope in schools and colleges, upon every class and nationwide." Continuing his wide-ranging defense of the power and integrity of this movement fueled by prayer, he chided,

> Citations in newspapers and journals of the time confirmed, and nothing in those of the following fifty years contradicted, that the Great Awakening of 1857–58 was one of the greatest in history. But it seemed too perfect as an example of the "outpouring of the Holy Spirit" to warrant the objective attention from those historians whose philosophy or theology rejected such a claim.[4]

Timothy Smith's chapter on this phenomenon is entitled "*Annus Mirabilis*"—Year of Wonders. His descriptor of it says, "The Awakening of 1858 spread from New York to every city in the North by means of daily interdenominational prayer meetings. It drew serious support from all denominations—including even the most liberal and liturgical ones—and stamped devotion to evangelistic measures deep on the Protestant mind."[5] He traced

---

[3]   J. Edwin Orr, *The Event of the Century: The 1857–1858 Awakening* (Wheaton: International Awakening Press, 1989), 338. Surprisingly, Orr attributed the phrase to Perry Miller, in *the Life of the Mind in America*, as something of a reprimand to historians who minimized the formative importance of this revival.

[4]   Orr, *The Event of the Century*, 337.

[5]   Timothy L. Smith, *Revivalism and Social Reform in Mid-Nineteenth-Century America* (New York; Nashville: Abingdon Press, 1957), 11.

the impact that this revival made on a variety of social movements in America, including a war on poverty and the anti-slavery campaigns.

In the 1996 publication of his ThD dissertation, *When Heaven Touched Earth*, Roy Fish looked at the impact that this event made on the strength, growth, and missiological progress in Baptist churches and denominational life. His work concentrated on Baptists, digging deeply into the minutes of associations in twenty-seven states, and also state convention minutes. Necessarily, however, he established the study of Baptists in the larger evangelical context. He gave this summary evaluation of the sweeping phenomenon of prayer and evangelism:

> The mysterious effects of the Holy Spirit in a time of revival can never be controlled or explained. Neither can they be foreseen. But they can be recognized and embraced when they occur. This certainly happened in the 1858 God-sent revival when powerful prayer resulted in countless conversions to Christ, when whole cities were transformed, and fervent praise to God ascended to heaven from the nineteenth-century American soil. We must learn from looking back and must emulate the example given us of prayer and faith by American believers in 1857–1858. And we must begin to cry as they did then: "Revive thy work in the midst of the years; in wrath remember mercy. Lord, do it again![6]

HISTORICAL CONTEXT

Bennet Tyler, in writing about the revival that occurred in New England in the first two decades of the nineteenth century, said, "The revivals of those days were eminently pure, as time has abundantly evinced, and eminently salutary in their influence

---

[6] Roy Fish, *When Heaven Touched Earth*, ed. Mack Tomlinson (Azle, TX; Need of the Times Publishers, 1996) 199.

upon the churches, and upon the community at large."[7] Tyler's book contains thirty-five accounts of revival, mainly in 1799, but it includes two from two years earlier, six from 1801 to 1806, and two from 1812 to 1814. Tyler was determined to contrast these revivals with those that had occurred under the influence of Charles Finney, beginning around 1820. Tyler wrote that "the converts in these revivals, were not made in that easy way, in which many professed converts in more recent times have been made, without any struggle in their minds, and without feeling any sensible opposition to God and the claims of the gospel." Instead, they endured great conflict in their conviction of sin and the knowledge of the plague of their own hearts and their experiential knowledge that "the carnal mind is enmity against God."[8]

Not only did saving experience plumb the depths of human sin and the sensible need of converting grace, but the doctrine was consistent with the historic confessional commitments of the Presbyterian, Congregational, and Baptist churches. They preached the doctrines of grace and dwelt with urgency on "the entire depravity of man by nature—the necessity of regeneration by the special agency of the Holy Spirit—justification by faith alone—and the sovereignty of God in the dispensation of his grace." They were not negative toward the converting power of these doctrines nor suspicious that they operated contrary to the interests of revival. As a matter of personal observation, they had seen the powerful effects of setting forth plainly the entire dependence of the sinner on the pleasure and power of God. At the same time, Tyler testified, they "set before them their obligation to obey every Divine command—demolished all their vain excuses, and pressed upon them with great plainness, the duty of immediate repentance. Under such preaching awakened sinners were brought to see their true character and condition."[9] Sinners

---

7   Tyler, *New England Revivals*, vii.
8   Tyler, *New England Revivals*, x.
9   Tyler, *New England Revivals,* ix–x.

saw from Scripture that their hearts were "enmity against God" and thus were not lulled into placid but false assurance of their safety. Their own conscience must rise to testify that "real change had been wrought in them." In addition, when "they became the subjects of renewing grace, they were 'born into the truth.'" The truths of all "the great fundamental doctrines of the gospel" were embedded both in mind and heart.

DECLINE AFTER THE SECOND GREAT AWAKENING

The Panic of 1837, twenty years before a similar financial panic at the beginning stages of the Prayer Revival, brought financial ruin to thousands. The Tappan brothers, deeply involved in Christian social action, became bankrupt. This panic resulted in a growth of a spirit of worldly mindedness in business as people scrambled to rebuild their finances and engineered schemes of protection. By contrast, the Panic of 1857 did not so aggravate a spirit of worldliness. The Prayer Revival was already forming a more heaven-oriented worldview.

In the sphere of religious fervor, a Baptist pastor, William Miller, predicted the coming of Christ between March 21, 1843, and March 21, 1844. An alternate date, October 22, was set after the passing of the March date. The failure of this prediction of Christ's personal appearance produced disillusionment from within the church and ridicule from secularists. It also eventuated in an entire system of reinterpretation of the nature of the advent, saying that it really had occurred in the "heavenly sanctuary," a presently unseen realm where judgment is proceeding. James and Ellen White crystallized several doctrinal idiosyncrasies and founded a distinct denomination in 1860 with the name Seventh-day Adventist.

Socio-politically, denominations were involved in an increasingly contested disagreement on the biblical legitimacy of slavery. In 1845, after a dozen years of suspicion and polemical interaction, Baptists in the South formed the Southern Baptist Convention. The year prior, the Methodist Episcopal Church,

215

South, separated from the Methodist Episcopal Church over the same issue. Presbyterians, already divided into New School and Old School over issues of revivalism, divided again into North and South (New School in 1857 and Old School in 1861). Theodore Weld went to Lane Theological Seminary in 1832 and formed a strong abolitionist group. The group was expelled in 1834. These "Lane Rebels" then went to the newly organized Oberlin college, where Charles Finney had become professor of theology. Weld became an agent of the newly formed American Anti-Slavery Society.

Another highly agitated and divisive issue concerned the impact that emigration was making on the American ethos. Concern over this led to the rise of nativism. The New York Protestant Association, founded in 1831, adopted a newspaper called *The Protestant* as its official voice. They sponsored debates such as that between John Breckenridge and John Hughes dealing with the question, "Is the Roman Catholic / Protestant religion in any or all its principles or doctrines inimical to Civil or Religious Liberty?" In 1836, the Protestant Reformation Society was founded and adopted the newspaper *American Protestant Vindicator* to inform the public of the evils of Catholicism and to convert Roman Catholics to Protestantism.

The fear of immigration from historically Roman Catholic countries triggered stories of conspiracy and immorality. They centered on Catholic convents and led to the burning of the Ursuline convent outside Boston in 1834. That came after three anti-Catholic sermons by Lyman Beecher. Samuel F. B. Morse added to the sense of threat to Protestantism and the American way of life in his works *Foreign Conspiracy against the Liberties of the United States* and *Imminent Dangers to the Free Institutions of the United States Through Foreign Immigration.*

Adding to these threats, the early decades of the nineteenth-century found Christianity in a complex religious atmosphere with several challenges to historic orthodoxy. Transcendentalism presented a spirituality independent of an acceptance of divine revelation and all the details of historic confessional Christianity. In 1836, Ralph Waldo Emerson (1803–1882) published *Nature*, which challenged the authority of the Bible and all institutions built on it. God was in all of nature and in all men, and we should learn to engage nature's God without a mediator. George Ripley (1802–1880) graduated from Harvard in 1826 and was ordained as a Unitarian pastor the same year. He left the ministry in 1841 after controversy with the more conservative Unitarians. In that year he established Brook Farm nine miles from Boston in West Roxbury, beginning an experiment in communal living. The farm ceased to be solvent in 1847 and the idea was abandoned. In 1841, Theodore Parker (1810–1860), also a Unitarian minister, wrote *The Transient and the Permanent in Christianity*, arguing that the historic creeds and their highly polemical content were mere passing ideas not to be identified with true Christianity. Rather, the ethical standards of Jesus tapped into the intuitive sense of equality, justice, and love that was present in the higher faculties of humanity.

Those years, billowing with the possibilities of newness as American independence and rapid westward expansion pressed the borders of traditional stability, saw the invention of some new religions. Mormonism arose when Joseph Smith published the Book of Mormon in 1830, a new revelation from the angel Moroni with a new view of Jesus Christ, God, the world, ethics, the family, and eternity. Communitarian and perfectionist groups such as Oneida formed in 1844 under John Humphrey Noyes. They saw humanity as free from sin, practiced what they defended as "Bible Communism," and practiced complex marriage. If that were not enough of a perplexing challenge to historic views of law and sin, Charles Finney developed the doctrine of perfectionism at Oberlin in conjunction with Asa Mahan. Finney responded with clear opposition and criticism to ministers who resisted him or sought to correct him at this point. Many of his former supporters began to distance themselves from him. Such theological/experiential puzzlement was complicated and extended by Phoebe Palmer's holiness meetings and teachings of perfectionism. Her meetings brought a revivalistic camp-meeting ambience from 1850 through 1857 to Canada and the eastern United States.

PRAYER REVIVAL IN ITS NEW YORK BEGINNING

Jeremiah Calvin Lanphier's name is not listed in the *Dictionary of Christianity in America*, though his name does occur in the article on the "Prayer Meeting Revival (1857–1859)."[10] Lanphier was converted at Broadway Tabernacle in 1842 under the preaching of Charles Finney. He was a member of the congregation of J. W. Alexander, Tabernacle Church, for eight or nine years. In 1857, he was employed by the North Reformed Protestant Dutch Church to look to the spiritual welfare of the people in the lower wards of the city. This church had six doctrinal standards. Three of these were patristic: the Apostles' Creed, the Nicene Creed, and the Athanasian Creed. The three others were specifically Dutch Reformed: the Belgic Confession, the Heidelberg Catechism, and the Canons of the Synod of Dort.

Changing patterns of physical space for business, warehouses, offices, and places of residence led to many in the congregation moving and no longer able to participate in the church. "It was evident," wrote Chambers, "that something must be done with a direct view to carry the gospel to the masses of the down town population." The region east of Broadway was of particular interest as it was relatively untouched by gospel witness and "was white unto the harvest."[11] In June of 1857, the consistory of the church pursued measures "conducive to an increased interest in and attendance upon the Divine Word." The result was a series of resolutions, one of which called on the church to "employ a suitable person or persons to be engaged in visiting the families in the vicinity, and inducing them to attend the services" of the

---

[10] Daniel G. Reid, ed., *Dictionary of Christianity in America*, (Downers Grove, IL: InterVarsity Press, 1990), 922.

[11] Chambers, *The New York City Noon Prayer Meeting*, 27.

church.[12] With this goal in mind, they settled on Lanphier as the man to carry forward the vision. Lanphier was described as "tall, well-made, with a remarkably pleasant face." He was known to be "pleasant in disposition and manner" and at the same time "possessed of indomitable energy and perseverance." His piety was intense and infectious, and he was gifted in prayer and exhortation.[13] Though he had never engaged in ministerial work, he sensed the gravity of the call and resigned his business to invest himself and his gifts in the work.

He knew that a heavy, eternally significant task had been put before him. The spiritual welfare of "the neglected thousands in these lower wards" pressed on his heart with a sense of gravity combined with complete insufficiency. Lanphier had proceeded systematically, dividing the area under assignment into districts, going house to house and calling upon each family and, if possible, each individual. He took tracts in hand and went through the streets and spoke personally of the gospel and its importance to as many as would give an ear. Many began to attend the church and listened soberly to the preached word.[14]

All the while, he knew that something far beyond his capacities was needed. He prayed for guidance and came under a strong persuasion that only by prayer could this stewardship of the gospel be effectual. On July 1, 1837, Lanphier wrote in his diary, "As I was walking along the streets, the idea was suggested to my mind that an hour of prayer, from twelve to one o'clock, would be beneficial to business men, who usually in great numbers take that hour for rest and refreshment."[15] He conceived, therefore, that he would invite businessmen in the neighborhood to come to the church at noon once a week to pray. A sign was placed at

---

[12] Chambers, *The New York City Noon Prayer Meeting*, 28.

[13] Prime, *The Power of Prayer*, 6.

[14] Chambers, *The New York City Noon Prayer Meeting*, 31; Prime, *The Power of Prayer*, 5.

[15] Prime, *The Power of Prayer*, 8.

the gateway of the church that announced, "Daily prayer meeting from 12 to 1 o'clock. STOP 5, 10, or 20 minutes. Or the whole hour. As your time admits." A handbill was circulated in hotels, factories, shops, boarding houses, financial offices, and individual homes. It contained a reminder of the circumstances that called for prayer, a description of the proposed hour of prayer, and some familiar poetry about prayer. The top of the bill asked, "How often should I pray?" It answered: "As often as the language of prayer is in my heart; as often as I see my need of help; as often as I feel the power of temptation; as often as I am made sensible of my spiritual declension, or feel the aggression of a worldly, earthly spirit. In prayer we leave the business of time for that of eternity, and intercourse with man for intercourse with God." The bill announced that the time to meet for prayer was Wednesday from noon to one o'clock. Here is a verse from one of the poems:

> Prayer is appointed to convey
> The blessings God designs to give:
> Long as they live should Christians pray,
> For only while they pray they live.[16]

The first meeting occurred on September 23, 1857. Lanphier prayed alone for the first half hour. Eventually he was joined by six men.[17] At the second meeting, twenty men came, and on October 7, there were forty. Lanphier consulted the consistory, and they decided to make the prayer time a daily event. Soon the prayer meetings grew exponentially, and many unconverted people were attending. By October 23, Lanphier reported these events to the religious press and in February 1858, the meetings began to be covered by the secular press. Horace Greely of the *New York Daily Tribune* eagerly took reports from Lanphier. Eventually reporters attended the meetings and had a regular column entitled "The Progress of the Revival." The coverage aided in the popping up

---

[16] Chambers, *The New York City Noon Prayer Meeting*, 36.
[17] Chambers, *The New York City Noon Prayer Meeting*, 35.

of other prayer meetings throughout the city. More than twenty became active, starting at different times but following the same format. Some congregated in the morning, some made the mid-morning around ten o'clock their optimum time for the gathering, and others maintained the noontime lunch break.

The order was both flexible and rigidly maintained. There were to be no controversial points or polemical differences introduced, and a balance between requests, exhortations, testimony, and prayer was pursued intentionally by the person moderating. The rules were exhibited in the prayer room:

Please Observe the Following Rules.

BE PROMPT

Commencing Precisely at 12 O'clock

The leadership is not expected to exceed ten minutes in opening the meeting.

1st. Open the meeting by reading and singing from three to five verses of a hymn.

2d. Prayer

3d. Read a portion of the Scripture

4th. Say the meeting is now open for prayers and exhortations, observing particularly the rules overhead, inviting brethren from abroad to take part in the services.

5th. Read but one or two requests at a time—REQUIRING a prayer to follow—such prayer to have special reference to the same.

6th. In case of any suggestion or proposition by any person, say this is simply a prayer meeting, and that they are out of order, and call on some brother to pray.

7th. Give out the closing hymn five minutes before one o'clock. Request the Benediction from a Clergyman, if one be present.[18]

The books by Chambers and Prime, written virtually in the midst of this extensive awakening of the need to lay before the triune God the direction for lives and eternal well-being of our friends and family, contain large numbers of anecdotes about requests for and answers to prayer. Letters came from all parts of the nation and from other nations. Early participants were deeply conscious that a "kind of superstitious feeling" might prompt some of the communications. Also, they were conscious that the simplicity of faith in God and earnest request and submission toward Him could give way to "a sense of self-complacency" in the minds of those who received this increasingly numerous body of requests. One participant wrote, "We are in danger of spiritual pride, because so many eyes are turned to the Fulton street Prayer Meeting, and because so many requests for prayer come to us from all parts of the land."[19] Some felt that the letters occupied too much attention, while others were disturbed that too much expectation was focused on Fulton Street as *the* place where prayers were answered. The earnestness of the letters demanded a sincere and faithful stewardship to pray. "I hope we shall never be unwilling that such requests shall come here, and feel lifted up because they come."[20]

At the same time, participants could not anoint themselves as a "Holy Sepulcher" of miraculous power but must be humbled, not exalted, because such requests come from burdened souls. "We lie

---

[18] Chambers, *The New York City Noon Prayer Meeting*, 38.

[19] Chambers, *The New York City Noon Prayer Meeting*, 73.

[20] Chambers, *The New York City Noon Prayer Meeting*, 74.

low before God, while he alone is exalted." The note concerning the danger of spiritual pride summarized their duty in saying, "Let us cherish the true spirit of fervent humble prayer, and let our faith and prayer go out after all these cases, and bear them up to the throne of heavenly grace." Contemplation of the results should encourage sacrificial application to this opportunity, for, "Who can tell the results of our petitions? . . . We have to do with the perishing. We pray for their salvation. We learn here the power of prayer in the signal answers which are given"[21]

Chambers recorded this: "Christian friends—A young man, who frequently attends this Meeting, desires you to return thanks for the conversion of his father and three sisters. All have been subjects of prayer."[22] Talbot Chambers included a seven-page narrative from an "infidel lawyer" about all the circumstances that culminated in his conversion—a remarkable chain of external events and mental contemplations that included his attendance at and perceptions of the prayer meetings. He closed the narrative, "From thence, hitherto, I have, by God's grace, rejoiced with thankfulness in the blessed assurance of His willingness and ability to pardon and save to the uttermost all who come to him through Jesus Christ my Saviour."[23] The narrative was published and the meeting received this request as a result:

> The reading of an Infidel Lawyer's Experience has awakened an anxiety for my soul's salvation. Without being an unbeliever, I am still in the bonds of iniquity. My object in writing is to solicit the earnest prayers of the members of the Globe Hotel and Fulton Street Prayer Meetings, that these bonds may be sundered, and that God in his infinite mercy will convert me and enable me to find peace in believing in Jesus.[24]

---

[21] Chambers, *The New York City Noon Prayer Meeting*, 74.

[22] Chambers, *The New York City Noon Prayer Meeting*, 83.

[23] Chambers, *The New York City Noon Prayer Meeting*, 69.

[24] Chambers, *The New York City Noon Prayer Meeting*, 70.

Other requests and reports included prayer for the conversion of a husband, a sister, children, people in the penitentiary, scoffers, atheists, destitute churches, or persons contemplating crimes and suicide. Often these were accompanied by statements of the quick answers to those prayers or the answers to prayers that had been lifted up for decades. Samuel Prime, in *The Power of Prayer,* gave chapters 5–24 to letters, requests, answers to prayer, testimonies of conversion, and endurance of hardship. Chapter 17 narrates the conversion of a Roman Catholic and the consequences within his Roman Catholic community. After a brief statement of the deportment of the priest toward him—"a priesthood as despotic and absolute as death"—we learn that his "wife has become so disgusted with this exhibition of the bitter malignity of those of her own faith, and so satisfied of the truth and sincerity of her husband, that she has declared her intention to go with her husband and bear his persecutions with him. . . . He has confidence in the Lord, who allows him to be tried, will also provide."[25]

Chambers warned against two errors. One, given the absence of a leading figure such as Edwards, Whitefield, or Spurgeon, one must avoid leaping to the conclusion that preaching is a "worn out and obsolete instrumentality" and that a union prayer meeting has become the chief means of bringing in "the latter-day glory." Such a notion must immediately be dismissed, for "the ministry of the word and ordinances is and ever has been, and . . . ever will be the grand means of conviction, conversion, and sanctification." All else is subordinate and accessory. Though prayer, conversation, and exhortation were immediately instrumental in the conversion of many and in the spread of the hope and efforts for sustained revival, nothing can replace the "authority, the systematic presentation of truth, the power to illuminate the understanding which the pulpit, honestly managed, always possesses." Other means presuppose "previous indoctrination by the ministry."[26]

---

[25] Prime, *The Power of Prayer,* 147.
[26] Chambers, *The New York City Noon Prayer Meeting,* 132–133.

Second, he noted again the temptation to superstition and exaltation of place—the sacramental ambience of the consistory building where the prayer meetings started. Though sentiment may attach to places and specific procedures, that does not justify giving to those the "honour which is due to God alone." All of our efforts, no matter how vigorous and apparently earnest, need to be "sprinkled with atoning blood." God is justly a jealous God and will share His glory with no other. When, in the history of Christianity, any have sought to undercut His honor even the slightest, "his outraged dignity has avenged itself to the confusion and dismay of those who rashly invaded the crown rights of Zion's great King."[27]

Effective Features

Chambers noted with clarity and insistence that the revival was purely an expression of the providence and power of God. No self-congratulatory spirit was allowable for "there is no room for human merit to insinuate itself." From this earliest report of the Prayer Revival, Chambers anticipated the kinds of explanations that future analyses would present. He gave a rational consideration to them, gave a disqualifying analysis to each, and maintained that it was the finger of God. "One of the distinguishing characteristics of this work, is not only that the Lord has done it, but that it is so manifest that he has done it."[28]

Another appealing feature that allowed the central issues concerning salvation to dominate was its non-sectarian approach. Smith observed, "Distinctions between the sects and between ministers and laymen were ignored. The joyous liberty of the camp meeting 'love feast' was thus transferred to an urban setting."[29] Keith J. Hardman summarized, "Sectarian differences

---

[27] Chambers, *The New York City Noon Prayer Meeting*, 134–135.

[28] Chambers, *The New York City Noon Prayer Meeting*, 121.

[29] Smith, *Revivalism and Social Reform*, 64.

were set aside and Christians cooperated so wholeheartedly that Methodists, Baptists, Lutherans, Congregationalists, and New School Presbyterians worked together, alongside Episcopalians, Old School Presbyterians, and even Universalists and Unitarians." He pointed to the example of James W. Alexander, an Old School Presbyterian preacher, who changed from an attitude of opposition to one of enthusiastic approval. He wrote a friend that the "openness of thousands to doctrine, reproof, etc. is undeniable." His lecture, given regularly in his church, was "crowded unendurable." He even mentioned that one of the sermons of Charles Spurgeon, published regularly in America, had sold one hundred thousand, according to the publisher. "You may rest assured," Alexander judged, "there is a great awakening among us."[30]

Chambers reported that from the beginning the plan, as conceived by Lanphier, was to appeal to "Christians as such, without respect to denominational distinctions." None were expected to deny their distinctives or replace their church connections with something else. Given the centrality of the concern as it related to all Christians, "Arminians and Calvinists, Baptists and Pedo-Baptists, Episcopalians and Presbyterians, and Congregationalists and Friends, sat side by side on the same benches, sang the same hymns, said Amen to the same prayers, and were refreshed and comforted by the same exhortations."[31] J. Edwin Orr summarized, "The general 'zeal for souls' blurred denominational lines and diminished the denominational ambitions for aggrandizement. . . . So striking was this manifestation of Christian love that it was regarded by various contemporary observers as the most significant characteristic of the revival."[32]

This characteristic had a two-fold thrust, one affirming and one dubious. That the central Christian truths so reside in the

---

[30] Keith J. Hardman, *Seasons of Refreshing* (Grand Rapids: Baker Books, 1994), 177.

[31] Chambers, *The New York City Noon Prayer Meeting*, 122.

[32] Orr, *The Event of the Century*, 276.

heart that Christians may worship with, pray with, and rejoice with other denominations testifies to the clarity of the biblical witness to God, Christ, sin, the cross, the new birth, and the grace of intercessory prayer. That such evident joyful practice can be engaged in by Unitarians and Universalists makes one desire a more defining doctrinal basis for what Chambers called "the true theory of Christian Union."[33] The leveling impact of this awakening had repercussions for the distinctness of confessional commitments among American denominations.

A third effective feature was the "place of the Lay Element in the diffusion of the gospel."[34] Orr devoted two pages to this element, giving a brief history of the effectiveness of lay ministry in revivals since the Wesleys.[35] Lanphier himself was a layman and developed a schedule and a method for the meetings that would give opportunity for laymen in spiritual, gospel-centered, prayer-rich, and ministry-oriented engagement. "The Noon Prayer Meeting was a laymen's meeting from commencement," Chandler reminded, "and its success acted directly upon laymen in revealing to them the immense amount or unemployed talent which lay wrapped up in a napkin, and in stimulating them to an active, diligent and conscientious use of their facilities and opportunities."[36]

Finally, convinced of the reality of God's interaction with His people through prayer, the most effective means was the relationship between earnest, plain, precise prayer and obvious answers. Answers often were quick and precisely aligned with the substance of the prayer. God showed His people that He was indeed involved in the world, in their lives, and that He would be inquired of.

---

[33] Chambers, *The New York City Noon Prayer Meeting*, 124.

[34] Chambers, *The New York City Noon Prayer Meeting*, 124.

[35] Orr, *The Event of the Century*, 270–271.

[36] Chandler, 146.

RESULTS

Kathryn Long argued that the Prayer Revival narrowed Christian piety to diminish the social concerns and leave them to prayer rather than action. Overall, she claimed, it "had very little direct social impact." She judged that the prohibition of controversial topics (such as abolition versus defense of slavery) gave a quality of isolation to spiritual experience, rejecting its connection with moral reform "that had been a part of the New England Calvinist tradition since the colonial revivals."[37]

Timothy Smith argued at length that the ideas of revival in general and the Prayer Revival in particular gave strength, perseverance, and optimism to efforts to solve all sorts of social ills. In closing his chapter on "The Church Helps the Poor," Smith made this observation: "Individual churches soon joined the interdenominational societies in distributing food and clothing, finding employment, resettling children, and providing medical aid for the lowest classes. The revival of 1858 was in many respects the harvest reaped from the gospel seed. It convinced churchmen that the story of the Good Samaritan was a parable for their times."[38]

The revival generated growth in the churches, including virtually all denominations, both North and South. Baptists and Methodists, including black congregations, reaped significant membership benefits and a deepening sense of the urgency of evangelism and productive Christian life. Looking at the years 1853 to 1856 compared to 1856 through 1859, Kathryn Long gave these statistics, which show a net increase in membership during the respective periods for which some degree of reliable denominational statistics is available: Methodists, North and

---

[37] Kathryn Long, *The Revival of 1857–58 Interpreting an American Religious Awakening* (New York: Oxford Press, 1998). Long also wrote the article on the "Revival of 1857–1858" in the *Encyclopedia of Religious Revivals in America* (Westport, CT: Greenwood Press, 2007), 1:362–366.

[38] Smith, *Revivalism and Social Reform*, 177.

South, went from 111,098 to 250,365; "Regular Baptists," 88,711 to 122,984; Presbyterians (Old School and New School), 12,781 to 52,971; Episcopal, 14,404 to 20,071. Congregationalists added 27,840 during the years of the revival, giving a total increase for these churches of 474,231. Several observers and researchers say that probably one million people were converted during this one-and-a-half-year span.

The awakening had the unusual double result of creating a deeper sympathy between the Northern and Southern states and also hastening the coming civil conflict. William Warren Sweet said the Prayer Revival functioned as a temporary preventative of war because of the common sense of divine visitation. William G. McLoughlin said feelings of animosity between North and South were exacerbated. There is observable evidence for both. Around 1898, Orr recorded the observation of Leonard Bacon in a "State of Religion" report:

> Like the Great Awakening [in 1740], it was the providential preparation of the American church for an immediately impending peril, the gravity of which there was none at the time far-sighted enough to predict. Looking backward, it is instructive to us to raise the question how the Church would have passed through the decade of the 1860s without the spiritual reinforcement that came to it amid the Pentecostal scenes of 1857 and 1858.[39]

The common experience of the powerful effects of prayer and truth in the infinitely important work of conversion and submission to divine prerogative in the matter of salvation created endearing ties to fellow Christians across denominational and sectional lines. They were all sons of God by divine grace. At the same time, the demands for social equality and the elimination of human bondage grew more intense and fueled the already ardent

---

[39] Orr, *The Event of the Century*, 317.

spirit of abolition. We see this in the great optimism for radical intrusion of divine justice into human society that fired Union troops in the Civil War. "Mine eyes have seen the glory of the coming of the Lord; He is trampling out the vintage where the grapes of wrath are stored; He hath loosed the fateful lightning of His terrible swift sword; His truth is marching on." Julia Ward Howe, the author of that hymn, was a committed and active abolitionist.

Kathryn Long posited that the Prayer Revival altered the revival tradition by introducing advertising, including newspaper reporting, consumer-sensitive methods, and highly managed orderly meetings of prayer assisting the time of proclamation. Urban evangelism fused the "decorum and respectability of earlier Calvinist revivals with the mass appeal of Methodist and Baptist revival practices."[40] Long's contention that it blurred the distinction between revivals and mass evangelism introduced a false dichotomy. Concern for both true conversion and increased holiness have been twin commitments in the ministry of those who defended, prayed for, and preached for revival from the days of seventeenth-century Puritans to the present.

The 1858 Prayer Revival gave palpable demonstration of the biblical connection between divine purpose and human intercession. The prayers of Jesus give mysterious and powerful witness to the necessity of prayerful interaction with God in seeking His blessing and accomplishing His sovereign decrees. Paul told the Philippians, when considering the outcome of his imprisonment, "I know that this will turn out for my deliverance through your prayer and the supply of the Spirit of Jesus Christ" (Phil. 1:19). The revival also demonstrated the Christian's posture of confident repose in divine provision in the context of prayer: "Be anxious for nothing, but in everything by prayer and supplication, with thanksgiving, let your requests be made known to God" (Phil. 4:6). In confronting the variety of difficulties faced

---

[40] Long, "Revival of 1857–1858," 364.

in a fallen and broken world, and the earnestness engendered by these difficult circumstances, this revival was a manifestation of the biblical truth that "the effective, fervent prayer of a righteous man avails much" (James 5:16). It served to show that one of the signs of true repentance and faith is earnest attention to prayer, as the Lord instructed Ananias, "Inquire at the house of Judas for one called Saul of Tarsus, for behold, he is praying" (Acts 9:11).

CHAPTER 9

┝━━━━━━━ • ━━━━━━━┥

REVIVAL IN THE CIVIL WAR

"As for [John A. Broadus's] preaching, I had appointments
for him three times every day, and occasionally four times.
He drew large crowds, and as he looked into the eyes of
those bronzed heroes of many a battle, and realized that
they might be summoned at any hour into another battle,
and into eternity, his very soul was stirred within him, and
I never heard him preach with such beautiful simplicity and
thrilling power the old gospel which he love so well."

—A. T. Robertson[1]

THE HISTORICAL FACT OF THE REVIVAL

The Prayer Revival of 1857–1858 prepared both sections
of the country for the fratricidal carnage of the next half
decade. Within the Northern army, through the work of the
YMCA and several itinerant chaplains and distributors of
literature, large numbers of conversions were reported. Daniel
Stowell summarized,

> The best estimates of the number of conversions in
> wartime revivals range from 100,000 to 200,000 men in
> the Union armies and as many as 150,000 in the smaller
> Confederate armies. Thousands more of the already
> converted and the curious participated in the religious
> meetings held in army camps across the theaters of war.

---

[1]   A. T. Robertson, *Life and Letters of John A. Broadus* (Philadelphia:
American Baptist Publication Society, 1909), 208.

In no other American war did so many soldiers actively participate in evangelical revivals.[2]

This narrative will focus on the revival in the Southern army.

In 1876, W. W. Bennett published *The Great Revival in the Southern Armies*[3] eleven years before J. William Jones published another account, entitled *Christ in the Camp*. In the preface of that latter book, Jones commended the work of Bennett, "late President of Randolph-Macon College." Jones also used war files of several newspapers, letters, and documents furnished to him in 1865 and 1866 by chaplains, missionaries, and other army workers.[4]

Recognizing the surprise, even resistance, that some feel toward an account of revival in the army of rebels, Bennett wrote, "To thousands in the North this book will be an enigma. That God should appear in the midst of men, to bless and save them, who, as they believe, rushed to arms without just cause, may be almost beyond belief. To all such persons we can only say, read the narrative, weigh the facts, and then make up your verdict."[5]

CULTURAL AND RELIGIOUS CONTEXT OF THE REVIVAL

In his description of the religious condition of the men of the army in relation to the general religious atmosphere of the South, Bennett noted a broad generality of religious knowledge in all levels of society in the South. There already were strong evangelical underpinnings to all the inhabitants due to seasons of religious refreshing that had been operating intermittently since the

---

[2] Daniel W. Stowell, "Civil War," in *Encyclopedia of Religious Revivals in America*, ed. Michael McClymond, (Westport, CT: Greenwood Press, 2007), 1:118.

[3] W. W. Bennett, *A Narrative of the Great Revival which Prevailed in the Southern Armies* (Harrisonburg, VA: Sprinkle Publications, 1976).

[4] J. Williams Jones, *Christ in the Camp* (Harrisonburg, VA: Sprinkle Publications, 1986).

[5] Bennett, *A Narrative of the Great Revival*, iv.

seventeenth century. The union of Separate Baptists and Regular Baptists brought evangelistic energy as well as doctrinal coherence to the Baptist movement. The missionary impulse of the Second Great Awakening had prompted not only zeal for the conversion of the nations but evangelistic and church-planting conviction at home, especially in the expansion into newly populated territory.

In addition, however, many manifestations of sinfulness endemic to the existence of slavery were present. Also, the social life and privilege that developed in the upper levels of society and the poverty and dependence at the lower levels carried their specific forms of moral challenge into the larger society. Valiant and insistent efforts of many to evangelize their slaves ameliorated inconsistency in this work of continuing concern. Despite inadequacies in promoting Christian knowledge, including prejudicial concepts of intellectual potential, many patterns of evangelization through preaching, catechizing, worship, singing, and recognizing gifted preachers among the slaves set a foundation of evangelical doctrines that undergirded revival in the slave population as well as in the Confederate armies.

An advantage for a strong and widespread development of evangelical fervor in the South lay in the virtual theological unanimity of the denominations. Bennett noted, "The four or five leading Christian denominations which occupied the South have never been seriously disturbed by any of those false theories which, among other people, have drawn away thousands from the true faith."[6] There was little influence of Unitarianism or Universalism or the developing sectarian radicalism of the North and Midwest that made any impact on the South. William Lloyd Garrison in *The Liberator* was radically intent on the abolition of slavery even if it meant the ruining of the South; Southerners believed that his abolitionism was fueled by his theological instability. In addition, Universalists and Unitarians, as well as Charles Finney, were active

---

[6]   Bennett, *A Narrative of the Great Revival*, 23.

abolitionists—these facts made Southerners suspect of all the fringe developments in Christianity.

The large number of Trans-Mississippi conversions led to the formation of "The Church of the Army," prompted largely by a Methodist Episcopal preacher named Marvin. They adopted a confession of faith that asserted the central commitments of evangelical Christianity.[7]

> The Christian men of the army, believing that the habitation of God by his Spirit constitutes the Church, agree, for the edification and conversion of their fellow-men, to organize the Church of the Army, with the following articles of faith and constitution:
>
> I. We believe the Scriptures of the Old and New Testament to be the Word of God, the only rule of faith and obedience.
>
> II. We believe in God, the Father, the Son, and the Holy Ghost; the same in substance; equal in power and glory.
>
> III. We believe in the fall of Adam, the redemption by Christ, and the renewing of the Holy Spirit.
>
> IV. We believe in justification by faith alone, and therefore receive and rest upon Christ as our only hope.
>
> V. We believe in the communion of saints, and in the doctrine of eternal rewards and punishments.
>
> The Christian men who have been baptized, adopting these articles of faith and constitution, in each regiment shall constitute one church; who shall choose ten officers to take spiritual oversight of the same.

---

[7]   Jones, *Christ in the Camp*, 553–554.

> Of the officers so elected the chaplain, or one chosen by
> them for that purpose, shall act as moderator.

Both Bennett and Jones described a variety of moral difficulties that produced a spirit of scoffing toward religion but at the same time provided clear evidence for the need of converting grace and spiritual conviction. Issues concerning sectional conflict, internal family dissension, and denominational divisions created a climate of spiritual depression. Strongly worded moral condemnation, written and spoken by Christian observers of the times, revealed some of the worst of human responses in a decline of spiritual interest, and an increase of profanity, gambling, and general worldliness. Drunkenness, get-rich-quick schemes, and general promiscuity increased. J. W. Jones gave clear notice of the "wicked and thoughtless companions, who spent their time in gaming, drinking, and frivolous conversations."[8]

One could judge James Petigru Boyce's perception about prospects of revival as being less than enthusiastic. Not only were lamentable vices seeping into the camps, but spiritual things seemed far from the minds of those wrought up in such political intensity. Animosity and concentration of a sound defeat of the enemy characterized the early war atmosphere. Boyce wrote John Broadus, "You cannot know how tenderly my heart yearns over them." He felt alarm at the prospects of how many "must go unprepared into the presence of God." He said that he felt like "preaching all the time," and would do it but for "the unwillingness of men to hear the gospel." Such an exuberant practice would only "frustrate all the good" he would do, and he asked for guidance to "help and aid me in what I can do!" He showed bewilderment in looking on the "indifference of men." He illustrated his concern with an anecdote of a "half-witted" young man saying, "We ought all to be converted before going to battles. It had been told as a joke, but how fearfully true it is. And how singular that such a

---

[8] Jones, *Christ in the Camp*, 40.

remark should have come only from such a one and how much more so that it should be spoken of as a funny thing." Though ready to preach and earnest in intent, Boyce was discouraged by the spiritual ennui of the men.[9]

This religious nonchalance was soon replaced with intensity of interest and depth of awareness of the need of a right standing before God. In August 1863, Broadus wrote to his wife, Charlotte, that in Mahone's Brigade "they have been holding prayer meetings all the week and had last night five hundred present, with much appearance of interest." Three days later he wrote that "sixty preachers were present of the different denominations" and that "there is a great work going on."[10] In September of 1863, Broadus wrote in the *Religious Herald* of Virginia:

> It is impossible to convey any just idea of the wide and effectual door that is now opened for preaching in the Army of Northern Virginia. . . . In every command that I visit, or hear from a large proportion of the soldiers will attend preaching and listen well; and in many cases the interest is really wonderful. . . . A much larger proportion of the soldiers attend preaching in camp than used to attend at home; and when any interest is awakened the homogeneity and fellow-feeling which exists among them may be a powerful means, as used by the Divine Spirit, of diffusing that interest through the whole mass. Brethren, there is far more religious interest in this army than at home. The Holy Spirit seems everywhere moving among us. These widespread camps are a magnificent collection of camp-meetings. Brethren, it is the noblest opportunity for protracted meetings you ever saw. The rich, ripe harvest stands waiting. Come, brother, thrust in your sickle, and, by

---

[9]   A. T. Robertson, ed., *Life and Letters of John A. Broadus* (Philadelphia: American Baptist Publication Society, 1909), 188–189.

[10]   Robertson, *Life and Letters,* 204–205.

God's blessing, you shall reap golden sheaves that shall
be your rejoicing in time and eternity.

THE EFFECTUAL USE OF FITTING MEANS

How did such a radical shift in religious disposition and
expectation occur? What prompted such seriousness of mind?
Concerned Christians across the South observed this shallow
transiency of mind and sought to find measures to counteract the
general decline in churches and society, as well as reap a harvest of
wheat when it seemed that only tares were being sown. Another
type of seed was needed. This attempt at a more healthful harvest
included distribution of religious intelligence among the soldiers.
Colporteurs, Bible societies, and camp preachers began to effect
results in a great ingathering of converts in both armies. Baptists
were particularly active and aggressively sought to capture the
momentous events for eternal purposes. What occurred, however,
far exceeded by large measure anything that could be explained by
any one factor or even the combination of them all.

It would be informative to show the specific use of means that
God had designed for such a spiritual harvest. One, circulation of
the Word of God laid the foundation. Bibles were distributed from
chaplains, from churches, and from individuals as armies would
march through towns and villages. Bennett recorded the offer
made by a chaplain at the close of a service to find New Testaments
for any soldier who would like one. They should provide him their
name at the close of the service. "Scarcely had the last words of
blessing died on the minister's lips," Bennett wrote, "before the
war-worn heroes charged on him almost as furiously as if storming
the enemy's breast-works."[11] Jones let H. G. Crews describe his
work of tract distribution in "the hotels, and saloons, . . . as well
as on the streets, to the hundreds who come in from the camps

---

[11] Bennett, *A Narrative of the Great Revival*, 50.

around." He called it a "blessed work to care for the souls of our brave boys."[12]

Officers desired chaplains whose first interest was faithful presentation of the gospel. If chaplains were not available, churches were requested to send ministers with the singular intent of gospel proclamation. Stonewall Jackson expressed with some urgency a desire for each branch of the Christian church to send into the army some of its most prominent ministers. He wanted men "distinguished for their piety, talents, and zeal." They should focus particularly on regiments without chaplains and convince them to take steps to get chaplains. "As a general rule," Jackson noted, "I do not think that a chaplain who would preach denominational sermons should be in the army." As Jackson saw it, the specific need faced by men who were always staring at death was not what denomination a preacher represented but "does he preach the gospel?"[13]

An unusual contribution to the spiritual resurgence among Confederate soldiers was the work of Dwight L. Moody among the Confederate prisoners. When nine thousand prisoners arrived at Camp Douglas, Moody organized workers (after receiving the proper permission) to form prayer groups among the prisoners and start preaching services. Also, one-on-one spiritual counseling was regularly exercised. Thousands of the Southerners—those rebels—heard the gospel and found salvation in Christ through Moody's ministry and the providence of wartime internment.

Another factor that operated to keep the gospel and the cause of eternal truth before the soldiers was the creative zeal of Christian women. Women worked among both the wounded and those in camp to provide clean linens, meals, and blankets, as well as prayers, hymns, words of witness, and spiritual encouragement. One woman maintained a private hospital in her home, named "The Samaritan." Her house accommodated twenty in one room.

---

[12] Jones, *Christ in the Camp*, 213.

[13] Bennett, *A Narrative of the Great Revival*, 51–53

In addition to comfortable and tasteful decor, including greenhouse plants, she had a library of religious books and pictures hung all around the walls. A dining room for convalescent patients was catered by private families, and tea and coffee were made in the room. Worship services were held morning and evening composed of Scripture reading, singing, and prayer. The lady led those unless she could gain the help of a gospel minister. She began this service in April 1861and regularly saw conversions to Christ.[14]

More work with the wounded both physically and spiritually was done in hospitals. W. F. Broaddus wrote: "The interest of our soldiers in the hospitals here, in the great things of eternity, is exceedingly encouraging. Several have professed conversion, while many others are evidently asking, 'What must I do to be saved?'" The soldiers were eager to have preaching in their respective wards. Their interest, which he judged to be in earnest, led Broaddus to comment, "What a luxury, to press the cup of salvation to one who is physically unable to inquire for it by going to the Lord's house!"[15] In light of that, Broaddus expressed, "There are some signs of religious awakening among the soldiers here. . . . I am not without hope that we are about to be favored with an ingathering of souls to the Lord."[16]

James B. Taylor agreed with this sense of rare privilege, stating, "What an opportunity for the child of God! Christian reader, your Saviour 'went about doing good.' He went where there was sickness and misery and death. This was His great concern, His meat and drink. He never faltered, not wearied, nor turned aside." Followers of Christ, Taylor insisted, should do all they could, either personally or in support of workers, to go "into this field, so vast and so inviting. Thus shall you win souls who shall deck the diadem of your Redeemer—who shall be stars to glitter in your crown of rejoicing for ever and ever." In a hospital of three hundred

[14] Bennett, *A Narrative of the Great Revival*, 59.
[15] Jones, *Christ in the Camp*, 211.
[16] Jones, *Christ in the Camp*, 222.

inmates, Taylor made it his business "to converse individually with most of those to whom I had access."[17]

Another powerful means of this revival was the distribution of select Christian literature. One anecdote among many was related by a soldier who had avoided any religious services but spent his time gambling. A chaplain, aware that he regularly missed listening to preaching to pursue his evil pastime, gave him a tract entitled "The wrath to come." The request to read the tract was so polite that "I promised him I would, and immediately went to my tent to give it a hasty perusal. I had not finished it until I felt that I was exposed to that wrath, and that I deserved to be damned. It showed me so plainly where and what I was." He knew that if he failed to find a remedy for his sin, wrath certainly would be in his eternity. The tract, however, did not leave him in despair but "pointed me to that glorious Refuge which has indeed been a refuge to me from the storm, for I now feel that I can trust in Christ." Bennett commented, "The history of this little tract is the history of thousands of like character that preached silently but powerfully and successfully, in camp and hospital, in tent and bivouac."[18]

In our day, the religion of social justice would find it difficult to consent to the godly influence of officers in the Confederate Army. In God's sovereign disposal of His purpose, however, he did use the witness of officers who sincerely believed the gospel and desired the salvation of their men in uniform. J. W. Jones had the studied opinion that "no army . . . was ever blessed with so large a proportion of high officers who were earnest Christ men, as the Army of Northern Virginia."[19] Robert E. Lee's piety ran in a parallel above his leadership and bravery. Jones in particular noted the deep-toned and unobtrusive piety of Lee. In 1864, following the lead of Jefferson Davis in calling for a day

---

[17] Jones, *Christ in the Camp*, 214–216.

[18] Bennett, *A Narrative of the Great Revival*, 84.

[19] Jones, *Christ in the Camp*, 42.

of fasting, humiliation, and prayer, Lee wrote his men, "Soldiers! Let us humble ourselves before the Lord our God, asking through Christ the forgiveness of our sins, beseeching the aid of God of our forefathers in the defence of our homes and our liberties, thanking Him for His past blessings, and imploring their continuance upon our cause and our people." Then after the war, upon hearing a sermon by John A. Broadus preached at the college, Lee observed, "It was a noble sermon—one of the very best I ever heard—and the beauty of it was that the preacher gave our young men the very marrow of the Gospel, and with a simple earnestness that must have reached their hearts and done them good."[20]

The unanimous testimony of those who knew T. J. "Stonewall" Jackson points to an other-worldly piety and abandonment to divine sovereignty. A soldier on the field reported, "I saw something today which affected me more than anything I ever saw or read on religion. While the battle was raging and the bullets were flying, Jackson rode by, calm as if he were at home, but his head was raised toward heaven, and his lips were moving evidently in prayer." Jackson never entered a battle without invoking God's blessing and protection. Another close associate judged, "The dependence of this strange man upon the Deity seems never to be absent from his mind, and whatever he says or does, it is always prefaced, 'By God's blessings.'" Jones recalled an incident in the tent of Jackson some days before Chancellorsville in which the conversation was on the blessings of personal piety. The group of men was discussing the obstacles to growth in grace in the army, the best means of promoting true piety, and other related subjects. Jackson engaged the discussion with such eloquence and heartfelt earnestness that Jones felt he must "lay aside my office as teacher in Israel and be content to 'sit at the feet' of this able theologian, this humble, earnest Christian, and learn of him lessons in the Divine life." Jackson "accepted fully the precious promises of God's word, walked by a living faith in Jesus, and was guided by the star of

---

[20] Jones, *Christ in the Camp*, 58–60.

hope as he trod firmly the path of duty." Jones believed that the "glorious revivals with which we were favored were in answer to the prayers, and in blessing on the efforts of 'Stonewall' Jackson." Eternity alone will fully reveal those interactions between prayer, desire, and the gracious blessings of divine sovereignty.[21]

Both Bennett and Jones commented on the deep concern that J. B. Gordon had for the souls of the soldiers. He chastened the churches for the lack of aggressiveness in sending men to the camps. He suggested that the "good people at home" showed a "criminal indifference" to the eternal well-being of these men, supposing that "preaching to a body of soldiers is 'casting pearls before swine.'" He observed, however, the intense eagerness of the men to hear the gospel, the rapt attention that up to two thousand men gave to the preaching of the occasional missionary that came, and the conversion of both young and seasoned men under gospel preaching. "Men, grown old in sin, and who never blanched in the presence of the foe, are made to tremble under the sense of guilt, and here in the forests and the fields are being converted to God." Young men, prayed for and feared for, turned to Christ, making the bitter tears of parents turn to tears of rejoicing. "I close by telling you," Gordon told A. E. Dickinson, "that in the last few weeks nearly two hundred in this single brigade have been added to the different churches."[22]

Bennett reported the observation of a writer noting the religious influence in the Army of Tennessee. Bennett preached in a place prepared for preaching in the center of the division of General Cleburne. Cleburne, a brave leader and hero on many battlefields, and most of his officers were present. Bennett was assisted by General M. P. Lowry. Lowry was a Baptist preacher, and, like Cleburne, a hero of many well-fought battlefields. Lowry held the rank of brigadier general in Cleburne's division, Hardee's corps, in the Army of Tennessee. He was from north Mississippi

---

[21] Jones, *Christ in the Camp*, 96–97.
[22] Jones, *Christ in the Camp*, 104–105.

near Kossuth, and he was a self-educated preacher who had experience in the Mexican-American War at age eighteen. One man who knew him well opined, "A braver soldier never graced a battlefield." Cleburne introduced him to General Hardee as "the bravest man in the Confederate army." According to Foster's *Mississippi Baptist Preachers*, "during his soldier life he did a great deal of preaching. He frequently said that he did not think that he did more good as a preacher during any four years of his life than [he] did during his four years in the army." One of his soldiers said that he would "pray with them in his tent, preach to them in the camp and lead them to the thickest of the fight in the battle." He was frequently referred to as "the fighting preacher of the Army of Tennessee." He did not believe in slavery, but he did believe in the South and in state's rights, and he fought for his convictions "with all the ardor of a patriot." After the war, Lowry continued to serve as a preacher for several small churches in north Mississippi and founded Blue Mountain College for women.[23]

WAS IT A WORK OF THE SPIRIT? DID IT LAST?

Bennett narrated the events of the revival in the army year by year from summer 1861 through spring 1865. He constructed the narrative with anecdotes from soldiers and reports and letters from chaplains, pastors, and lay workers. Writing in 1876, Bennett asked whether the fruits of the army revivals were enduring. He affirmed, after more than a decade of observation and interviews and correspondence with others, that the apparent work of grace was far more than merely apparent—it was real. He had documented that "in all the churches of the south there are earnest, devout and active Christians, who date their spiritual birth from some revival in Virginia, in the West, or in the far South" during the trials of the war. They recalled vividly "the rude camp church, the gathering throngs from the various commands, the hearty singing,

---

[23] L. S. Foster, *Mississippi Baptist Preachers* (St. Louis: National Baptist Publishing Company, 1895), 460.

the simple and earnest prayers, the tender appeals of the loving chaplain, urging all who stand on the perilous edge of battle to fly for refuge to the Friend of sinners." They recalled not only the tears but the lives of repentance and the joy of the new birth. Those seasons of conversion and spiritual renewal were "the bright spots to which memory returns and delights to dwell upon in the dark period that drenched the land in blood and put a load of grief up on every household." Taking off the sword of steel, scores of those converts took the sword of the Sprit to confront the powers of spiritual darkness. Bennett asserted, "The seed they sowed in trench and camp and hospital, in the bivouac, and on the weary march, was watered from above and has borne a rich harvest. And may we not hope that the full fruition of this work is to be realized in that era of peace and goodwill which is even now descending upon our common country?"[24]

J. W. Jones gave testimony to his personal efforts to ascertain the fruit of this revival. "If the personal allusion may be pardoned," he wrote, "I will say that I have taken especial pains— by correspondence, by inquiries of pastors, and by personal interviews with many of them, as I have travelled in every state from Maryland to Texas—to ascertain the after-lives of the four hundred and ten soldiers whom I baptized in the army, and I have heard of only three (there were doubtless others) who had gone back to the world." One pastor of a leading church in the Southwest told him, "I am indebted to you for baptizing in the army the best and most efficient men in my church."

Jones closed his book with a chapter of seventy-five pages entitled "Results of the Work and Proofs of Its Genuineness." He estimated the number of converts at fifteen thousand in Lee's army. Given Bennett's figures, however, the number could be increased to fifty thousand. Jones sought always to underestimate so as not to exaggerate in the least. Even in his day, many asked, "Was this a *genuine* and *permanent* work of grace? Was it not a

---

[24] Bennett, *A Narrative of the Great Revival*, 426–427.

mere animal excitement produced by the dangers to which the men were exposed, and liable to pass off when those dangers were removed? Are not the accounts of this army work exaggerated?"[25]

After acknowledging the presence of much wickedness and the spurious nature of some professions, Jones stated, "And yet I do not hesitate to affirm—and think that I can abundantly prove—that the revivals in our camps were as genuine works of grace as any that occur in our churches at home—that as large a proportion of the converts proved the reality of their professions as in any revivals which the world ever saw."[26]

In gathering his reasons to refute any accusation of "animal excitement," he noted that ministers of every denomination and of different temperaments cooperated in these revival efforts. If any "were disposed to get up any undue excitement, or to use improper 'machinery,'" others would quickly restrain him. He gave evidence of this by citing reports from a large number of denominational presses, including *Old School Presbyterian*. Not only did Jones make self-sacrificing efforts to follow up on those whom he baptized during the conflict some years subsequent to the war, but he told scores of stories from others about the conduct of men who were converted during the war and their usefulness after it.

B. T. Kavanaugh, instrumental in the great Trans-Mississippi revival, made this note: "To show the genuineness of this work of grace upon the lives of these converts, we have to remark that after our camp was broken up, and the army was put upon the march to distant fields, wherever we went into camp but for a night our boys held prayer-meetings every night, greatly to the astonishment of the people in the country who were witnesses of their devotion."[27] Prayer, rather than carousing, gambling, drinking, and engaging

---

[25] Jones, *Christ in the Camp*, 392.

[26] Jones, *Christ in the Camp*, 392.

[27] Jones, *Christ in the Camp*, 553.

in loud profanity-laced talk, was seen as evidence of a work of the Spirit of God.

OBSERVATIONS

Even with the admitted Confederate bias of each author, the narrative of the revivals is sober and understated. Though a large amount of the evidence is anecdotal, the amount of material and the representative nature of it is powerful documentation for a true revival. The anecdotal information itself comes from seasoned and theologically sound observers, and the large amount of it shows that none of the accounts is an isolated phenomenon that, taken alone, could distort the overall picture. The distance of the books by Bennett and Jones from the close of the war—one eleven years and the other twenty-two years—and the nature of the ongoing involvement of each author in religious life in the South serves as further evidence of the persevering character of the revival.

As late as 1895, upon a memorial service for John A. Broadus, thirty years after the close of the Civil War, Jones related an event of the war in which Broadus preached on Proverbs 3:17, "Her ways are ways of pleasantness and all her paths are peace." Scarcely a dry eye could be seen among the thousands who gathered, so moving and captivating was the sermon. Jones continued his recollection, "At the close of the service they came by the hundreds to ask an interest in the prayers of God's people, or profess a new-found faith in the Lord Jesus Christ, and I doubt not that our beloved brother has greeted on the other shore not a few who heard him that day or at other points in the army."[28]

When the content of the bowls of incense, "which are the prayers of the saints" (Rev. 5:8), is revealed, an earthly incongruity will be seen as heavenly harmony. Union "watchfires of a hundred circling camps" joined in final truth with preaching by the light of pine-knot fires in camps of the Southern Army and Confederate

---

[28] Robertson, *Life and Letters,* 209.

prayer meetings, in the uncontrollable and invincible grace of God, were made effectual to the redemption and eternal emancipation of people "out of every tribe and tongue and people and nation" (Rev. 5:9). Doubtless, this includes many of those whose earthly emancipation depended on the defeat of the Confederate Army, of those whose prayers for the kingdom of God transcended the constricted perceptions of their culture.

We are still short of heaven and must struggle as fallen people in a fallen world. This revival, nevertheless, left a legacy of faith in the gospel, submission to the truth of the Bible, and love of the kingdom of God that progressively worked through subsequent generations. Its deep-seated power molded the culture, challenged the society, and pointed the relation between heirs of owners and owned, masters and slaves, free and bound, toward true Christian fraternity and a growing common commitment to eternal truth. These blessings were in the "golden bowls of incense."

CHAPTER 10

Dwight L. Moody

"You ask me to explain regeneration. I cannot do it. But one thing I know—that I have been regenerated. All the infidels and skeptics could not make me believe differently. I feel a different man that I did twenty-one years ago last March, when God gave me a new heart."

—Dwight L. Moody[1]

Dwight Lyman Moody (1837–1899) was born in Northfield, Massachusetts, February 5, 1837, the sixth of nine children, impoverished by a father's careless use of finances. Edwin Moody, married to Betsy Holton on January 3, 1828, was a brick mason and died suddenly on May 28, 1841, when Dwight was four. Edwin's death left his wife with seven children to care for and twins, a boy and a girl, to be born within a month.[2] The family was destitute and owed a yearly mortgage on the home, so creditors came and hauled off anything they could find of worth in the household. Betsy had managed to hide a few things of value and of necessity. Through the help of uncles, neighbors, and a

---

[1] D. L. Moody, "The New Birth" in *The Best of D. L. Moody,* ed. Wilbur Smith (Chicago: Moody Press, 1971), 92.

[2] Lyle W. Dorsett, *A Passion for Souls* (Chicago: Moody Press, 1997), 29. Also see Wiliam R. Moody, *D. L. Moody* (New York: Macmillan, 1930), 6–9. Also, Kevin Belmonte, *D. L. Moody: A Life* (Chicago, Mody Publishers, 2014), 20–21; Richard S. Rhodes, *Dwight Lyman Moody's Life Work and Gospel Sermons . . . With a Biography of His Co-Laborer Ira David Sankey* (Chicago: Rhodes & McClure Publishing Co, 1904), i–ii.

compassionate Unitarian pastor, Reverend Oliver Capen Everett, the family survived intact.[3]

While Edwin was alive, the family had only sporadic contact with any religious training. Betsy felt compunctions of conscience about this. The kindness and paternal attention Oliver Everett gave to the Moody children prompted her to send them to the Congregational church where Everett was pastor. He baptized all the children. He was caught in the roiling controversy within New England Congregationalism over orthodoxy, Unitarianism, transcendentalism, and spiritualism. His views, a pious Unitarianism, probably were influenced by William Ellery Channing.

Moody's mother found the strong confessional Calvinism of New England intensely distasteful and welcomed the more benign, good-natured, and kind doctrine of Reverend Everett. She taught her children a Bible lesson each day, and they attended the church each Sunday. Asked later in life if the baptism at the hands of a semi-evangelical Unitarian had troubled his conscience, Moody responded, "I found I was baptized in the name of the Father, Son, and Holy Ghost. I couldn't see that anyone could add to this." Everett was replaced by a pastor more forcefully committed to the rationalistic side of the theological debates and less committed to any friendly personal interaction with his parishioners, especially the children of the Moody family. Dwight looked upon Sunday as a day of dread, unnoticed by his pastor unless he went to sleep. Everett's friendly greeting, regular benevolence, and pat on the head gave way to a detached glare and a demeanor of unconcern. Moody's son, William, concluded, "In his religious background, therefore, there was no doctrinal teaching in the Christian faith."[4]

---

[3] William Moody, *D. L. Moody*, 14; Dorsett, *A Passion for Souls*, 30; Belmonte, *D. L. Moody: A Life*, 23.

[4] William Moody, *D. L. Moody*, 14–19. Dorsett, *A Passion for Souls*, 32, 33; Belmonte, *D. L. Moody: A Life*, 23, 24;

Moody's guided education ended when he was thirteen years old. One biographer surmised that Moody "went through as many as a dozen terms at the little district schoolhouse; but very little of the schools ever went through him."5 His education was punctuated with working on a neighborhood farm for a penny a week. He led his peers in pranks that at times were destructive, he learned to swear without compunction, he had little guidance and less respect for it, and though he loved his mother deeply, he knew that the distribution of her personal attention had severe challenges with the number of siblings and the constant need for survival labor. In addition, her emotions were deeply affected by the desertion of the family by her oldest son, Isaiah, who gave no warning, no note of explanation, and was gone without a trace. He returned thirteen years later.6

Leaving the Farm, Finding the Faith

Moody moved to Boston in 1854 to work with his uncle. Tired of the soul-killing, body-numbing, marginally sustaining labor that sapped time and energy day after day, he determined that the city would offer a more powerful opportunity for his ambition for success and material advancement. Undeterred by all family warnings and arguments to the contrary, Moody planned to set out on his journey even if he had to walk the one hundred miles.[7] His brother George's attempt to dissuade him proved vain, but Dwight's determination to go earned a five-dollar donation from the older brother to fund the trip.[8]

---

[5] Belmonte, *D. L. Moody: A Life*, 28, citing W. H. Daniels *D. L. Moody and his Work* published in 1875.

[6] Rhodes, *Dwight Lyman Moody's Life Work*, ii–iii; Dorsett, *A Passion for Souls*, 33.

[7] William Moody, *D. L. Moody*, 24; Dorsett, *A Passion for Souls*, 37; Belmonte, *D. L. Moody: A Life*, 31.

[8] William Moody, *D. L. Moody*, 24; Belmonte, *D. L. Moody: A Life*, 31.

After days of discouragement and failing in one job, he consented to conditions that his uncle, Samuel Holton, set for employment at his retail shoe store. He would follow instructions and would attend Mount Vernon Congregational Church.[9] At the church he became a member of a Sunday school class taught by Edward Kimball.[10]

Having greater affinity with Kimball than with the pastor, E. N. Kirk, Moody learned to trust Kimball and sensed his transparent love for Christ. After a year of attending the church and the class, Moody received an unexpected visit from Kimball in the shoe store. Tactfully and with deep sincerity and evident emotion, Kimball told Moody of "Christ's love for him, and the love Christ wanted in return."[11] On that day, April 21, 1855, and at that interview, Moody surrendered to the appeal, sensing the sincerity of Kimball and the power of such unconditional love from Christ. Moody said simply, "I was brought into the Kingdom of God."[12] His son William wrote this about his father's conversion:

> Apparently there was no deep conviction of sin or wrestling of spirit. His allegiance was a reasonable service joyously rendered. The few words wisely spoken achieved what sermons and class work had failed to bring about. That one conversation was the turning point in Moody's life. There was a new incentive, ultimately revolutionizing all his early objectives.[13]

---

[9] William Moody, *D. L. Moody*, 26–27; Belmonte, *D. L. Moody: A Life*, 35. Rhodes, iii.

[10] Dorsett, *A Passion for Souls*, 47; Belmonte, *D. L. Moody: A Life*, 40–43.

[11] Belmonte, *D. L. Moody: A Life*, 42; Dorsett, *A Passion for Souls*, 47.

[12] See Dorsett's discussion of the time of Moody's conversion as he perceived it, and his eventual reception into membership of the Mount Vernon Congregational Church (47–49).

[13] William Moody, *D. L. Moody*, 33.

His first attempt at church membership ended with rejection. When asked what Christ had done that "entitles Him to our love and obedience," he responded, "I think He has done a great deal for us all, but I don't know of anything He has done in particular."[14] Kimball stayed loyal to Moody, instructed him, observed him, and persuaded him to go before the committee. Even though the committee still had doubts concerning the clarity and precision of his understanding, they were convinced of his sincerity and his true sense of repentance for sin and loyalty to Christ. He was received as a member on May 3, 1856.

Leaving Boston, Embracing Chicago, Finding Ministry

Moody had tasted success in business and felt that the burgeoning city of Chicago would provide both an opportunity and a challenge for his ambition and his developing skill in commerce and investment. Feeling restrictions on his energy in both church and business in the finely finished and organized city of Boston, he moved to Chicago in September 1856. Moody became a member of Plymouth Congregational Church in May 1857. He rented four pews that he filled each Sunday with young boys from the streets of Chicago. Unsatisfied with the limited opportunities for work and fellowship in just one congregation, soon Moody began to do the same work at the First Methodist Episcopal Church and the First Baptist Church. He was unbothered by, or perhaps unaware of, any prohibitive doctrinal differences but reveled in the expansive opportunity for getting young boys and men to attend church, fellowship, and prayer. His zeal for the destitute children that he observed in "The Sands"—also known as "Little Hell"—along with his methods of enticing them to his Sunday school classes and other weekday evening services, gained for him the nickname "Crazy Moody."

---

[14] William Moody, *D. L. Moody*, 33. Dorsett, *A Passion for Souls*, 47–49.

As a Christian worker, he cut his teeth on the principles that he observed in the Prayer Revival of 1857–1858. Stan Gundry saw this influence as prominent in making Moody very hesitant about the use of measures and giving him a deeper reliance on the ministry of prayer and the work of the Spirit. Moody started a Sunday school class in the Wells Street Mission and went along the Chicago River getting indigent and orphaned children to come to the class. He worked in other mission endeavors starting classes and providing aid to hundreds of needy people. One writer noted,

> His ardent spirit soon impelled him to set up a mission for himself, in a neglected and degraded section of North Chicago. He paid for the hire of an empty tavern, and gathered together the unclean and rude children of the neighborhood for Sunday-school services, while the intemperate and ignorant adults were reached in the evening meetings. The poor little ones were won over to attention by gifts of maple sugar, and a liberal lot of hymns and stories.[15]

Two of his helpers in those outreach and teaching ministries were Emma Revell and John V. Farwell. Moody consecrated himself to full-time evangelistic work in 1860, quit his job, did without a home, slept on a bench in the YMCA, and minimized his meals. Emma became his wife on August 28, 1862. The ceremony was held in First Baptist Church. He soon was domesticated to a small home that became a haven of hospitality for Christian workers and "reclaimed prodigals."[16]

From 1861 to 1865, he worked with the US Christian Commission on the front lines in the Union Army doing evangelistic work.[17] He made nine trips to the front lines and

---

15 Rhodes, *Dwight Lyman Moody's Life Work*, v–vi.

16 Rhodes, *Dwight Lyman Moody's Life Work*, viii.

17 See Dorsett, *A Passion for* Souls, 87ff.

often was called to the cots of dying men to give counsel in the time of death. He prayed and pointed them to the dying Jesus as the Savior of sinners. Into the confines of Confederate wounded he also went with consoling evangelistic purpose. Even with opposition from some who argued for a different approach to the wounded and dying, Moody maintained his intention of pointing to the gospel.[18] His work with the soldiers and his work on the streets of Chicago combined with his retentive memory and lively perceptions to give an unending source of apt illustrations and stories that permeated his sermons.

LEARNING TO PREACH

In 1863, Moody organized and built a non-denominational church, Illinois Street Church, at a cost of $20,000 and served as its senior pastor. In 1866, he became president of the Chicago chapter of the YMCA. His manic busyness brought him to the edge of an emotional collapse; that combined with his wife's sickness prompted a trip abroad to England.

For four and a half months in 1867, Moody and Emma visited England. Moody's frank manner and unpredictability in public speech made him a sensation and gained many speaking invitations during this visit. He met Charles Haddon Spurgeon, one of his heroes, and heard him preach several times. He admired the variety of Spurgeon's work but felt that he was behind on Sunday schools. He also had conversations with George Müeller. He greatly admired the orphanage work that Müeller supported and felt genuine appreciation for the faith demonstrated in the way the orphanages were supported. Moody wanted to print stories of answered prayer in a periodical entitled *Heavenly Tidings*. He also met with the Plymouth Brethren and J. N. Darby, who were probably influential in his adopting certain views of premillenialism. He was impressed with the book-by-book

---

[18] Dorsett, *A Passion for Souls*, 87–98

exposition they practiced. Later, in America, Moody and Darby had a public disagreement over Calvinistic doctrine and Moody's emphasis on "free will." Darby closed his Bible and walked out of the meeting during a "Bible reading" time at Farwell Hall in Chicago, never to return.[19]

Among the Brethren, a West Londoner named Henry Varley took a personal interest in Moody. Varley was a butcher by trade but had become a man of deep prayer and an effective evangelist. He opened many doors for Moody to speak in Brethren halls. On a visit to Ireland, another influential friendship was begun with F. C. Bland, a law officer who was High Sheriff of Kerry County. Bland, "bright, articulate, and well-educated," had been converted in 1861. He developed into an ardent student of the Bible and became Moody's friend and also his Bible consultant. As Moody neared the time of departure to the United States, he heard words from Varley that haunted him and drove him for the next three decades of his ministry: "The world has yet to see what God will do with and for and through and in and by the man who is fully and wholly consecrated to him."[20]

In late July 1867, the Moodys returned to Chicago and became extraordinarily busy. Dwight was speaking in his church on Sundays and at many places during the week, along with his work as president of the YMCA.

Henry Moorhouse was a twenty-seven-year-old, boyish-looking preacher who had gone across the Irish Sea to hear Moody preach in Dublin.[21] He invited himself to preach for Moody in Chicago. From there he believed he would find other places of itinerant ministry. Moody was not enthusiastic about the idea

---

[19] Dorsett, *A Passion for Souls*, 137.

[20] Dorsett, *A Passion for Souls*, 141; Torrey, 10. Rhodes, *Dwight Lyman Moody's Life Work*, xi. Also R. A. Torrey, *Why God Used D. L. Moody* (Chicago: The Bible Institute Colportage Association, 1923), 10.

[21] Dorsett, *A Passion for Souls*, 137; Rhodes says Moorhouse was 17, *Dwight Lyman Moody's Life Work*, xi.

and sought to put brakes on Moorhouse's insistence. Eventually Moorhouse showed up in Chicago and pressed for the opportunity to preach. Moody hesitated but allowed him to preach on a Thursday evening while Moody was absent. He returned to find his wife quite impressed with Moorhouse's message and insistent that Moody himself would like him. From the attendance Moody saw that the sermon and presentation had pleased the congregation.

Moorhouse preached for seven straight nights on John 3:16, emphasizing the love of God for all men. In each sermon he took a different approach, going through the Bible demonstrating the manifestations of divine love throughout Scripture. He changed Moody's perception of the nature of preaching and the nature of the message to be preached. Whereas Moody was initially skeptical of this emphasis on God's universal love as a dominant theme, at the end of the series, Moody decided to shift his own emphasis. Now he did not press the sinner with the warning to "flee from the wrath to come," but he set forth the wooing atmosphere that "God is filled with undeserved grace for every sinner if only you will come."[22]

Moorhouse advised Moody to spend more time in learning his English Bible and follow through themes by using a concordance. The influence of this method on Moody is obvious, and it gave the sense of simple biblicism to his sermons. The method also helped with Moody's emphasis on themes rather than exposition of specific texts. Also, in the diary of Moorhouse, there is evidence that Moody's synopsis of "ruin, redemption, and regeneration" was learned from Moorhouse.

While engaged in a flurry of speaking opportunities in churches and YMCA meetings, Moody's friend and benefactor John Farwell gave the Moodys a new home, furnished and rent

---

[22] Dorsett relates this series of events, *A Passion for Souls*, 137–140. See also Stanley and Patricia Gundry, *The Wit and Wisdom of D. L. Moody* (Chicago: Moody Press, 1974), 19.

free. This came on New Years Day, 1868.[23] Less than a week later, on January 7, 1868, the YMCA burned. The new Farwell Hall was destroyed by flames. Several difficult situations, combined with feverish activity, speaking, destitution for his mother and brother, and an inability to do all that he felt was needed, brought Moody to a point of depression. In 1871, two ladies—a young widow, W. R. Hawkshurst, and Sarah Cooke—began to pray that Moody would be given the "baptism of the Holy Ghost and of fire." With an eerie literalness, in October 1871 the fire that burned Chicago came. It destroyed over eighteen thousand buildings and left more than a hundred thousand people homeless. The fire destroyed four square miles, including virtually all of the business district, grain elevators, warehouses, boats in the river. The second Farwell Hall, the Illinois Street Church, and Moody's home were all burned. Moody used this as an illustration in the sermon "There is no Difference."

> It seems to me I got a glimpse in the Chicago fire of what judgment will be, when I saw that fire rolling down the streets of Chicago, twenty and thirty feet high, consuming man and everything in its march that did not flee. I saw there the millionaire and the beggar fleeing alike. There was no difference. That night our great men, learned men, wise men, all fled alike. There was no difference. And when God comes to judge the world, there will be no difference.[24]

Four months after, Moody experienced an infilling of the Spirit while walking down Wall Street in New York. "I had such an experience of his love that I had to ask him to stay his hand." Dorsett observed from subsequent episodes in the life of Moody that his experience "left him profoundly changed. Inner peace, disappearance of spiritual depression, focused goals, a calmer

---

[23] Rhodes, *Dwight Lyman Moody's Life Work*, ix; Dorsett, *A Passion for Souls*, 145

[24] Rhodes, *Dwight Lyman Moody's Life Work*, 170–171.

demeanor, and preaching with new power now characterized the man."[25]

BACK TO ENGLAND—TWICE

So invigorating to Moody, biblically and spiritually, was the initial visit to England that he scheduled another trip in 1872. He wanted to "sit at the feet" of some of the great Bible teachers he had met in 1867. Given this propensity to learn from others, Gundry found it remarkable that no evidence exists of discussion between Moody and Charles Finney, or Moody ever seeking out Finney for advice. Nor has Gundry found evidence that Moody read Finney.[26] While in England, Moody was asked to preach in a North London church where an apparent powerful work of revival occurred. He became convinced that his opportunity to preach, and the strong presence of divine mercy, were due to the prayers of a young crippled girl, Marianne Adlard. He was invited to return the next year for a larger preaching tour; he agreed to go home, get someone to sing, and return to make the experiment.

A part of his flurry of activities during this visit was attendance at the Mildmay conference sponsored by William Pennefather. The conference gave concentrated attention to seeking of the gift of the Spirit. Pennefather asked Moody to speak. These conferences were preparatory to the Keswick conferences. Moody returned to America to prepare to return to England.

Moody went back to England from 1873 to 1875, this time with full intent of preaching in large evangelistic meetings. He had been invited by three friends, including Pennefeather, who promised to support him and his company while there. Unknown to Moody, they had died before he arrived. Ira Sankey and his wife had come along as singers, adding to Moody's unexpected

---

[25] Dorsett, *A Passion for Souls*, 156, 173. Torrey, *Why God Used D. L. Moody*, 53.

[26] Stanley Gundry, *Love Them In* (Chicago: Moody Press, 1976), 77–78.

obligation to find support.[27] He quickly contacted places that had corresponded with him about the trip and had asked him to speak. Among these was a preaching engagement in Scotland. That became an extended engagement characterized by conversions and enthusiastic acceptance from the Scots. A publication called *The Christian* referred to the meeting as a "work of grace" and reported that it had a remarkable "absence of excitement even at that time of greatest interest." By "excitement," the report meant humanly contrived emotional exuberance. The high spiritual interest was indicated by "crowded churches and halls, most earnest preaching, fervent, hearty singing, and many moved to tears of penitence." Gratefully absent were "articulate wailings" and falling; there were no "sudden outbursts of rapture, of which we have heard in former revivals." It certainly sounded the right note in Moody's perception when the paper judged, "We account for this by the fact that the Spirit of God has done more, and man less, in this work than in any similar awakening since the days of the Reformation."[28]

F. B. Meyer reflected on Moody's impact during this visit by noting that his unconventional and natural manner of organizing and speaking drew people to hear him and had a great impact on Meyer personally as a young pastor, for he was "bound rather rigidly by the chains of conventionalism." "Fresh and unexpected" ways were startling but not off-putting to the masses. Meyer recalled, "There was never the slightest approach to irreverence, fanaticism, or extravagance."[29] Horatius Bonar summarized, "They fully deserve our confidence; the more we know of them in private the more do we appreciate them and the more do we feel inclined to cast in our lot with them." He observed that "these men have the most definite of all definite aims—winning souls to

---

[27] William Moody, *D. L. Moody*, 141–142.

[28] See Dorsett, *A Passion for Souls*, 197–203, for a discussion of this Scotland campaign. I have lost the reference material for the quote from *The Christian*.

[29] William Moody, *D. L. Moody*, 144.

everlasting joy." He informed those who read his analysis, "They have in view no sinister nor sordid motives, as their past history shows. . . . Beside all this, it is vain to try to stop them. They will work and they will speak whoever shall say nay. Let us work along with them."[30]

Moody's preaching in England gained the support and participation of Charles Spurgeon; Spurgeon even defended Moody's simple message in a *Sword and Trowel* article about the doctrine of justification by faith. The criticism that Moody and Sankey were wicked for "they were the means of saving the lower orders" suited precisely; so was Spurgeon. During the 1873 Moody Crusade in Scotland, Spurgeon expressed his delight "to hear of the Lord's work in Newcastle and in Edinburgh. May the Lord prosper our brethren Moody and Sankey more and more."[31]

In April 1874, Spurgeon gave eight full pages to report the awakening in the north, the Moody-Sankey crusade in Scotland. The writer, simply referred to as "an eye-witness," refuted reports of "irreverent fanaticism" and spasmodic and spurious concoctions of religious fervor. He pointed rather to the merging of a growing common desire for religious awakening with the spiritual gifts of the evangelists. The evidence pointed to a true working of the Spirit, far from any false fervor generated by mere mesmerizing influence of the revival atmosphere. The reporter gave positive evidence of Moody's skill at preaching, knowledge of human nature, thorough knowledge of Scripture, and the precision and practical wisdom of a businessman. Moody exhibited a father's affection and had a burning zeal without being one-sided. The writer attributed Moody's broad appeal to his true tenderness and compassion, on the one hand, and his stern and uncompromising application of truth on the other. The attractiveness of the man was in some ways mysterious. The *Sword and Trowel* writer saw

---

[30] William Moody, *D. L. Moody*, 168.

[31] Charles Spurgeon, ed., *The Sword and the Trowel 1874* (London: Passmore & Alabaster), February 1874, 93.

it arising from the wisdom, simplicity of presentation, and sense of empathy that came from Moody's work during the American Civil War. Without these deeply embedded traits, Moody's style would be "barely tolerable to correct ears." Lack of fitting grammar and presence of colloquial abruptness, and a full menu of Americanisms, made his style unprepossessing in itself, yet "it exercises the most perfect control over an audience." The reporter noted that "an infinity of striking illustrations" gave rise to "heights of natural impassioned eloquence." The element of kingly authority and sovereignty emanating from his preaching can only be explained by "sitting long at the feet of divine wisdom."[32]

Later in 1875, Spurgeon preached for Moody at Bow Hall in London to an immense crowd; he would have done so oftener had the effort not been so exhausting. Spurgeon appeared again at Camberwell Hall and expressed his strong approval of the blessed work "which our American brethren have been privileged to carry on." Though Spurgeon felt that they had charted a frenetic pace for themselves that could enervate their strength and power, he expressed his great pleasure in being able to assist "our brethren Messrs. Moody and Sankey at Camberwell Hall, and we would have done far more, only our own enterprises demand our constant attention." He lamented the bigotry shown by the national establishment in casting indignity toward the true-hearted Americans with epithets of schismatics and ranters.[33]

In June, on the approach of the time when Moody and Sankey would come to London, Spurgeon encouraged his people to do all they could "to make this movement a success." They should pray, attend, take their friends, neighbors and children, and do all they could to win souls "as the Holy Spirit shall enable you." Spurgeon made support of the Moody-Sankey mission virtually a matter of conscience. He pointed to the reports in Glasgow, Edinburgh,

---

[32] Spurgeon, *The Sword and the Trowel*, April 1874, 156.

[33] Charles Spurgeon, ed., *The Sword and the Trowel 1875* (London: Passmore & Alabaster), June 1875, 283.

and Newcastle "that souls were saved in large numbers, that the Churches were edified and the tone of religious feeling improved." People must not hold back because of the "simple instrumentality" being effective in this phenomenon of gospel success, but rather celebrate it.[34]

Spurgeon responded to the criticism of the simplicity of the message of justification by faith with a strong defense of the doctrine.[35] Though it calls for an efficacious operation of the Spirit, neither the doctrine nor the act of believing is complicated. Some criticized Moody for the straightforward manner of his call to believe in Christ. It seemed that they were afraid that "the doctrine of immediate salvation through faith in Christ Jesus is a very dangerous one" that will lead to the deterioration of public morality. Spurgeon's sermon on "Justification by Faith" addressed the unfair and unfounded charges against Moody and argued for the virtuous tendency of the doctrine of justification by faith alone. "We are not so dastardly as to allow our friends to stand alone in the front of the battle, to be looked upon as peculiar persons holding strange notions from which the rest of us dissent."[36] Like Moody, Spurgeon preached the atoning blood, and had done so all his ministry, and considered it a teaching that had "the general consent of Protestant Christendom." It was an attack not only on Moody but on the Protestant faith and the Bible itself. "Deny inspiration," Spurgeon proposed, "and you have ground to stand on; but while you believe the Bible you must believe in justification by faith." The objection to Moody and Sankey on these grounds, in Spurgeon's mind, amounted to a contest "between the Popish doctrine of *merit* and the Protestant doctrine of Grace!"[37]

---

[34] Charles Spurgeon, *The Metropolitan Tabernacle Pulpit, 1875* (London: Passmore & Alabaster), 334, 335.

[35] Spurgeon, *The Metropolitan Tabernacle Pulpit, 1875*, 337.

[36] Spurgeon, *The Metropolitan Tabernacle Pulpit, 1875*, 338.

[37] Spurgeon, *The Metropolitan Tabernacle Pulpit, 1875*, 338–339.

Of course, some brief opposition came from some of the Scots to Sankey's music and his small cabinet organ. They considered it a "kist fu' o' whistles."[38] Soon, however, the unobtrusive manner of Sankey, the ease with which he involved the congregation, and the veracity and simplicity of both text and tune in his music won them over. Sankey's music created a seamless continuum with Moody's preaching. The inviting musical lines of "The Ninety and Nine" embedded a message of the tender care of Jesus in seeking wandering sheep deep in the memory of its singers.[39]

Spurgeon did not, however, throw all caution to the wind on account of his affection for Moody. One of Spurgeon's hesitations about the Moody revival efforts was the lack of increase of church membership. In the beginning of 1876, Spurgeon was pensive about what seemed to be "a mere surface motion, and not a deep ground-swell of grace." Crowds were large, professed converts were many, but churches only slightly increased, and the tone of religious feeling seemingly had fallen rather than risen. He said that the past year was "disappointing," for what began with a flourish "did not revive the churches" and had "left the masses very much as they were." Perhaps he began to regret that he had given such strong encouragement to the Moody-Sankey campaigns. In a sober and hesitant frame of mind, Spurgeon warned that "nations are not to be enlightened with a flash, nor cities sensationalized into religion in a month."[40]

All was not as depressing as it seemed, however. Given a few more months to observe, Spurgeon's evaluation improved. In November 1876, Spurgeon mentioned that "during the last few

---

[38] Charles R. Erdman, *Dwight L. Moody* (New York: Fleming H. Revell Company, 1949), 12.

[39] For a brief and highly sympathetic biographical statement about Sankey, see Rhodes, *Dwight Lyman Moody's Life Work*, xlii–liv. Also see Dorsett for observations about the Moody-Sankey relationship, 173–176.

[40] Charles Spurgeon, ed., *The Sword and the Trowel 1876* (London: Passmore & Alabaster), January 1876, 2.

months we have met with more converts from Messrs. Moody and Sankey's meetings than in all the time before." "We could not believe," Spurgeon indicated, in defense of Moody, "that such earnest gospel preaching could be without saving result, but we feared that the converts would remain separate, and not unite with the churches."[41]

Spurgeon did not turn sour toward Moody. During Spurgeon's trip to Mentone at the close of 1881, Moody and Sankey took the services at the Metropolitan Tabernacle for a Sunday. More than twelve thousand people sought to gain entrance to a building whose maximum capacity was six thousand. Spurgeon's seat-holders left their tickets to others for the evening service, but that did nothing to relieve the pressure of people. "We see clear evidence," Spurgeon observed, "that if Messrs. Moody and Sankey again visit London no building will be sufficiently capacious to hold the crowds who will gather to hear them." Without regret or envy, he added, "May the Lord send a great blessing upon their efforts, and may London, on this occasion, have a double portion of the resulting benefit."[42]

In 1884, at Spurgeon's fiftieth birthday celebration, Moody gave a tribute remembering the times that he came to hear Spurgeon preach in 1867. The experience encouraged Moody to try to preach. He attended again in 1872. He had read Spurgeon's sermons for twenty-five years. Giving sincere commendation of the multiplicity of ministries that Spurgeon's faithful preaching had spawned, Moody concluded, "If God can use Mr. Spurgeon, why should He not use the rest of us, and why should we not all just lay ourselves at the Master's feet and say to Him, 'Send me, use me?'"[43]

---

[41] Spurgeon, *The Sword and the Trowel*, November 1876, 530.

[42] Charles Spurgeon, ed., *The Sword and the Trowel 1882* (London: Passmore & Alabaster), January 1882, 42.

[43] Wilbur E. Smith, ed., *The Best of D. L. Moody* (Chicago; Moody Press, 1971), 8. See the account of this event and the full quote by Moody

In the 1891 volume of *The Sword and the Trowel*, several entries entitled "The Work of an Evangelist" by Thomas Spurgeon are included.[44] Most of the months for that year carry reports of evangelistic ministries. Due at least in part to the influence of Moody, Spurgeon had come to give public notice of the work of an evangelist and valued it highly.

AN EXPANDED AMERICAN INFLUENCE

Back to America again, Moody's level of revival and evangelistic activity increased in volume. Moody held meetings in many large cities in the United States from 1875 to 1879. He took another tour of England from 1881 to 1884 and returned to his labors in the United States and Canada from 1884 to 1891. Back to England he went in 1891 and 1892.

The New York promoters had a plan to invite Moody and Sankey for a series of meetings there, even at the time they were in England. Those meetings began in February 1876. When an atheist wrote an objection and accused Moody of driving people insane, an editorial in *The New York Times* came to his defense. "In this city," the editorial said, "they may be said to have checked insanity" by bringing numbers of men to sobriety. In addition, the impact had not been one of excitement or sensationalism, and "the audiences have been singularly calm and still." But the lack of physical and emotional exuberance did not mean a lack of deep-seated conviction, change of heart, and determination to inculcate true belief and loving action. The writer commented that "the drunken have become sober, the vicious virtuous, the worldly and

---

in C. H. Spurgeon, *Autobiography: Volume 2, The Full Harvest,* Autobiography (Edinburgh; Banner of Truth, 1976) 393–400. Moody's remarks are found on 396–398.

[44] Charles Spurgeon, ed., *The Sword and the Trowel 1891* (London: Passmore & Alabaster), 10, 55, 19, 216, 506.

self-seeking unselfish, the ignoble noble, the impure pure," among other evidences of deep change of character and conduct.[45]

An important element of Moody's genius was his ability to motivate Christians to seek and do the ministry that lay before them. He had deep convictions about personal usefulness in whatever sphere of influence one had. "My prayer has been for years," Moody preached, "that God will let me die when the spirit of revival dies out in my heart, and I don't want to live any longer if I can't be used to some purpose." He told his listeners, "Let us do all the business we can. If we can't be a lighthouse, let us be a tallow candle." This usefulness included the determination to speak to people about their need to be saved. Some people, Moody chastened, would delight to speak to thousands "but are not willing to take their seat beside one soul, and lead that soul to the blessed Jesus." Revival that would bring cultural transformation would follow upon the faithful stewardship of personal witness.

> If people, instead of merely coming to these meetings, folding up their arms and enjoying themselves, without personal effort, would wake up to the fact that they have a work to do, what a wonderful work could be done! . . . We need ten thousand men and women that are willing to say, "Lord, here am I, use me." Ten thousand of such people would revolutionize this city. . . . The trouble is, we are afraid to speak to men about their souls. Let us ask God to give us grace to overcome this man-fearing spirit.[46]

Women should speak to their husbands about their souls and fathers should speak to their sons. Waiting to do the great thing and putting aside the one thing means that nothing will be done.

---

[45] William Moody, *D. L. Moody*, 268.

[46] Garth Rosell, ed., *Commending the Faith: The Preaching of D.L. Moody* (Peabody, MA.: Hendrickson Publishers, 1999), 131, 133–134.

Moody's ministry, having begun with the ragged and unkempt boys of the street, left its mark permanently through the founding of conferences, schools, and a variety of organizations. Moody established the Northfield School for Girls and the Mount Hermon School for Boys. The Northfield Bible conferences began in 1880, with the Keswick emphasis on seeking the Lord for emptying of any confidence in the flesh and filling of power for holiness and service. Other than setting a time, the conference involved very little planning, but it included prayer and impromptu sermons and Bible lessons from people whom Moody would appoint on the spot. David Bebbington observed, "The Northfield Conferences were organized partly for his own benefit, so that he could absorb the teaching of the eminent preachers of the day."[47] Arising from these conferences, the Student Volunteer Movement originated in 1886. Moody called on A. T. Pierson to preach. Pierson called for "the evangelization of the world in this generation."[48] Eventually over five thousand college students were sent through various mission organizations and denominational agencies as a result of the influence of the movement. In 1889, Moody established a Bible school that became Moody Bible Institute.

DOCTRINAL THEMES

Stan Gundry summarized several of the doctrinal themes that governed Moody's preaching. Moody did not have a well-developed system but manifested a basically conservative propensity. Early in his Christian life Moody had Methodist influences that gave him sympathy for some aspects of Arminianism. He greatly admired the Wesleys and believed that their zeal and skill in organization reflected some true and imitable perceptions of gospel ministry. He employed a mild dispensational scheme in the handling of

---

[47] David Bebbington, "Moody as a Transatlantic Evangelical" in *Mr. Moody and the Evangelical Tradition*, ed. Timothy George (London and New York: T & T Clark International, 2004), 83.

[48] Dorsett, *A Passion for Souls*, 353.

certain passages and sweeping ideas. This came from his contact with Darby and the Plymouth Brethren. He believed in a separate baptism of the Spirit subsequent to conversion and promoted the deeper life through Keswick speakers he brought to the Northfield Bible conferences. His ministerial involvement with R. A. Torrey gave reinforcement to this concern. He respected certain aspects of Calvinism through his contact with Spurgeon, Moorhouse, and Andrew Bonar, particularly the permanent safety of the one who has come into union with the saving work of Christ by faith.

He highlighted the principle of love above the principles of fear and duty. It seems that he did not investigate closely enough the relationship of these three elements of human affection. "I am tired of the word duty," Moody proclaimed, "tired of hearing duty, duty, duty. . . . Let us strike for a higher plane. God loved the world when it was full of sinners and those who broke his law. If he did so, can't we do it, and love our fellowmen?"[49] Early in his career as an evangelist, Moody shifted his emphasis from fear of wrath as motive to receive the gospel to divine love as the impetus for the sinner's surrender to God. His son wrote, "Early in his public work his emphasis had been upon retribution, a relic of the early Calvinistic views, representing God as a vengeful deity. This was followed by the influence of Henry Moorhouse and from that time the emphasis was wholly upon the love of God."[50] William contrasted his father's views with those of Jonathan Edwards in "Sinners in the Hands of an Angry God," and cited Moody's view that "God will not punish us. We shall punish ourselves. When we come before God, He will turn us over to ourselves. 'Go and read the book of your memory,' He will say." William went on to recall, "In later years he seldom referred to future punishment."[51]

---

[49] Gundry, *The Wit and Wisdom*, 23. This quote is from *Glad Tidings: Compromising Sermons and Prayer Meeting talks Delivered at the New York Hippodrome* (New York: E. B. Treat, 1876), 55.

[50] William Moody, *D. L. Moody*, 438.

[51] William Moody, *D. L. Moody*, 441–442

Moody preached with clarity, and with earnest appeal, but often was incomplete in his presentation of gospel truth. He did not risk enervating his gospel preaching through polemical engagement. The avoidance, even the ignorance, of metaphysics arguably does not detract from Moody; that which is disturbing is his occasional lack of theological discernment in pursuit of broadly expanded lines of fellowship. The virtual absence of a continuity and connection in presenting the logic of thought within a biblical text made Moody think he was preaching the gospel when sometimes its truncated presentation belied the results he thought were present.

In the winter of 1898–1899, a year before his death, Moody read an article about him that said his preaching no longer had the effect that it used to. He determined to take note and make an experiment. He preached the next Sunday in the Mormon Tabernacle in Salt Lake City to around seven thousand people. His subject for the message was sin, for he believed that "Mormons are just as much sinners as the rest of us." Having given an impassioned and energetic description of the destructive nature of sin, he said, "You have heard this. Do you want to break with sin? Are you tired and sick of sin?" He asked them not to act on impulse but with sober consideration. Then he challenged them, "*If* there is one in this house that wants to break with sin, I am going to ask you to rise and stand while I pray." His lament about sin and its tendency was sincere and "fair and square." He gave five minutes for them to consider before he brought them to a decision. "Do you know, almost the whole crowd rose!" And also, "Tears rolled down their cheeks."[52] He repeated the same sermon in three more places with virtually the same results. Issues of the person and work of Christ

---

[52] Dwight L. Moody, *Moody's Latest Sermons*, 120–121. This is in a sermon entitled "Revivals," in which Moody presents an impassioned defense of itinerant revivalism, claims that perhaps four out of five persons who are Christians in America were converted in revival meetings, and expresses a deep revulsion at the controversy over revivals and their supposed extravagances and sensationalism.

and the eternal and immutable nature of God would have been fitting.

According to most observers of Moody's recurring emphases in his sermons, the themes of "ruin, redemption, and regeneration" constitute an accurate summary. Mankind in general, and all men in particular, were ruined morally and spiritually in the fall of Adam. "Paul brings in the law to show man that he is lost and ruined. . . . The law stops every man's mouth. God will have a man humbled himself down on his face before Him, with not a word to say for himself."[53] Preaching on the text "there is no difference," from Romans 3, Moody testified, "If you want to find out what man is by nature, all you have to do is read the third chapter of Romans." He went on to explain, "I have to give out the law as well as the gospel" because "man is being deceived by his own heart. Man is bad by nature." He saw the biblical principle of law as requiring a singular obedience. "There are not ten different laws," Moody taught. "They are one law." The person who violates one of these laws has broken them all, for they are a unit of necessary and fully rational obedience to God. "If you have broken one of them, you have broken the law and are therefore guilty." The law shows man his guilt and his need of salvation but has no power to provide salvation. He proclaimed Paul's dictum, that the law is a "schoolmaster to bring him to Christ" (see Gal. 3:24). But it must bring him, for it cannot save him. "The law never saved a man, never will, and never can. The law condemns me, shows me my guilt, but Christ comes and saves me from the curse of the law."[54]

Moody employed his tendency toward dispensationalism in showing how humanity had failed in each dispensation of God's dealing with men. Mankind failed in the state of innocence, covenant, law, government, prophets, Christ, and now grace. "And now we are living under the dispensation of grace—a wonderful

---

[53] Smith, *The Best of D. L. Moody*, 100.

[54] Rhodes, *Dwight Lyman Moody's Life Work* 158–166. These quotes are from the sermon "No Difference."

dispensation. . . . But what is man under grace? A stupendous failure. . . . Look at the vice and crime that fester everywhere, and tell me is it not true that man is a *failure* under grace?" Moody then looked to the other side of the millennium and saw Satan loosed and still able to deceive man in his ruined condition. "What man wants is another nature; he must be born again."[55]

Moody left himself in a quandary. He saw and asserted the persistent failure of man and attributed this failure to his moral ruin. Even under the dispensation of grace and the millennial reign of Christ, man persists in refusal of God's operations of discipline, revelations of increasing truth, manifestations of judgment, and appeals for repentance and return. Examples of forgiveness do not move man, and in the context of every overture of mercy, he fails to respond. How then, without a prevenient operation of invincible grace in the human heart, will any person believe? Failure regularly plagues human appeal, even spiritual conviction, unless this ruined sinner receives the new heart. How can it be otherwise unless, by intrinsic persuasion connected to a spiritual resurrection, one runs to the crucified Savior in full trust of His finished work? Like Finney (although there is no evidence that Moody read Finney), Moody allowed for the necessity of immediate repentance and faith based on the justice of the universal command and the reality of man's natural ability to believe and respond to commands and invitations. Like Finney, he put out of sight the concept of moral inability, a deadness as well as active resistance to the prerogatives and holy character of God. "I do not believe," Moody insisted with force and clarity, "He wants us to come and preach to you the gospel, and then does not give you power to believe it; do you?" He reinforced this view with another rhetorical question: "Do you think the Lord sends His messengers out all over the earth to preach His glorious gospel, and then has constituted man so he cannot believe it? That is what many people tell us. . . . Away with

---

[55] Smith, *The Best of D. L. Moody*, 102–104.

such doctrine!"[56] He seems to have imbibed a Wesleyan concept of prevenient grace while also maintaining the power of natural ability to overcome the sinful disposition of unbelief.

Redemption by the blood of Christ follows closely on the concept of ruin. Moody viewed the redemptive work of Christ in terms of substitution—Christ was punished for sin in the stead of the sinner. Citing 1 Corinthians 15:3 ("Christ died for our sins according to the Scriptures"), Moody warned against modern attempts to give something new and said, "Bear in mind there is no new gospel. Christ died for our sins. If he did not, how are we going to get rid of them? Would you insult the Almighty by offering the fruits of this frail body to atone for sin? If Christ did not die for our sins, what is going to become of our souls?"[57]

Moody contrasted the ideas of moral influence and martyrdom to the purposeful substitutionary death of Christ. He did not die just to "convince men that he loved them" or in an act of uncompromising loyalty to His principles and doctrines. No, "He died as man's substitute" to redeem the world. At the judgment, believers have confidence that "the judgment has already passed to the believer, and I was judged in Christ. Christ took my place. He died in my stead. He suffered for my sins. He became the sinner's substitute." His substitution was necessarily penal in its nature. "If Christ was punished for me, I am not going to be punished. God is not going to demand payment twice is he?"[58] It seems, however, that in Moody's embrace of both penal substitution and universal atonement, God does require payment, first at the hands of Christ to render forgiveness possible, but then at the hands of the sinners who refuse what Christ already has paid.

---

[56] From a sermon called "Preach the Gospel," in Rhodes, *Dwight Lyman Moody's Life Work*, 318.

[57] D. L Moody, *The Way Home* (Chicago: The Bible Institute Colportage Association, 1904), 39, 40. See also "Saved by Grace Alone," in D. L Moody, *Sovereign Grace* (Chicago: Fleming H. Revell, 1891) 16-21.

[58] Rhodes, *Dwight Lyman Moody's Life Work*, 311, 316,

A sermon entitled "The Death of Christ" used Isaiah 53 as its text. "Five times that little word 'our' is used," Moody pointed out. "*Our* sorrows, *our* griefs, *our* iniquities, *our* transgressions, and the chastisement of *our* peace—there is a Substitute for you!"[59] Moody frequently cited the verses that emphasize substitution and concluded, according to Titus 2:12, that God has provided salvation for all. He came from the throne of heaven and redeemed us from the law. "He bore our sins in his own body on the tree. . . . He was wounded for our transgressions, bruised for our iniquity, and by his stripes we are healed." Christ took the penalty of the law upon Himself and tasted death for every man. Christ was the end of the law by giving up His own life. "Sinner, will you have him as your Savior? Will you let him redeem you for the curse of the law tonight? Will you pass from death unto life? You can, if you will have him."[60] In Smith's version of "There is No Difference," Moody gave an oft-used illustration of substitution from Napoleon's army of a soldier whose death was recorded as the death of another person. He drew the application, "You ask me what my hope is; it is that Christ died for my sins, in my stead, in my place, and therefore I can enter into life eternal. . . . The Emperor of heaven recognizes the doctrine of substitution. Christ died for me; that is my hope of eternal life."[61]

The third prominent theme from Moody was his concept of regeneration. Regeneration comes in response to faith, according to Moody. God's sovereign grace consists of the death of Christ in the stead of sinners. Grace also comes in the sending of gospel preachers to proclaim the gospel and urge the hearer to repent of sin and take Christ in His substitutionary atonement as His assurance for eternal life. But regeneration follows upon faith and constitutes the assurance of eternal life in the preservation of the

---

[59] Moody, *The Way Home*, 52.

[60] From a sermon called "No Difference," in Rhodes, *Dwight Lyman Moody's Life Work*, 174.

[61] Smith, *The Best of D. L. Moody*, 110.

one who has believed. Moody asked a Mr. Radstock, "Have these friends the power to believe?" Mr. Radstock answered, "They are commanded to believe. They can believe it just as well as they can believe any other fact, if they only listen to God's voice."[62]

In a dialogue in which Moody gave instructions on how to give an invitation and the value of inquiry meetings, he offered this analysis of their effect: "If you can get a man to walk across a church before all the people and go into an inquiry room, it means a great deal." Such a move in itself indicates that effective resolution already is at work, for "no human power can get a man to do that. Only the Spirit of God can do it." The journey itself virtually constitutes an act of saving belief because "nine-tenths of the men surrender their will before they get there. That is the advantage of the Methodist altar. People surrender their will before they get that far."[63]

In the Smith version of "There is No Difference," Moody closed with two illustrations about Jesus raising the dead—the son of the widow of Nain and Lazarus. He did this to illustrate the power of Jesus to forgive the greatest sinner, not to show the absolute spiritual impotence that makes the irresistible grace of effectual calling necessary. "And therefore, my friend," Moody addressed the congregation, "you need not complain that Christ cannot save you. Christ died *for the ungodly*, and if you turn to him at this moment with an honest heart, and receive Him simply as your Saviour and your God I have the authority of His Word for telling you that He will in *no wise cast you out*."[64]

Moody was aware that large numbers of professions were not genuine. "I have been forty years in Christian work," he preached in 1899, "and I have never known God to disappoint any man or woman who was in earnest about their soul's salvation. I know lots

---

[62] Moody, *Sovereign Grace: Its Source, Its Nature and Its Effects* (London: Fleming H. Revell, 1891), 123.

[63] *D. L. Moody at Home* (Chicago: Fleming H. Revell, 1886), 74.

[64] Smith, *The Best of D. L. Moody,* 111.

of people who pretend to be in earnest, but their prayers are never answered."[65]

Perhaps three extra "R's" could be added: revelation, return, and retribution. Moody emphasized revelation. As creatures and as sinners we are dependent on revelation for knowledge of God and how to be rightly related to him. In a sermon on heaven, Moody pointed out that all we can know about this subject is a matter of divine revelation. After quoting 2 Timothy 3:16, he preached, "Here then is our guidebook, our text-book—the Word of God. If I utter a syllable that is not justified by the Scriptures, don't believe me. The Bible is the only rule. Walk by it, and by it alone. . . . I say then that the Scriptures are our sole guide in seeking for any information about heaven. Take up the Word of God prayerfully and reverently, and the Holy Spirit will reveal unto us the things of God."[66]

Moody also emphasized the premillennial return of Christ as the sinner's final hope and the guarantee of his eternal safety. Though Moody emphasized heaven and divine love more than the subject of hell, invoking the motive of escaping divine wrath, he nevertheless believed that retribution was certain for those who ended life unjustified, in unbelief, and thus in a Christless state. At a memorial service for P. P. Bliss at the close of 1876, Moody noted with urgency and pathos, "I haven't said much about death. Perhaps I haven't been faithful in this regard. I'd always rather tell about life; perhaps there's not been warning enough in my preaching. But I feel that if I should hold my peace this afternoon, and not lift up my voice and warn you to make ready for death, God might lay me aside and put someone else in my place; I must speak and forewarn you."[67]

---

[65] Dwight L. Moody, *Moody's Latest Sermons* (Chicago: The Bible Colportage Association, 1900), 15.

[66] D. L. Moody, *The Way Home* (Chicago: The Bible Institute Colportage Association, 1904), 94.

[67] From "On the Death of Mr. P. P. Bliss," in Smith, *The Best of D. L. Moody*, 211.

Distilling Traits of Greatness

Lyle Dorsett listed ten traits that were the key to Moody's consistency in the Christian life and his effectiveness as an evangelist. In summary, these are: commitment, willingness to take risks, vision, a sense of the Holy Spirit, a high view of Scripture, a Christ-centered life, confidence in young people, teachability, humility, and love for souls.[68]

R. A. Torrey, in *Why God Used D. L Moody*, said, "I shall not seek to glorify Mr. Moody, but the God Who by his grace, His entirely unmerited favor, used him so mightily, and the Christ Who saved him by his atoning death and resurrection life, and the Holy Spirit Who lived in him and wrought through him and Who alone made him the mighty power that he was to this world."[69] He listed and discussed seven traits about Moody: he was a "fully surrendered man," and a man of prayer. He was a deep and practical student of the Bible and a humble man. Though zealous for business and profit early in his professional life, Moody gained entire freedom from love of money while his consuming passion was for the salvation of the lost. Finally, all of these traits were elevated by his being definitely endued with power from on high.

Of all the nineteenth-century evangelists, none has had more staying power in the affections of modern evangelical thought than D. L Moody. A friend of Spurgeon, a friend of Boyce, an opponent of ungodliness and the developing worldliness of the end of the nineteenth century, an honest, sincere, plain-spoken layman, Moody was high in unction and in compassion. He had great appeal to the masses. They seemed convinced that he was sincerely concerned about them. And he was.

---

[68] Dorsett, *A Passion for Souls*, 388–399.
[69] R. A. Torrey, *Why God Used D. L Moody,* 6.

Brief Harvest of Ideas

Moody serves as an example of the extraordinary work that God does through the self-emptying devotion of a person who desires to see the gospel embraced by every person. From the time of his conversion he sought to establish situations in which people could be brought into the grace of prayer, the privilege of Bible knowledge, and a confrontation with the urgency of faith in Christ.

His experiences in the Civil War and the Chicago fire pressed on him the reality that no mortal can assume tomorrow, or even the next moment, for repentance and faith. You should repent now; you should believe in Christ now. And then you should work for the conversion of others without hesitation.

His habits of personal study and listening well to others produced a pervasive, broad, and at times deep knowledge of Scripture and refinement of communication skill. His narrative and illustrative style of preaching connected with his congregations and engaged people of every level of education and knowledge with intrigue and earnestness. His sense of the weakness of the human attention span, his commitment to the preeminent importance of his subject, and his emotional integrity engaged every level of education and sophistication with attention fitting for the nature of his subject.

His sense of the fleeting nature of personal life led him to be a beginner and builder of evangelical ministries that would outlive him. These were not to be institutions that doted on themselves but ministered givingly to others for the perpetuation of biblical truth coherently fixated on gospel presentation.

Though fiercely devoted to central evangelical and evangelistic truth and practice, his breadth of affection, his minimizing of creed, and his desire for creating an ever-expanding circumference of fellowship and participation led to a confusing and sometimes contradictory combination of ideas.

Moody set standards to be admired and emulated. He exhibited energy combined with practicality that garnered observable spiritual results. He embodied weaknesses to be overlooked and set off a few alarms of ideas and practices to be avoided.

CHAPTER 11

BILLY SUNDAY

"As the Lord of hosts liveth, before whom I stand . . .' cried the prophet. That ought to be the preacher's cry every time he walks into the pulpit. That kind of faith makes the devil get up and dust every time! Such confidence in God as the prophet had as he stood before Him would make granite out of soapstone. And to know God as Elijah knew Him, and to have the same unbroken sense of His presence, is better preparation for a great career in the ministry than a degree from any college you can name."

—Billy Sunday[1]

A COMPLEX FIGURE

William T. Ellis said in 1914, evaluating Billy Sunday (1862–1935), "That he is God's tool is the first and last word about Billy Sunday." Putting all the issues aside, or perhaps in answer to all the detractions of culture, politics, burgeoning entertainment enterprises, liberal political and theological thought, international unrest, relativistic morality, and other contextual complexities, Ellis continued his messianic evaluation of Sunday: "He is a 'phenomenon' only as God is forever doing phenomenal things, and upsetting man's best-laid plans. He is simply a tool of God. For a special work he is the special instrument. God called, and he answered." This was written twenty-one years before Sunday's

---

[1] Billy Sunday, "Broken Down Altars," in *21 Sermons by Evangelist Billy Sunday*, Hope Faith Prayer, https://www.hopefaithprayer.com/books/billysundaysermons.pdf.

death and seven years before Sunday achieved his highest level of national influence.[2]

On the other hand, William H. Cooper Jr., in 2010, saw little if any of God in the histrionic ministry of Billy Sunday.

> Revival became unabashedly dramatic performances where the audiences laugh at, cry over, and are entertained by the histrionics of a master showman. America's great ability to trivialize the important finally occurs here in the religious realm. And sadly, it is in the story of Billy Sunday that we see in clear detail what man hath wrought; the supernatural aspects of revivalism disappear, the methodology is exalted, and the minister himself becomes corrupted by the very system he uses.[3]

Back to 1914, Elijah ("Ram's Horn") Brown wrote, in the midst of a variety of accolades, "I know that however unconventional his language may be, his preaching has in it the spirit of Christ and the power of Christ, and that it accomplishes what Christ commissioned his disciples to do." As to Sunday's biblically founded courage, Brown testified, "I know that he believes the Bible to be the word of God, and believes himself to be a messenger from God. I know that he fears neither man nor devil when he stands in the pulpit, and if it came to a test would go to the stake for his faith. A more honest or zealous man I have never known."[4]

In 1986, Doug Frank presented Sunday as the invincible personification of American evangelical fear, hubris, and triumphalism. "One would think," he reasoned, "that these

---

[2]   William T. Ellis, *"Billy" Sunday: The Man and His Message* (Philadelphia: The John C. Winston Company, 1914), 16. I will cite also from an edited version of this work published by Moody Press in 1959.

[3]   William H. Cooper, Jr. *The Great Revivalists in American Religion, 1740–1944* (Jefferson, NC: McFarland & Company, 2010), 128.

[4]   Elijah P. Brown, *The Real Billy Sunday* (Dayton: The Otterbein Press, 1914), 12.

evangelicals might have reflected on their history and might have slowly apprehended the full extent of their surrender to human arrogance in the form of the American national mythology, bringing them to repentance, mourning, and an attitude of waiting." Sunday, however, in Frank's view was perfectly fitted to forestall such a turn of humility and honest reflection. "The half-heartedness of their relinquishing worldly power," Frank surmised, "becomes evident in their enthusiastic support for an evangelist like Billy Sunday, who overtly symbolized a new lease on life for evangelical hegemony in America and tantalized them with the possible re-establishment of the power they had lost." Willing to sidestep truth for power, "they happily overlooked all doctrinal inconsistencies in their rush to identify themselves with this powerful champion who told them they were the true Americans, destined by virtue of their morality and manliness to rule over their country and their history once again."[5]

Roger Bruns caught the radical ambivalence in judgments concerning the character and impact of Sunday the person and the nature of the influence of the "sawdust trail." To many caught in the dizzying changes in late nineteenth-century America, Sunday provided "a voice harkening back to simpler times, to true moral values, fundamentalist theology, to the American way." He was the incarnation of "truth and decency and all that remained good." In the same man, others saw a "religious grafter, his Jesus spiel straight from savage, right-wing, conservative dogma, his words mind-numbing pabulum, fed to masses of middle-class followers—the words of a reactionary." If you are patriotic, if you work hard, if you stay away from booze, and if you are loyal to family, country, and bosses, "your reward waits for you in heaven." Bruns saw that the judgments could not be conflated into any kind of balanced evaluation. "At this time of social and political upheaval, the preacher stood to some as a rock of assurance, a

---

[5]   Douglas W. Frank, *Less Than Conquerors* (Grand Rapids: Eerdmans, 1986), 227.

mighty figure of morality and righteousness; to others he loomed as a wretched symbol of right-wing oppression."[6]

The Twig is Bent

William A. Sunday was born November 19, 1862, in Ames, Iowa. He gloried in identifying himself with those who struggled in life. As Wiliam T. Ellis noted, "He learned life's fundamental lessons in the school of poverty and toil."[7] "I know all about the seamy side of life," he wrote for *Ladies' Home Journal.* "If you knew the hardships and struggles and mountains of difficulties I have climbed, and the distance I have come, you would be surprised that I do as well as I do."[8] In a sermon entitled "The Three Groups," he said, "I was a rube of the rubes, a hayseed of the hayseeds, and malodors of the barnyard are on me yet. . . . I have greased my hair with goose grease and blacked my boots with stove blacking. I have wiped my old proboscis with a gunny sack towel; I have drunk coffee out of a saucer, and I have eaten with my knife." After references to several grammatical errors of his upbringing, he added, "I have crept and crawled out from the university of poverty and hard knocks, and have taken postgraduate courses."[9]

His parents were William and Mary Jane Sunday. He had two older brothers, Allen and Ed. His mother, called "Jennie," was in her mid-teens when she married. She was the daughter of Martin (Squire) Cory and had seven younger siblings. Billy's father's

---

[6]   Roger Bruns, *Preacher: Billy Sunday and Big-time American Evangelism* (Urbana and Chicago: University of Illinois Press, 2002), 16–17.

[7]   Ellis, *The Man and His Message* (1914), 24.

[8]   William A. Sunday, *The Sawdust Trail* (Iowa City: University of Iowa Press, 2005), 9. This book first appeared in serial form in *Ladies' Home Journal* in September through December 1932 and February and April 1933.

[9]   Ellis, *The Man and His Message* (1914), 24–25. See a slightly amended version of the same self-description in Billy Sunday, "The Three Groups," in *Billy Sunday Speaks*, ed. Karen Gullen (New York: Chelsea House Publishers, 1970), 148.

parents had emigrated from Germany and originally were named Sonntag. On August 14, 1862, four months before the third son's birth, his father enlisted as a private in the 23rd Iowa Infantry. The elder William died of a respiratory illness on December 22, 1862, a little more than a month after his namesake was born. He never saw the son who was to lift the "Sunday" name from obscurity to nationwide fame.[10]

Though surviving with the aid of her parents, Jennie needed family completeness and independent financial stability.[11] She remarried in 1868 and had two more children, Roy and Mary Elizabeth. The second husband, James M. Heizer, did not provide the stability Jennie and the children needed; he paid more attention to alcohol than to family responsibility. He disappeared in 1871 never to be present in the family again. In 1872, unable to handle the rearing of three sons on a farm, Jennie sent Willie—now preferring to be called Billy—and his brother Ed to an orphanage established for children of fallen Union soldiers in Glenwood, Iowa. He recalled fondly, "There we had the freedom of the fields and the woods that surrounded the home."[12]

Later they were transferred to a similar home in Davenport. Though life was sterner in Davenport, the results in character development were remarkable in a positive way. Mr. and Mrs. S. W. Pierce operated the home as superintendent and assistant superintendent. Mr. Pierce used stern methods of discipline in

---

[10] Ellis, *The Man and His Message* (1959), 14–15. See also William G. McLoughlin Jr., *Billy Sunday Was His Real Name* (Chicago: University of Chicago Press, 1955), 1–2. He gives December 23 as the date of William Sunday's death.

[11] During the days of living with Squire Cole in these early years before his mother's second marriage, and then again when he and Heizer failed to have any kind connections, Sunday had many happy memories and starkly sad events. He lived with him a third time when he left the orphanage. Many of these events are recorded in Sunday, *The Sawdust Trail*, 3–21.

[12] Sunday, *The Sawdust Trail*, 20.

keeping order; Mrs. Pierce used tender pleading, prayer, and appeals to conscience. The townspeople treated the boys with sympathy and generosity when they were allowed to go to town on Saturday. They would return to town Sunday for church. Teaching in the orphanage included Bible memory, basic evangelical doctrine, prayer, tidiness, specific responsibilities in caring for the facilities, and the normal curricula of specific grade levels. Sunday reported, "At both homes, religion had an important place in our training. All our teachers and officers were Christians. I never knew a boy from either home to be an infidel or a criminal. Of those of whom I have kept track, some became lawyers, merchants, farmers, railroad men, educators. I was the only one who ever became a big-league baseball player."[13]

Sunday greatly admired his grandfather. He was inventive, industrious, unrelenting in his work ethic, and the fastest man in the town. He taught Billy to ride a horse bareback standing up. Billy would stand on his grandfather's shoulders while going through the middle of town "while everybody looked with open-eyed wonder at the free performance."[14] Sunday also worked as a fireman and a janitor, and he helped work a farm. His speed attracted some of the community baseball teams. "Cap" Anson discovered him at a sandlot game in Marshalltown, Iowa, and signed him to a professional contract.

He played professional baseball from 1883 to 1891 for the Chicago, Pittsburgh, and Philadelphia teams.[15] He struck

---

13 Sunday, *The Sawdust Trail*, 22.

14 Sunday, *The Sawdust Trail,* 10.

15 Robert F. Martin, *Hero of the Heartland* (Indianapolis: Indiana University Press, 2002), 65–79. Martin gives insight into the way that baseball informed Billy Sunday's perception of life and of evangelism. He closed that chapter with this paragraph: "Although extraordinarily advantageous, the fusion of sports and religion in Billy Sunday's ministry was not mere opportunistic showmanship. Rather, it was, at least in part, a logical expression of his own experience. In the 1880's, baseball and the evangelical gospel of the Pacific Garden Mission had converged to engender in

out his first thirteen at-bats in Chicago.[16] His personality and showmanship made him popular, and his speed was a marvel. Though he was only mediocre as a hitter, his agility in the outfield and his sideshow potential in racing local track stars made him a valuable asset for the White Stockings (who became the Chicago Cubs). "Because of my speed and ability to judge fly balls," he recorded, "I was the only country boy who played on the 'town' nine."[17] He used certain aspects of the game as illustrations when he preached: "I am vehement," he would proclaim, "and I serve God with the same vehemence that I served the devil when I went down the line."[18] He was the first man to run the length of the baseball diamond in fourteen seconds, "from a standing start, touching all bases."[19] The lasting affection that Sunday had for the game is clear in the memory he cherished about being the recipient of a silver ball with solid gold stitches. As a special production for their winning the National League pennant, the team threw dice for possession of the ball. Sunday won. Writing in 1933, he remembered that one of his teammates offered him $100 for the ball, but Sunday refused. "I have the ball yet; and every time I look at it, I become young again, and the faces of the old team pass in panorama before my eyes, and the scenes of other day flit by like a butterfly. The great umpire of the universe has called most of the 'out!'"[20]

---

him a sense of confidence and self-worth at a time when he felt profoundly rootless and insecure. Given the meaningful role they had played in his own personal development, it was only natural for him to weave these two integrating forces in his life into the fabric of his evangelism."

[16] Ellis, *The Man and His Message* (1914), 33.

[17] Sunday, *The Sawdust Trail*, 33.

[18] Ellis, *The Man and His Message* (1914), 150.

[19] Sunday, *The Sawdust Trail*, 43.

[20] Sunday, *The Sawdust Trail*, 47.

CONVERTED

In 1886, Sunday was converted through the street preaching of Harry Monroe and the personal witness of a Mrs. Clark of the Pacific Garden Mission in Chicago.[21] Sunday heard the preaching and the singing of hymns with which he had become familiar as a child. He attended several services. He stopped going with his teammates to the bars, stopped playing cards, and began attending Jefferson Park Presbyterian Church. Following his conversion, Sunday denounced drinking, swearing, and gambling, and he changed his behavior—which was recognized by both teammates and fans.

Shortly thereafter, Sunday began speaking in churches and at YMCAs. He met Nell Thompson and, through sheer determination, he overcame the objections of her father, won the affections and approval of her mother, and married her in 1888. On several occasions, Sunday said, "She was a Presbyterian, so I am a Presbyterian. Had she been a Catholic, I would have been a Catholic—because I was hot on the trail of Nell."[22] She became the organizer and administrator of the campaigns, salvaged them from financial ruin, and gave a comprehensive program of beneficial spiritual activity to each campaign.[23]

In describing the kind of emotion often expressed in conversion in some contexts, Sunday said, "I wasn't converted that way, but I do not rush around and say, with gall and bitterness, that you are not saved because you did not get religion the way I did. If we all got religion in the same way, the devil might go to sleep with a

---

[21] Ellis, *The Man and His Message* (1914), 40. He gives the year as 1887. Sunday, *The Sawdust Trail,* 50; McLoughlin, *Billy Sunday Was His Real Name*, 6.

[22] McLoughlin, *Billy Sunday Was His Real Name*, 6. See this quote in a slightly different wording in Homer Rodeheaver, *Twenty Years with Billy Sunday* (Nashville: Cokesbury Press, 1936), 49. "My ma was a Methodist," he added, "but I am a Presbyterian."

[23] Rodeheaver, *Twenty Years with Billy Sunday,* 116.

regular Rip Van Winkle snooze and still be on the job." He looked at the simplicity of the call Jesus gave His disciples and remarked, "How long did that conversion take? How long did it take him to accept Christ after he had made up his mind? And you tell me you can't make an instant decision to please God?"[24]

TO THE WORK

In 1891, Sunday rejected a $3,500-per-year contract (one article said $5,000) to remain in professional baseball. Instead, he opted for $83 a month for a position in the YMCA. His sermons quite often have anecdotes of events and persons that he encountered while he worked in the Y. He soon left this work to become full-time assistant to J. Wilbur Chapman (1859–1918). He served as "one of his most trusted and effective campaign confidants" from 1893 to 1895. Chapman, at that time, was one of the best known evangelists in the United States. He was well educated and was a meticulous dresser, noted as being "suave and urbane." Chapman was shy personally but commanding in the pulpit. His voice was strong and his manner sophisticated. Sunday served as his advance man and learned the techniques of organizing large campaigns. He would organize the prayer meeting, arrange for choirs, secure the location, rally the churches, and even erect a tent when needed. Chapman gave time to critique and construct the sermonic preparation and theological consistency of Sunday, allowing him on occasions to preach when Chapman was unable to answer the call.[25]

Billy Sunday pursued relentlessly the calling of evangelism from 1896 to 1935. Not only was Chapman a major influence, but he had the immediate impact of the final three years of D. L. Moody's revivalist career. Sunday had the experience of personal witness and some grueling street work in his position with the

---

[24] Ellis, *The Man and His Message* (1914), 151–152.

[25] Bruns, *Preacher*, 61–64

YMCA. He obviously paid attention to the theories of Charles Finney. He adopted Finney's ideas of the relation of means in the pursuit of revival. Sunday wrote:

> Somebody asks: "What is a revival?" Revival is a purely philosophical, common-sense result of the wise use of divinely appointed means, just the same as water will put out a fire; the same as food will appease your hunger; just the same as water will slake your thirst; it is a philosophical common-sense use of divinely appointed means to accomplish that end. A revival is just as much horse sense as that.[26]

Sunday described cause and effect relationships in nature as perfectly analogous to revival and just as naturally produced. As a light bulb produces light when energized in all its parts by a dynamo, "religion can be judged on the same basis of cause and effect. If you do a thing, results always come." "Horse sense" informs us of this truth, and to live in the world or in religion by any other understanding will kill both crops and religion. "I believe," Sunday certified, "there is no doctrine more dangerous to the Church today than to convey the impression that a revival is something peculiar in itself and cannot be judged by the same rules of causes and effects as other things." God is sovereign over crops in the same way He is sovereign over revival. The results of both crops and revivals are bound up in the divinely ordained but humanly applied means—follow the instructions and reap the crop. Reflecting on the concept of God's sovereignty over revival and conversion, Sunday instructed, "The churches have been preaching some false doctrines and religion has died out."[27]

Sunday frequently interspersed his discussion of revival with a defense of his promotional methods and the litany of abuses he endured. A revival may be expected when Christians confess their

---

[26] Ellis, *The Man and His Message* (1914), 290.

[27] Ellis, *The Man and His Message* (1914), 291.

sins, including any mental hesitation concerning his methods. If they were with clear conscience before God, they would be "willing that God shall promote and use whatever means or instruments or individuals or methods he is pleased to use to promote them." God cannot "provide a revival" if the people "are sitting on the judgment of the methods and means that God is employing to promote a revival." Persons who expect the blessing of a revival must "let God have his way" and realize that they are not running it. When they consent that God may use whom He chooses and any method that He chooses, they will not "growl if I use some things that you don't like. You have no business to. How can you promote a revival? Break up your fallow ground, the ground that produces nothing but weeds, briars, tin cans and brick-bats. Fallow ground is ground that never had a glow in it."[28]

To those who criticized his occasional use of poor grammar, he responded that "literary excellence, . . . a nice adjective or noun, . . . and a little bit of grammar" is all right, but "you cannot be saved by grammar." Those who sat around and criticize over the wrong use of words have their heads "filled with buck oysters and sawdust." Truth and escape from the effects of sin were far beyond more important, and "some won't come to hear me because they are afraid to hear the truth." They want "deodorized, disinfected sermons" and could not stand to be "stuck over the edge of the pit and get a smell of the brimstone. You can't get rid of sin as long as you treat it as a cream puff instead of a rattlesnake." The drunkard who was sobered, the wayward girl who was restored, the housewife who had grocery money would not listen to the complaint, "'Oh, he's sensational.' Nothing would be more sensational than if some of you were suddenly to become decent. I would rather be a guide-post than a tombstone."[29]

In illustrating the idea that suffering in the cause of Christ is a part of our "reasonable service," Sunday went through the difficult

---

[28] Ellis, *The Man and His Message* (1914), 294–295.
[29] Ellis, *The Man and His Message* (1914), 196.

service given by biblical characters with the final affirmation that each of them "is satisfied." He concluded,

> It was a hard thing for me when God told me to leave home and go out into the world to preach the gospel and be vilified and libeled and have my life threatened and denounced, but when my time comes, when I have preached my last sermon, and I can go home to God and the Lamb, he'll say, "Bill, this was the reason." I'll know what it all meant, and I'll say "I'm satisfied, God, I'm satisfied."[30]

In closing his famous and oft-repeated sermon on "Booze," in which the trafficking in alcoholic beverage was severely and impressively denounced as the root of virtually all crime and domestic woes, Sunday ended by saying, "I've stood for more sneers and scoffs and insults and had my life threatened from one end of the land to the other by this God-forsaken gang of thugs and cutthroats because I have come out uncompromisingly against them." He continued by affirming his willingness to endure all of that in order to rescue people from such devastation. "I've taken more dirty, vile insults from this low-down bunch than from any one on earth," he proclaimed, "but there is not one that will reach lower, or reach higher up or wider, to help you out of the pits of drunkenness than I."[31]

In 1896, Sunday began to itinerate on his own, scheduling meetings on the "kerosene circuit," small towns that still were outside the developing electrical grid of America. Soon, the size of the crowds made expansion necessary. He purchased a tent, which he helped erect at each stop on the revival circuit. In 1906 in Colorado, a snowstorm destroyed Sunday's tent. After that, he required that towns build a tabernacle. Sawdust was put on the floor as an acoustical device and to minimize the dust generated

---

[30] Ellis, *The Man and His Message* (1914), 342.
[31] Ellis, *The Man and His Message* (1914), 120.

by the construction and the normal bareness of the site, usually dirt floors. The increasing size of the meetings, the necessity of sponsorship from the city churches, arrangements for choirs, up-front business matters, the development of "delegations," and other *ad hoc* matters led Sunday to have twenty-six paid staff, musicians, custodians, advance men, and Bible teachers.[32]

Two of the most noted staff were Homer Rodeheaver (1880–1955), who was much younger than Sunday and noted as an excellent vocal and choral musician, and Virginia Asher, a vocalist and also the one who directed women's ministries. Rodeheaver served with Sunday for twenty years (1910–1930) after having served with Presbyterian evangelist W. E. Biederwolf (1867–1939) from 1904 to 1910. Rodeheaver used a trombone that he called a Methodist trombone because often it would "backslide." He organized choirs that on occasion involved six thousand people. He wrote a book entitled *Song Stories of the Sawdust Trail.*[33] In it, he included text and music of eleven songs used in the campaigns, along with stories of the spiritual impact these songs had.

From 1910 to 1915, Sunday went to smaller cities where he usually stayed for a month. After a tent collapsed under the weight of a three-foot snowfall in Salida, Colorado, Sunday began using exclusively tabernacles for his meetings. The first had been constructed in Perry, Iowa, and became a model for all those built afterward. The dimensions could be increased according to the pattern and in light of the expected attendance. They were never large enough to accommodate all who desired to attend.

Between 1915 and 1917 he began to go to large cities like Detroit, New York, Philadelphia, Boston, and Buffalo. The Philadelphia campaign in 1915 and the New York campaign in 1917 were perhaps the most notable of his career. The New York revival meetings lasted over ten weeks, and a significant portion of

---

[32] Rodeheaver, *Twenty Years with Billy Sunday,* 119–139.

[33] Homer Rodeheaver, *Song Stories of the Sawdust Trail* (Milford, NJ: Melick's Agent Supply House, 1918).

the money collected was given to Wilson's war effort, specifically to the YMCA and the Red Cross working in the war zone. One million people attended, and 100,000 conversions were reported.

For each professed convert, Sunday provided a four-page circular. He encouraged every person to paste it in their Bible and read it frequently. It defined a Christian as a person "who comes to God as a lost sinner, accepts the Lord Jesus Christ as their personal Saviour, surrenders to Him as their Lord and Master, confesses Him as such before the world, and strives to please Him in everything day by day."[34] If the professed convert had done each of these in a personal way, Sunday assured the walker of the sawdust trail, "If you have done **your** part . . . God has done HIS part." He then recommended seven points of instruction for them to grow, for "now that you are a child of God **your** growth depends upon **yourself.**" These seven keys to growth, with supportive Scripture passages, were "study the Bible, pray much, win someone for Christ, shun evil companions, join some church, give to the support of the Lord's work, and do not become discouraged."[35] The major player in the Christian experience of conversion and growth is the person himself.

Sunday was a relentless advocate for the need of "personal work," the art of personal evangelism for every Christian. Lack of involvement in this discipline was a cause of decline in the churches and an indication of disobedience and lethargy on the part of Christians. In 1916, Sunday produced *How to Do Personal Work: A Guide.* It contained a biblical defense of personal work with examples of its practice in Scripture. It gave advice on how to answer objections. Also included was guidance to the personal worker in Bible study, prayer, and personal holiness. The

---

[34] R. A. Torrey, "What It Costs Not to be a Christians," in *Revival Addresses* (Chicago: Fleming H. Revell, 1903), 147.

[35] From a "brochure given to people who committed their lives to Christ at Billy Sunday meetings," Wheaton University Billy Graham Center, https://www2.wheaton.edu/bgc/archives/docs/sunbro.html.

introduction said that the little book "has been compiled in the interest of the rapidly increasing ranks of Christians throughout the country who have been aroused to a quickened sense of active service in the Christian life, and to meet the demands of a multitude of enquirers in the special service of winning souls for Christ." Sunday said that the emptiness of worldly systems produced a situation where "human nature was never before more readily disposed to hear the appeal and accept the terms of the Gospel of our Lord, Jesus Christ."[36]

Sunday's highly confrontational style and amazing fluidity of speech in name-calling created great opposition among many in the scientific community, the liquor industry, and the upper levels of the academic industry. In fact, one strong supporter of Sunday noted with admiration, "He calls things by their right names, even if to do so he has to use words that almost burn and blister." His admirer added, "It is doubtful if any living preacher can pour out such a stream of red-hot and sizzling adjectives to show the scorn and withering contempt he feels for all that bears the name of sin as Billy Sunday." A reporter in Wilkes-Barre, Pennsylvania, wrote, "He has skimmed the literature of the English race for information and illustrations, and has a slang vocabulary that is simply astounding."[37]

Less than amused with this "outstanding" vocabulary, Carl Sandburg wrote,

> You come along squirting words at us, shaking your fist
> and calling us all damn fools so fierce the froth slobbers

---

[36] Billy Sunday, *How To Do Personal Work: A Guide* (Arranged and Copyrighted by Wm. A. Sunday, 1916), 5. The book contains ninety-six pages. Sunday wrote after the introduction, "This little booklet has been compiled under my personal direction and advice. I believe that the comments and suggestions offered will afford valuable assistance to those engaged in the work of winning the unsaved to Christ, as well as to the beginner in the Christian life."

[37] Brown, *The Real Billy Sunday,* 107, 110.

over your lips, . . . always blabbing we're all going to hell straight off and you know all about it. . . . Go ahead and bust all the chairs you want to. Smash a whole wagon load of furniture at every performance. Turn sixty somersaults and stand on your nutty head. If it wasn't for the way you scare the women and kids, I'd feel sorry for you and pass the hat. I like to watch a good four-flusher work, but not when he starts people puking and calling for the doctors. . . . I'm telling you this Jesus guy wouldn't stand for the stuff you're handing out.[38]

The year before this expression of outrage on the part of Sandburg, William Ellis included a chapter in his book on Sunday entitled "Acrobatic Preaching." Contrary to the judgment of Sandburg's later evaluation, he observed, "I never yet have met a layman who has been through a Billy Sunday campaign who had a single word of criticism of the platform gymnastics of the evangelist."[39]

To the End

Sunday's attraction declined during the last years of his ministry. After 1921, major cities sent no invitations for revival meetings and he had to cut back on staff. Rodeheaver wrote, "The great tabernacle campaigns under Mr. Sunday's leadership had their peak time between the years 1910 and 1920." He believed the Philadelphia campaign of 1915 was the "greatest single meeting."[40]

He handled his money well and became highly solvent financially and was never accused of any misdealings with the money. Elijah Brown, writing in 1914, testified that "he hasn't a drop of mercenary blood in his veins," that he "tithes every dollar of his income," and that "religiously and quietly he is continually

---

[38] See Bruns, *Preacher*, 193–194 for a summary of Sandburg's literary confrontation with Sunday. The poem originally appeared in *The Masses*, Vol. 6 (September 1915), 11. It was entitled simply "To Billy Sunday."

[39] Ellis, *The Man and His Message* (1914), 139.

[40] Rodeheaver, *Twenty Years with Billy Sunday*, 141.

doing good with his money."[41] After Sunday's death, Homer Rodeheaver recorded the generosity of Sunday concerning Winona Lake, the Pacific Garden Mission in Chicago, and other places but also admitted, "In the later years there may have been a tendency to acquisitiveness."[42] Sometimes he would give the entire offering from a campaign to some local charity. He dressed well, following the manner of Chapman, and dressed his family well. He expected his associates to look neat and tastefully dressed. His home in Winona Lake, Indiana, was adequate but modest. Nevertheless, his income was many times that of the average person to whom he was preaching, and newspapers often sought to generate disdain for him on that account.

Sunday had sadness with his children. Some of the decline in the appeal of his meetings after 1921 might have been connected to the emotional distraction this presented. His daughter, Helen Haines, died of pneumonia in 1932 possibly connected with multiple sclerosis. She was conscientious, stable, and grateful. One son committed suicide in 1933 after Sunday had bailed him out of debt. The other two sons created scandal, and Sunday actually paid off informants not to make their indiscretions public.[43] Robert F. Martin noted that the Sundays spent a "substantial portion of their wealth" rescuing their sons from debt and sexual scandal. Billy wanted the "Sunday" name clean but found that his sons' conduct "made a mockery of the version of the gospel to which their father had committed his life." For almost fifteen years, his public demeanor of confidence, aggression, unflappableness, and unperturbed stability was maintained by the pure talent of performance. In private he was distressed, doubting, weepy, and haunted in conscience.[44]

---

[41] Brown, *The Real Billy Sunday,* 12.

[42] Rodeheaver, *Twenty Years with Billy Sunday*, 117.

[43] See Cooper, Jr. *The Great Revivalists*, 135–136 for the distressingly sad summary of some of these difficulties.

[44] Martin, *Hero of the Heartland*, 121–125. Martin gave a sensible and sensitive narrative of the mental and spiritual affects that these diffi-

During his last years. though surrounded by sorrow, diminished in strength, and more isolated to smaller venues, Sunday was faithful to his call to evangelism to the end. He was eclipsed by the growth in the entertainment industry, the expansion of radio preaching, and his own increasing weakness. Early in 1935, he had a mild heart attack, and his doctor advised him to stay out of the pulpit. Sunday ignored the advice. He died on November 6, a week after preaching his last sermon on Acts 16:30—"What must I do to be saved?"

Political and Social Issues

Within the range of a large number of social issues Sunday addressed, he was most noted for his opposition to "booze." Isolating alcohol intake as perhaps the most calamitous, destructive practice any person could begin, he said that "the saloon is the sum of all villainies. It is worse than war or pestilence. It is the crime of crimes. It is the parent of crimes and the mother of sins. It is the appalling source of misery and crime in the land. And to license such an incarnate fiend of hell is the dirtiest, low-down, damnable business on top of this old earth. There is nothing to be compared to it."[45]

Because of the moral, financial, and domestic havoc wrought by alcohol, Sunday proclaimed himself as "the sworn, eternal and uncompromising enemy of the Liquor Traffic. I have been, and will go on, fighting that damnable, dirty, rotten business with all the power at my command." Sunday played a significant role in arousing public interest in prohibition and in the passage of the Eighteenth Amendment in 1919. When the tide turned against

---

culties had on the Sundays. He made this thoughtful observation, without dismissing the personal responsibility of the sons: "Just as their father had been scarred by a childhood characterized by death, poverty, and failure, they were impaired by childhoods distinguished by affluence, success, and popular acclaim" (125).

[45] Ellis, *The Man and His Message* (1914), 89.

the amendment, Sunday still spoke vociferously in its favor, and called for its reintroduction after it was repealed in 1933.

In his sermon on booze, Sunday likened Jesus casting the devils into the swine to his own opposition to the liquor traffic. He pictured the hog-keepers going back to report the events to the "peanut-brained, weasel-eyed, hog-jowled, beetle-browed, bull-necked lobsters that owned the hogs." They said, according to Sunday's dramatic rendition, that a "long-haired fanatic from Nazareth, named Jesus, has driven the devils out of some men and the devils have gone into the hogs, and the hogs into the sea, and the sea into the hogs, and the whole bunch is dead."[46]

Even if not preaching on alcohol directly, the subject appeared in a high percentage of his sermons. In a sermon on "The Three Groups," Sunday promised, "If I had a hundred tongues, and every tongue speaking a different language, in a different key at the same time, I could not do justice to the splendid chaos that the world-loving, dancing, card-playing, whiskey-guzzling, gin sizzling, wine sizzling novel reading crowd in the church brings to the cause of Christ."[47]

Almost equally as devastating on the morals and usefulness of humanity was "the dance." Both boys and girls, as well as grown men and women, fell into immorality—and some into lives of promiscuity—through "the dance." A Catholic priest told Billy Sunday from his experience in the confessional, "We can trace the laxity of nineteen out of every twenty who have lost their purity to the ballroom." Sunday cited ministers from several denominations in their serious concern for the moral turpitude endemic to the waltz and the ballroom dance and surmised, "The dance is the moral graveyard of more girls than anything else in the world. The dance is the dry rot of society. I say it is immoral." Sunday called on people of all faiths, and of no faith, to join him in his immovable opposition to the dance. "This crusade against the

---

[46] Ellis, *The Man and His Message* (1914), 86.
[47] Gullen, *Billy Sunday Speaks,* 146.

dance is for everybody—not merely for the preacher or the old man or woman who couldn't dance if they wanted to, but for everybody interested in morals, whether in the church, or out of the church." In preaching a sermon highlighting the destructive influence of this specific passion of modern society, Sunday claimed, "I am preaching a sermon that Jew or Gentile, Catholic or Protestant, infidel or Christian, if he wants better morals, can indorse."[48]

Sunday was an advocate of woman's suffrage, and though muffled on most racial issues, he opposed Jim Crow laws. He fervently supported the war effort against Germany, considering it a clear case of wrong against right and hell versus heaven.

He had friends and supporters in big business and was an outspoken supporter of the capitalist system, but he opposed monopolies and the tendency to oppress the poor through price control. But a group that he called the "Reds" received some of the most violent invective in the vocabulary of Sunday. He was "bitter, vindictive, and increasingly hysterical" against them, for they not only were out to destroy him, they were aggressive in their desire to destroy America. These were anarchists, socialists, anti-capitalists, various kinds of academics, poets, and philosophers who joined in the judgment of George Bellows that Billy Sunday was "the worst thing that ever happened to America." Sunday left no doubt as to his pugilistic extremism toward them when, at the Cincinnati campaign, he gave this assurance: "They tell me I am a marked man by these God-forsaken anarchists and cutthroats. All right, let me be a marked man," he aggressively consented, "and if there are any of them here tonight they had just as well begin right now." Then the full power of his confrontational talent warned, "I'll shoot the first one of them that starts anything as full of holes that he'd pass for a sieve anywhere."[49]

---

[48] Ellis, *The Man and His Message* (1914), 442–451.

[49] Bruns, *Preacher*, 201. This chapter, "Red Emma Et Al.," narrates Sunday's engagement with this large and varied group of intellectuals and

THEOLOGICAL IDEAS

Sunday sought to educate himself in theology and infidelity. "I have read a great deal," he claimed, "not everything, mind you, for a man would go crazy if he tried to read everything—but I have read a great deal that has been written against the atonement from the infidel standpoint."[50] He mentioned Voltaire, Huxley, Spencer, Diderot, Bradlaugh, Paine, and his contemporary Bob Ingersoll. "I have never found an argument that would stand the test of common sense and common reasoning." Before he read Ingersoll, Sunday had four years of instruction in the Bible. While he was reluctant to do anything to insult the intelligence of Ingersoll, his personal study revealed that Ingersoll's objections did not arise from a profound knowledge of the Bible. "I have taken his lectures and placed them by the side of the Bible, and said, 'You didn't say it from your knowledge of the Bible.'" This tendency toward caricature and inaccuracy led Sunday to conclude that Ingersoll was not honest, particularly about redemption. How could he write and speak with such apparent intelligence and miss this vital Christian doctrine? "I have never considered him honest," Sunday admitted, "for he could not have been so wise in other things and such a fool about the plan of redemption." Had Sunday read Ingersoll before he read the Bible, he thought that perhaps "I would be preaching infidelity instead of Christianity. Thank the Lord I saw the Bible first."[51]

Sunday kept to simple theological formulas, mainly within the tradition of fundamental conservatism. One of his most quoted evaluations of the usefulness, or uselessness, of theology is this one: "I don't know any more about theology than a jack-rabbit

---

political radicals to whom he gave the name "Reds."

[50] Ellis, *The Man and His Message* (1914), 426–427. Also see Sunday, *Billy Sunday Speaks*, 20, where he mentions the names of several who either had low views of Scripture or were antagonistic to it.

[51] Ellis, *The Man and His Message* (1914), 430.

does about ping-pong, but I'm on the way to glory."[52] Sunday's defenders argued that he saw the purpose of all theology as the assurance of eternal life in heaven. Far superior was it to have that than to be skilled in the fine points of polemical theology. Botany may change, but flowers don't; astronomy may change, but stars remain in the sky. "Theology changes," he said, affirming that if it makes Christian truths clearer, we should not object, "but Christianity abides." Nobody is kept out of heaven because he does not understand theology. "It isn't theology that saves, but Christ; it is not the sawdust trail that saves, but Christ is the motive that makes you hit the trail." He reduced his theology to these immutable propositions: "With Christ you are saved, without him you are lost."[53]

He never entertained doubts about the inspiration of Scripture and the necessity of affirming all that it said. "The Bible is the Word of God. Nothing has ever been more clearly established in the world today, and God blesses every people and nation that reverence it." Its contents and claims render it impossible to have been written by evil men. They would condemn themselves in overwhelmingly precise language and predict for themselves an unbearable end with "the heaviest penalties against sin." If men wrote it apart from divine inspiration, they lied constantly, for they claimed to be inspired by God in their writing and speaking. If

---

[52] Frank, *Less Than Conquerors*, 181. He was citing McLoughlin, *Billy Sunday Was His Real Name*, 123, which gives no reference. Rodeheaver quoted it as "I know as much about theology as a jack rabbit does about ping-pong" (Rodeheaver, *Twenty Years with Billy Sunday*, 67). Cooper, with no source citation said, "I know no more about theology than a jackrabbit does about ping-pong or an elephant does about crocheting" (Cooper, *The Great Revivalists*, 140).

[53] Cooper, *The Great Revivalists*, 140; McLoughlin, *Billy Sunday Was His Real Name*, 123. See Ellis, *The Man and His Message*, 140. He added, "Are you saved? Are you lost? Going to heaven? Going to hell? I have tried to build every sermon right around those questions; . . . I want to say to you in closing, that it is the inspiration of my life, the secret of my earnestness."

they were *good* men—and good men tell the unvarnished truth—
then their testimony about the origin of the Bible must be true.
Given these options, "the only being left, to whom you or I or any
sensible person could ascribe the origin of the Bible, is God." The
Bible was written to be read and believed. Its content demands
that we believe that Jesus is the Son of God, and it all points to the
great "Star which was to rise as an atonement for sin." Those who
scoff it or ignore it, who minimize or trivialize its message, and
who refuse to give it the serious attention that its contents deserve,
will go to hell. In light of the Bible's inspiration and clear message,
Sunday snapped, "Don't blame God if you wind up in hell, after
God warned you, because you didn't take time to read it or think
about it." But Billy Sunday did take time to read it and think
about it and reached this conclusion: "I believe the Bible is the
word of God from cover to cover." The Bible taught him how to
live and how to die and for that reason, he affirmed, "I am here,"
that is, preaching in an evangelistic revival campaign, "sober and a
Christian, instead of a booze-hoisting infidel."[54]

Sunday contended that the one "who magnifies the word of
God in his preaching" is the one "whom God will honor." We see it
in the roll call of effective witness for Christ. "Why do such names
stand out on the pages of history as Wesley, Whitefield, Finney and
Martin Luther? Because of their fearless denunciation of all sin,
and because they preach Jesus Christ without fear or favor."[55]

He had a very straightforward acceptance of substitutionary
atonement that was present in most sermons. If some suggested
that a blood atonement was mere garbage unworthy of the human
intellect, Sunday responded, "What have you to offer that is
better?" Until a more relevant and pertinent argument on the
question of human sin and the possibility of forgiveness could be
offered, Sunday exclaimed, "I'll nail my hopes to the cross."[56] In

---

[54] Sunday, *Billy Sunday Speaks,* 17–24.

[55] Ellis, *The Man and His Message* (1914), 147.

[56] Ellis, *The Man and His Message* (1914), 426–427.

"Atonement by the Blood of Jesus," Sunday affirmed, "Jesus gave his life on the cross for any who will believe. We're not redeemed by silver or gold. Jesus paid for it with his blood [1 Peter 1:18–19]. When some one tells you that your religion is a bloody religion and the Bible is a bloody book, tell them yes, Christianity is a bloody religion; the gospel is a bloody gospel; the Bible is a bloody book; the plan of redemption is bloody." Christianity without the blood renders the Bible a book not "worth the paper it is written on. It would be worth no more than your body with the blood taken out. Take the blood of Jesus Christ out and it would be a meaningless jargon and jumble of words." The death of Christ is not just a charade of personal determination or dedication but a necessary transaction of payment, a penalty due for sin. "Without it not a sinner will ever be saved. Jesus has paid for your sins with his blood. The doctrine of universal salvation is a lie." Sunday asserted his consistent desire for the salvation of all people, but he knew that resistance to coming by the cross renders salvation impossible. "I wish every one would be saved, but they won't. You will never be saved if you reject the blood."[57]

As shown above, Sunday adopted Finney's insistence on the decisionistic character of immediate conversion. "My method is and always will be to obtain immediate decision and open confession of Christ."[58] He was more theological than fellow evangelist Sam Jones but still focused on the vital turning point of human decision. Each rejection of a gospel invitation would put a person closer to committing the unpardonable sin, which was the continued refusal to obey the call to accept Christ until that call has no attraction at all. "Not any one sin," he deduced, "is the unpardonable sin, but it may be the constant repetition, over and over again until God will say: 'Take it and go to hell.'"[59]

---

[57] Ellis, *The Man and His Message* (1914), 428–429.

[58] Sunday, *The Sawdust Trail*, 83.

[59] Ellis, *The Man and His Message* (1914), 376.

He combined the doctrine of the unpardonable sin with the urgency of immediate response. After a pugilistic verbal assault on those who questioned the lasting effectiveness of revival campaigns, Sunday warned, "If you are thirty and have not been converted, the chances are that if you are not converted at this revival you never will be converted." Since the majority of truly converted people were converted at revivals, "just think of what hell would be like" if not for revivals. "Then think of any low-down, God forsaken, dirty gang knocking a revival." After further assurance that God waits to forgive sins of all sorts for those who seek pardon, he warned again, "If you sneer and say it is not true, your sin may become unpardonable. If you don't settle it here, you never will settle it anywhere else." God wants to forgive, "but you have got to comply with his requirements." Though He does not will that any perish, "he has a right to tell me and you what to do to be saved."[60]

Sunday's confrontational style was designed for an immediate choosing of sides, not necessarily on the basis of remorse for sin, but to avoid being labeled a coward. "Now own up," he confronted his audience. "The truth is that you have a yellow streak. Own up, business men, and business women, and all of you others. Isn't it so? Haven't you got a little saffron?" After pointing to the example of Elijah being full of fear and wanting to die, he noted that God had other plans for Elijah—a chariot of fire. "God despises a coward—a mutt," he chided. "You cannot be converted by thinking so and sitting still."[61] He wanted men to have a special moment when fear had been overcome, hesitance had been ignored, neutrality had been exposed as obscene, and inaction had given way to obedience, "when they did just what God told them to do." He explained simply, "That is why I like to have people come down to the front and publicly acknowledge God. I like to

---

[60] Sunday, *Billy Sunday Speaks*, 86–88. From the sermon "The Unpardonable Sin."

[61] Ellis, *The Man and His Message* (1914).

have a man have a definite experience in religion—something to remember."[62]

Believing, like Finney, that the doctrine of regeneration was necessary to effect true faith caused delays in decision, Sunday urged, "Now, leave God out of the proposition for a minute. Never mind about the new birth—that's his business. Jesus Christ became a man, bone of our bone, flesh of our flesh. He died on the cross for us, so that we might escape the penalty pronounced on us. Now, never mind about anything but our part in salvation. Here it is: 'Believe on the Lord Jesus Christ, and thou shalt be saved.'"[63]

It may be argued credibly that immediate response is the only fitting way to regard God's absolute prerogative in demanding our repentance, faith, obedience, and pursuit of holiness. The simplistic contortion of Sunday, however, omitted poignant elements of human rebellion and spiritual deadness. "There is no need of struggling for hours—or for days—do it now," he retorted. One can hear Finney's take on "make yourself a new heart." Sunday continued, "Who are you struggling with? Not God. God's mind was made up long before the foundations of the earth were laid." He was not referring to unconditional election but to the immutable establishing of a plan. "The plan of salvation was made long before there was any sin in the world. That plan consists of this, in part: 'Let the wicked man forsake his way.'" He queried rightly, concerning how soon wickedness should be forsaken. Does the command imply that one may continue to engage in wickedness for a month, or a week, or a day? No, forsake it now! "The instant you yield, God's plan of salvation is thrown into gear. You will be saved before you know it, like a child being born."[64]

---

[62] Sunday, *Billy Sunday Speaks*, 104–105. The sermon is "A Plain Talk to Men."

[63] Ellis, *The Man and His Message* (1914), 147.

[64] Ellis, *The Man and His Message* (1914), 152–153.

The plan is God's business; He established it, Jesus executed it, and the Holy Spirit witnesses to it. Our action is necessary to set the plan in motion. It is not precisely the action of forsaking and receiving that saves us, Sunday conceded. Salvation is in Jesus alone. Sunday set forth a simple but necessary explanation of orthodox Christology as the true foundation of salvation. In His divinity, Jesus "understands God's side of it." In His humanity, He "understands our side of it." For that reason, no other person is "qualified to be the mediator." He explained it this way: "A lawyer is a mediator between the jury and the defendant. A retail merchant is a mediator between the wholesale dealer and the consumer." The mediator relates one party to the other through a special position and particular qualifications. Because of the uniqueness of His person, therefore, "Jesus Christ is the Mediator between God and man. Believe on the Lord. He's ruling today. Believe on the Lord Jesus. He died to save us. Believe on the Lord Jesus Christ. He's the Mediator."[65]

As Sunday saw it, though Jesus is uniquely qualified as Mediator, and therefore He alone can save, still the work He has done is of no avail unless we identify publicly with His mediatorial work. "Going to church doesn't make you a Christian any more than going to a garage makes you an automobile," Sunday quipped. Secrecy, however, will never do, so "public definite enlistment for Christ makes you a Christian."[66]

Sunday affirmed the doctrine of the Trinity, showing that the Bible gives extensive discussion of all three persons. God the Father is a person; God the Son is a person; God the Holy Spirit is a person. Each is divine and yet there is only one God. The Father has made the plan of salvation and sent His Son. The Son has died in our place so that sinners can be forgiven. The Spirit, though present in the two former dispensations (the Mosaic and the historical appearance of Christ), now is here in power and

---

[65] Ellis, *The Man and His Message* (1914), 155–156.

[66] Ellis, *The Man and His Message* (1914), 155.

no Christian work can be done without His power. "The Holy Spirit is ours. He is the promise of Jesus from the Father as a gift to the prayers of the Son." The church has more money, more finery, more intellectual sophistication than it has power. "There is no substitute for the Holy Spirit and you cannot have power without the Holy Spirit. The Holy Spirit is ours by the promise of Christ."[67]

Sunday put some theological points through prescribed contortions to wield them into sentimentality or weapons of shame aimed at generating decision. Public decision put one on a path of true manhood, or womanhood. In describing the Father's intention in the cross, Sunday set a dramatic scene. "Right where the two roads through life diverge God has put Calvary. There he put up a cross, the stumbling block over which the love of God said, 'I'll touch the heart of man with the thought of father and son.' He thought that would win the world to him, but for nineteen hundred years men have climbed the Mount of Calvary and trampled into the earth the tenderest teachings of God."[68]

In his sermon on manhood, based on "Shew Thyself a Man" (1 Kings 2:2 KJV), Sunday sought to describe the features of true manhood, referring to biblical men both in their strength and in their sinfully weak failures. For example, David did not desire a soft and luxurious life for Solomon, to be content with "a summer house in the valley"; he wanted his son to pursue the "very best estate in the country where the giants were." He sought to train his son with such rigorous instruction that he would not "be an old woman or a sissy sort of a fellow, but a man with knotted muscles on his arms, a big heart in his body and plenty of matter in his head." David wanted Solomon to "aim high, as a king's son should, knowing that if his aim was high his endeavor would not

---

[67] Ellis, *The Man and His Message* (1914), 309–310.
[68] Ellis, *The Man and His Message* (1914), 154.

be wasted." He wanted him to "look the sun in the face," and to that end, said, "Solomon, be a man!"[69]

Samson was not destroyed by the Philistines, but by himself. Every young man and boy must make a decision to avoid drink, bad company, bad habits—and do it now. A thread can be broken, but a rope will hang you. And while one is deciding on actions that will establish good character and a solid life here, he also should decide for life in eternity. "If you are not willing to run the risk of losing your soul take the only step that can make it safe by taking Christ into your heart and life at once. Join the church of your choice and commit yourself to a religious life."[70]

Both true manhood and eternal life are to be found in following Jesus. A man must learn "how to behold as in a glass His glory and so be changed into His likeness from glory to glory even as by the spirit of the Lord." Sunday urged his thousands of listeners to study Jesus, and soon they would find "that everything that is not like Him is unmanly and mean." He is the perfect man. "Spend three months in studying His life on its man ward side, and you will have a more exalted knowledge of what it means to be a man than you ever before possessed." This knowledge "will quicken and inspire you to live for God and man as you never lived before." Men should imitate the unwavering purpose of Christ, though for Him it meant Gethsemane and Calvary. Also, make time to study His "prudence and courage . . . His self control, faithfulness, charity, unselfishness, benevolence and sympathy." These things, as seen in Jesus, constitute true manhood. "Find anything in any man anywhere that everybody considers noble and manly, and then look for the same thing in Jesus, and see how it shines out in Him as the day above the twilight." So resolute and clearly focused on righteousness and the will of God was Jesus that "He never shows the white feather, and never in his whole life does He

---

[69] Billy Sunday, "Shew Thyself a Man," SermonIndex.net, https://www.sermonindex.net/modules/articles/index.php?view=article&aid=429.

[70] Sunday, "Shew Thyself a Man."

speak one single unmanly word, think an unmanly thought or do an unmanly deed." This man was the "Son of God and the most glorious promise for us ever given that when He shall appear we shall be like Him. 'Be thou strong, therefore, and show thyself a man.'"[71]

BRIEF SUMMATION OF SUNDAY AND REVIVAL

Billy Sunday fought for orthodoxy in an age of aggressive liberal thinkers and theologians. He was plain and clear on his belief in the Bible as the Word of God. He held to the general outline of historical evangelical Christianity. While he tended to minimize the importance of theology through careless analogies, emphasizing human courage and aggression more than mental comprehension, he taught that if one denied fundamental doctrines he was not a Christian.

Sunday identified the courage to take a public stand with the saving act of faith. Certainly, he knew that some who made public stances turned away and revealed their hypocrisy. He knew that he was saved and kept by God's power, but he had very little commitment to, and probably a trivialized understanding of, the depth of human depravity and the consequent dependence of effectual grace at every point of the Christian's experience of salvation from the new birth to glorification. Sinfulness, in his view, consists of an accumulation of choices made by humans contrary to God's revealed standard of morality. Jesus died that those sinful choices may be forgiven. As we made the choice to sin, so may we make the choice to be forgiven by placing faith in the atonement of Christ. Sunday was convinced that the doctrine of an efficacious call was both too complicated and wrong. The teaching that humans are born with an original moral corruption that can only be overcome by an invincible operation of divine

---

[71] Sunday, "Shew Thyself a Man."

mercy and power came from overthinking theologians whose judgment had been distorted by overmuch study.

He took seriously the task of the preacher to be clear about the perversity of sin, its corruption of society, its ruin of individual integrity and usefulness, and its eternal consequences. He confronted his listeners with the distinction between serving Christ and the gospel and pursuing one's personal pleasure and societal elevation. A break with sin must be immediate—no hesitation, no lamentation for its loss—and a failure to do so would result in eternity in the fire and brimstone of hell. Sunday was transparently earnest about matters of sin and forgiveness, heaven and hell. "We are all on a journey to eternity. What will be the end?"[72] This concern had the force of spiritual gravity behind it in Sunday's ministry.

God's grace undergirded individual salvation, spiritual growth, and corporate revival. His grace had full manifestation in an eternal plan, a historical provision, and present available help—Father, Son, and Spirit. The consummation of the saving experience, however, was up to man. All the grace of conversion and revival has been laid before us, and our personal determination produces its effectuality. That God would require immediate repentance and faith, while at the same time teasing us with the doctrine of inability, would make God a mocker and a cruel, merciless tyrant. The final word of salvation and of revival is in the mouth of mere mortals, not the everlasting God.

Endemic to Sunday's sermonic condemnation of sin was the amazing art of insult—"a rare gift of satire and scorn and invective and ridicule has been given to Sunday."[73] He was no respecter of persons in his archery of epithet; arrows were shot in massive numbers toward all levels of both public perversity and social dignity. The character of the average young girl was "foul and rotten and damnable." To the reverent Presbyterians, Sunday

---

[72] Ellis, *The Man and His Message* (1914), 396.
[73] Ellis, *The Man and His Message* (1914), 267.

scolded, "I don't expect any of those ossified, petrified, dyed-in-the-wool, stamped on the cork Presbyterians or Episcopalians to shout, 'Amen,' but it would do you good and loosen you up."[74] Evidence of the oppressive linguistic assault on boozers, pimps, dance-masters, abusive husbands, and theater magnates has been given. It was truly amazing.

One could argue, moreover, that hard verbal warnings are not without some biblical warrant from Jesus and Paul. Opening a person to the destructive potency and eternal danger of their present character may be just what some people need. Jonathan Edwards was full of serious and confrontive warnings, such as, "What account will you be able to give, when it shall be inquired of you, why you led such a sinful, wicked life? . . . Every time you indulge any lust, whether secretly or openly, you must give an account of it: it will never be forgotten, it stands written in that book which will be opened on that day."[75] Consciousness of sin, warnings of its damnable nature, and clarity on the biblical threats against it are fundamental to conviction, confession, and conversion.

Sunday celebrated virtue and lamented that his personal convictions and preaching could not mold the character of his male children. "To teach a child to love truth and hate a lie, to love purity and hate vice, is greater than inventing a flying machine that will take you to the moon before breakfast."[76] Women should set aside their pug-nosed bulldogs, their poodle dogs, the Spitz, and their card playing and give their affection and encouragement to a child. Sunday conceived of great moral power in a mother's love. In words of amazing relevance for our day, Sunday proposed, "You know a mother has to love her baby before it is born, . . . [and]

---

[74] Ellis, *The Man and His Message* (1914), 224, 269.

[75] Jonathan Edwards, "The Final Judgment," in Edwards, *Works* (Banner of Truth), 2:198–199.

[76] Ellis, *The Man and His Message* (1914), 239.

every child is put in a mother's arms as a trust from God, and she has to answer to God for the way she deals with that child."[77]

So will all persons have to answer to God for the way they have treated His law, His gifts, and His image-bearers. When revival comes, many of the emphases of Billy Sunday will be a part of the means that prompt it. Many of his idiosyncrasies and theological puerilities will necessarily be laid aside or even overcome in the pursuit of a God-honoring, God-dependent resurgence of purity in worship and life.

---

[77] Ellis, *The Man and His Message* (1914), 242–243.

CHAPTER 12

The Ends and Means of Revival

"The authenticity of any alleged revival is to be judged by the same tests by which the genuineness of all Christianity is to be tested. The normal mark of true grace consists in spiritual enlightenment producing love to God, reverence and obedience to Scripture, concern to serve Christ, personal holiness, compassion for others and so one. If revivals consist of more of what Christians already possess, then these same characteristics of character and conduct will be eminent in every true revival."

—Iain Murray[1]

Distilling principles from historical observation about revival and personal hunger for its reality, it seems self-evident that the ends and means of revival must closely align. Those things that Scripture teaches as evidences of powerful operations of the Spirit of God are the very things that should constitute a ministry intent on seeing joyful spirituality in the people of God and an extensive flood of repentance and faith in the world. If we desire revival, we must preach and practice the things that, by God's Word, we want to see. The ends of revival determine the means that are used.

In *The Distinguishing Marks of a Work of the Spirit of God*, Jonathan Edwards mentioned five substantial results of a true work of the Holy Spirit, condensed from 1 John 4. One, the Spirit in His operations will raise the esteem that people have for Christ in the flesh. This includes His incarnation; His life of

---

[1] Iain Murray, *Pentecost Today?* (Cape Coral: Founders Press, 1998), 31

human obedience; His death, resurrection, and ascension; and His bodily return. Two, the Spirit operates against the interests of Satan's kingdom and all that he uses to promote it. Three, the Spirit gives a greater regard for the Holy Scriptures, for the true apostolic witness to Christ. Both its absolute truthfulness and its content become precious to God's people. Four, the Spirit operates as a Spirit of truth and opposes error. Five, the Spirit operates as a Spirit of love to God and to man. This is a love that "arises from an apprehension of the wonderful riches of free grace and the sovereignty of God's love to us in Christ."[2] Edwards also discussed some things that should be avoided, such as spiritual pride, an expectation of special revelation, extraordinary gifts of the Spirit, and a spirit of censoriousness.

Taking these observations of Edwards as a starting place, those who desire revival should give clear, biblically derived expectations of how a Spirit-wrought, Christ-centered, biblically governed, and God-glorifying movement of truth would affect the churches and the world around them.

Revival will magnify the necessity and the perfection of the work of Christ. The Father and the Spirit concentrate their redemptive operations on the Son of God in the flesh, Jesus the Christ. As the Father spoke, "This is My beloved Son, in whom I am well pleased," the Spirit descended on Him in the form of a dove (Matt. 3:16–17). To see increased focus on Christ, we must intensify such focus in our lives. We want clearer and deeper convictions concerning the person and work of Christ and desire to see every aspect of His redemptive labors and His universal lordship embraced. Then we must manifest that devotion in our lives. Those who are in positions of teaching should give special attention to instruction about the Lord and encourage Christ-centered living.

We desire a revival in which the power of God and the greatness of Christ is demonstrated in the conversion of sinners. Edwards

---

[2] Edwards, *The Works of Jonathan Edwards, Volume 4*, 257.

saw large numbers of conversions; George Whitefield left a path of sinners slain to themselves but alive to God, snatched from hell and embraced for eternal life. If this is a result of revival, then we must work for the conversion of sinners. Christians should learn with an authentic purpose to build opportunities for gospel encounters with their neighbors, their families, and friends in the public square. Preaching must include the obligation of sinners to know God in truth, worship Him in Spirit, obey His laws with joy and love, and, therefore, repent of their sin in not doing any of these. They must see that the entire biblical message and the focal point of the incarnation in glorifying God is bound up in the gospel. It must be preached in the pulpits for the conversion of sinners. No matter how deep and instructive were their sermons, Jonathan Edwards, George Whitefield, Asahel Nettleton, and Charles Spurgeon, without fail, gave spiritual, emotional, and physical energy to instructing sinners in the gospel, their obligations to it, their desperate condition eternally without it, and the willingness of Jesus to receive them on the terms clearly established in Scripture.

> Lo! th' incarnate God, ascended,
> pleads the merit of His blood;
> venture on Him, venture wholly;
> let no other trust intrude.[3]

If we want greater love for Scripture, then particular attention must be given to the Bible's claims about itself as the "word of the Lord,"[4] its status of being breathed out by God, and its communication of the things that cannot be discovered by human means that God has prepared for those who love Him. The people of God should cherish its truths, read it frequently with intent to soak in its truth, and work to

---

[3] Joseph Hart, William Letton Viner, "Come, Ye Sinners, Poor and Wretched," 1759.

[4] See Jeremiah 1:2; 2:1; 33:19; 34:8; Ezekiel 32:1; 34:1, among other texts.

find ways to apply and teach its beauties to others. Ministers of the gospel should appropriate the pulpits God has given them to preach with obvious submission to the authority of Scripture and to give energetic presentations of the reasons for and advantages of a full commitment to biblical inspiration. As did Timothy Dwight and others, engaging in gracious but convinced polemical presentation of the revelation, inspiration, and authority of Scripture serves the cause of Christ and is foundational to revival.

When one highlights the full authority of Scripture, he implies a conformity of life and mind to all that is taught there. In revival, we hope for profit from the inspired Word to correct our lives and our thought and to instruct us in doctrine and holiness. Though fullness of assent to doctrinal knowledge does not ascertain transformation of affections, fullness of repentance, and richness of faith, these spiritual realities cannot thrive in the absence of doctrine. Faith feeds on truth. Revival necessarily assumes the alteration of viewpoint and enlargement of love through growing knowledge of the beauties, coherence, wisdom, and instruction in righteousness abiding within the meat of biblical truth—fullness of doctrine. If revival establishes increasing conformity to God's revealed Word, then teachers and preachers pursue it by rigorous instruction.

Revival will bring a more conscience-driven energy for cross-centered living, believing that those who benefit from the cross-work of Jesus must take their crosses and follow Him. If this is a desire, then we must consciously inquire of Scripture and conscience what this means—how does cross-bearing manifest itself in today's culture? The cross means that God has bound Himself in covenant determination and historical accomplishment to save a people from deserved wrath. Bearing the cross means cultivating a felt awareness of our intrinsic moral foulness in conjunction with the reality that we are not our own but have been bought with a price. Again, ministers of the gospel should pray and study and teach conscientiously on this, helping their people grasp the importance of this fundamental aspect of following Jesus.

Revival will bring to bear the full range of biblical evidences of conversion and the presence of the Spirit in the lives of believers. We would like to see and experience the fruit of the Spirit and the reign of Christ's peace in our lives. The Spirit of truth does this. To open the door for this reality, believers must study, memorize, and incorporate such passages as Romans 12:1–3; Galatians 5:17–26; Ephesians 5:1–5 and 6:10–18; Philippians 2:1–5, 3:8–16, and 4:4–9; Colossians 3:12–17; 1 Peter 2:1–3; and 2 Peter 1:4–9. Others obviously apply, but these revealed instructions as to the implications of Jesus's life and death, the presence and work of the Holy Spirit, and the call to live in imitation of God must be present in our minds with an intention of practicing them in conscience and in interpersonal relationships. Pastors must preach with the intent of seeing such fruit in their relation with the sheep and the world, accompanied by practical admonition concerning specific applications of that spiritual fruit. As Paul said of himself, we must so live and learn as to "press toward the goal for the prize of the upward call of God in Christ Jesus" (Phil. 3:14). We do it in the confidence that if we are in a state of being "otherwise minded" (Phil. 3:15 KJV), God will show through His truth the way forward and transform our minds for conformity to the way of Christ and truth.

A result of revival will be a deeper willingness to suffer for righteousness' sake. Godless culture will consistently bring challenges to the biblical norms for truth, holiness, righteousness, specific moral issues, and ways of conduct in society. Revival will give both the way and the determination for such engagement in the world. Christians must gird up the loins of their minds, love one another fervently, detect and avoid the deceit of the world, and practice the very righteousness for which they might well suffer.

Revival will bring a love for prayer and a confidence in its efficacy according to Scripture. The privilege of coming to the Father, saying "Abba, Father" by the Spirit, and manifesting a humble confidence in the willingness of God to hear because we have Jesus Christ the Righteous as our Advocate and Mediator, will grow increasingly dear in revival. Revival will make a praying people who approach the privilege with spiritual joy and expectation combined with confidence in God's sovereignty that governs all His relations with His people, all nations, and all creation. If we want such prayer, then we look for ways and times to practice it. We will actively seek to cultivate a delight in the presence of God. Consider the privilege of obeying His prescriptions as to how He is to be approached. Consider the mysterious interaction that sinful creatures may solicit His favor as the source of all good, believing that He cares for us. Ponder the unending advantage of resting in awe at His power, knowledge, and moral perfection that did not inhibit His coming to us with mercy. We join in the corporate call to God in the company of other believers; we set aside time for private invocation to God from whom all blessings flow. He alone can provide these things. Although He will do it in a sovereign way, He loves to see His redeemed people, His holy nation, call on Him so that he may show increasing manifestation of both power and mercy as a loving Father to His children. Paul asked his churches for prayer that "utterance may be given to me, that I may open my mouth boldly to make known the mystery of the gospel" (Eph. 6:19). He requested this immediately after he had established prayer as one of the necessary offensive weapons for Christians to be strong in the Lord and in the power of His might: "praying always with all prayer and supplication in the Spirit, being watchful to this end with all perseverance and supplication for all the saints" (Eph. 6:18).

Revival enhances a deeper level of assurance in those whom it finds. The joy of assurance gives boldness, confidence, and intrinsic delight in preaching and witness. The joyful security of knowing that we have eternal life, in light of all the divine work that brings that gracious status, tends to minimize earthly concerns and fears. It heightens confidence in the gospel's power to convert and in the unerring revelation given in Holy Scripture. Seeking assurance in a biblical way purges us of false spirituality and unbiblical contrivances and elevates a truth-centered walk before the triune God.

If we want revival and all of its salutary effects, then we must practice the very things that constitute the spiritual life engendered by revival.

A SUMMARY OF *RELIGIOUS AFFECTIONS* BY JONATHAN EDWARDS

Jonathan Edwards was instrumental in, and the most insightful observer of, a spiritual awakening in the town of Northampton, Massachusetts, from 1734 to 1736. He was pastor, having followed his grandfather Solomon Stoddard, who had witnessed five such awakenings in his fifty-seven years of ministry (1672–1729). Edwards recorded the events and his analysis in *A Faithful Narrative of the Surprising Work of God in the Conversion of Many Hundred Souls* (short title) in 1737. Another wave of awakening came from 1738 to 1741, a movement in which George Whitefield became a major instrument of God's Spirit. In light of the fallout as well as the powerful and lasting results in both of these, Edwards wrote *The Distinguishing Marks of a Work of the Spirit of God* based on 1 John 4. In this work, Edwards gave nine negative signs, that is, certain phenomena that are highly criticized but constitute "no argument that a work is not from the Spirit of God." He posited five marks from the 1 John text that are indicative of a true work of the Spirit, ending with "a spirit of love to God and man." This was followed in 1742 by another analysis entitled *Some Thoughts Concerning the Present Revival of Religion in New England.* Edwards said that the revival "ought to be acknowledged and promoted." Both of these works examined the evidences of genuineness, phenomena that were extraneous to any valid judgment, warnings against opposition, and encouragements to support and employ biblically warranted means for promoting revival. These writings and the consistent application of biblical analysis to human experience led to his 1746 publication of *A Treatise Concerning Religious Affections*.[1]

The first sentence of the preface to *Religious Affections* leaves no ambiguity as to the book's contents or the importance of the subject as Edwards viewed it: "There is no question whatsoever, that is of greater importance to mankind, and that it more concerns every individual person to be well resolved in, than this, what are the distinguishing qualifications of those that are in favor with God, and entitled to his eternal rewards?" To establish some confidence in the mind of the reader that the discussion has mature thought behind it, Edwards assured, "It is a subject on which my mind has been peculiarly intent, ever since I first entered on the study of divinity." Given the "dust and smoke" of controversy over the phenomena of the Awakening, Edwards described his long years of peculiar attention to this issue in terms like "long engaged me," "with the utmost diligence and care," "exactness of search and inquiry," and "my mind has been peculiarly intent." Even with that, he knew that many would be displeased with his analysis and his contextual admonitions. One party would be aghast that he approved the prominence of affections and affirmed the revival. Another would be disappointed that he condemned much that he saw as an evil and pernicious tendency.

The text was built on 1 Peter 1:8, giving exposition to the stated doctrine, "True religion in great part consists in holy affections." Love to Christ and joy in Christ were the two keys in the text that guided Edwards's doctrine. Edwards defined holy affections as the "more vigorous and sensible exercises of the inclinations and will of the soul." Edwards contended that the soul consists of two faculties: understanding and affections. Understanding includes perception and speculative thought achieving accurate notions. Identifying will, heart, and affections as virtually synonymous, Edwards used words such as *liking, disliking,* and *inclination.* Those

---

[1] Edwards, *Works, Volume 2* (Yale University Press), 84. All quotations and references in this appendix are from this work.

326

that are the more vigorous and sensible are, in this discussion, the affections.

The person who "has no religious affections, is in a state of spiritual death, and is wholly destitute of the powerful, quickening, saving influences of the Spirit of God upon his heart." In the person who has nothing but affection, no true religion exists. The person devoid of any godly affection also has no true religion.

Edwards gave ten areas of thought from the Bible that demonstrate that religion consists largely of the affections. He believed it was obvious that religion consists of the inclination of the will. God not only has given us affections but has made them the spring of action. Edwards pointed to David, Paul, and John to demonstrate that true religion consists very much in love, fear, hatred, desire, joy, sorrow, gratitude, compassion, and zeal. As Edwards argued in several writings (e.g., *Charity and its Fruits* and *The Nature of True Virtue*), these affections may be summed up in love. Jesus Himself was dominated by holy affection. Edwards's seventh argument said, "He whom God sent into the world, to be the Light of the World, and Head of the whole church, and the perfect example of true religion and virtue, for the imitation of all, the shepherd whom the whole flock should follow wherever he goes, even the Lord Jesus Christ, was a person who was remarkably of a tender and affectionate heart; and his virtue was expressed very much in the exercise of holy affections." The religion of heaven is a religion of affection. The biblical elements of worship—prayer, singing, and preaching—assume a major presence of affection.

Part two begins with a discussion of affections that are neither truly gracious nor exclusively carnal. They are "no certain signs that religious affections are truly gracious, or that they are not." We must learn to distinguish between the varieties of affections of which the human soul is capable and realize that they can be prompted by purely natural events, or they might manifest a genuine response to the power of saving grace and partake of its character.

First, that affections are raised very high is no sign either of reality or of passing excitement. High affections are to be expected if rightly connected to understanding, but they may be high and wrongly motivated or easily lost. So it was with the Israelites after the Red Sea who quickly turned to perverseness at Sinai.

Second, effects on the body are neither positive nor negative. Sometimes there is indeed a natural physical response to deep and real spiritual perception; sometimes such bodily responses merely express temporary or even contrived emotion.

Third, fluent, fervent, and abundant talking about religious ideas or biblical concepts may reflect a genuine renewal of understanding and spiritual interest or merely a temporary operation of the natural intellect.

Fourth, interest that is piqued apart from any personal contrivance may indeed be the effectual operation of the Holy Spirit opening to the mind the glory of Christ and the hope embedded within gospel promises. Alternatively, such involuntary perceptions could be prompted by Satan himself or by some heightened common operations of the Spirit of God.

Fifth, it is not a sign that affections are holy or unholy that they come to mind in a remarkable manner with texts of Scripture. Some may reason "that the Scripture is the Word of God, and has nothing in it which is wrong, but is pure and perfect: and therefore, those experiences which come from the Scripture must be right." On such considerations it is necessary to recognize the difference between Scripture as an occasion of certain feelings and Scripture as the proper and effectual cause of rising affections. Some people might be greatly encouraged that they are in a state of grace when a Scripture text comes into their mind, such as "I am my beloved's" (Song 6:3), with no attention to the original meaning. This amounts to reliance on a newly wrought special revelation, for it has no connection with the original meaning of the biblical proposition.

Sixth, it is no evidence that affections are either saving or false that there is an appearance of love in them. Love to God and man may be counterfeited; it often can be of a corrupt sort or become cold under trying circumstances. A kind of false love seems to have been present even in apostolic times as is indicated by Paul's benediction, "Grace be with all those who love our Lord Jesus Christ in sincerity" (Eph. 6:24).

Seventh, having religious affections of many kinds and accompanying one another is no sign that they are truly spiritual. Although one trait of true affections is the entirety and symmetry of parts as they all flow from true divine love, "so from counterfeit love in like manner, naturally flow other false affections."

Eighth, nothing can be determined about the character of the affections that comforts and joys seem to follow certain terrors, convictions, and mental distress in a certain manner. Edwards defended the system of preparationism, a law/gospel dynamic with many examples. This, however, can also be the generator of false assurance. On the other hand, Edwards warned, it is no evidence that comforts and joys are right because they succeed great terrors and amazing fears of hell. Edwards gave twelve pages of discussion to this issue, for it concerned the very heart of Puritan evangelism. Edwards's careful scrutiny of this issue is worth careful attention. His own experience of conversion did not follow the precise preparationist model. One of the sections of his *Faithful Narrative* was headed, "The manner of conversion very various, yet bearing a great analogy." Here he made the observation as a caution for minsters, "The Spirit is so exceeding various in the manner of his operating, that in many cases it is impossible to trace him, or find out his way."

Ninth, certain affections may dispose persons to spend much time in religion, and to be zealously engaged in the external duties of worship. Though true affections prompt a person to engage in reading the Bible, praying, singing praises to God with the congregation and in private, hearing sermons, desiring fellowship, and other edifying manifestations of sincere love for God and His truth, to be "zealously engaged in the external exercises of religion, and to spend much time in them, is not sure evidence of grace." Edwards told about living next door to a Jew, who, in his "acts of devotion, at the eastern window," appeared to Edwards to be "the devoutest person that ever I saw in my life."

Tenth, Edwards observed, as an extension of the last point, that praise by mouth, though sincere praise is desired, may be done within a mixed company—some sincere as arising from genuine conversion and others without root in the heart. Moving events combined with certain apparent advantages can dispose persons with their mouths, apart from true lasting affections, to praise and glorify God. Edwards gave many biblical examples of exuberant praise that arose from pure self-interest or naturally provoked conscience. Crowds uttered praise at the miracles done in their presence, Saul expressed deep remorse at his unfair hounding of David, and Darius was deeply affected at God's protection of Daniel, making a decree that "men must tremble and fear before the God of Daniel" (Dan. 6:25–27).

Eleventh, some impressions give rise to an exceedingly confident air of assurance apart from any true biblical warrant. Edwards gave a long discussion on the nature of assurance, affirming its possibility and goodness in the redeemed but showing that some can have confidence with no scriptural and spiritual ground for it. "It is manifest," Edwards explained, "that it was a common thing for the saints of whom we have a particular account in Scripture, to be assured." In the covenant of grace, God has made ample provision for the saints having an assured hope of eternal life while living here upon earth. Things are so ordered in that covenant and revealed with such clarity that he who has the Spirit of Christ may make his "calling and election sure" (2 Peter 1:10 KJV). At the same time, that some persons have abundant confidence that they are among the redeemed is not a sufficient reason to conclude that they are saved. Edwards warned, "When once a hypocrite is thus established in a false hope, he has not those things to cause him to call his hope in question, that oftentimes are the occasions of doubting to true saints." Such ill-convinced people do not consider their own blindness and the deceitfulness of their hearts. They do not share the low opinion that a true saint has of his own understanding. Nor do they find Satan assaulting their hopes as he does that of a true saint.

Twelfth, one can conclude nothing about the saving effects of the gospel in another person's life from this, that "the outward manifestations of them, and the relation persons give of them, are very affecting and pleasing to the truly godly, and such as greatly gain their charity, and win their hearts." Though saints know what true religion is from their own personal encounters through the Spirit, they can neither see nor feel those in the heart of another. Many poor judges are quick and peremptory in determining persons' states, claiming competence in discerning and distinguishing in these vitally important matters. They have not judged by the mature fruit of saving faith but by impressions, engaging language, and some sense of immediate revelation in the matter, as though all was open and clear to them. Such erroneous counselors encourage assurance on the part of silver-tongued hypocrites who are quick with words, high on pride and self-confidence, but void of any transforming work of the Spirit. One who manifests confidence that he can know another's true godliness arrogates to himself a power of discernment beyond that granted to the apostles. Their counsel may be summarized in the admonition of Paul, "Examine yourselves, as to whether you are in the faith. Test yourselves. Do you not know yourselves, that Jesus Christ is in you?—unless indeed you are disqualified" (2 Cor. 13:5).

Edwards reviewed all the signs given to that point and summarized, "I think it has been made plain, that there may be all these things, and yet nothing more than the common influences of the Spirit of God, joined with the delusions of Satan, and a wicked, deceitful heart. . . . How great therefore may the resemblance be, as to all outward expressions and appearances, between an hypocrite and a true saint!"

Before launching into his description of truly gracious affections, Edwards discussed preliminary assumptions about his detailed discussion of religious affections. One, we cannot distinguish true affections from false in others. Two, no one can discern their "good estate" who are in a low state of grace and have fallen into a "dead, carnal, and unchristian frame." He argued that it is "not God's design that men should obtain assurance in any other way, than by mortifying corruption, and increasing in grace, and obtaining the lively exercises of it." Three, it is difficult if not impossible to undeceive hypocrites.

Having given special attention to phenomena that neither rule against nor militate in favor of the presence of genuine religious affections, Edwards set forth an exposition of the ways "wherein those affections that are spiritual and gracious, do differ from those that are not so."

First, these affections do not arise from natural sources within or without the person, but from influences that are spiritual, supernatural, and divine. They are produced within the hearts of those who are born of the Spirit (John 3:6; Rom. 8:9–11). This indwelling Spirit produces spiritual fruit both as His proper nature and in His transforming operations on our spirit (Gal 5:18–6:1; Rom. 8:16). These are not the extraordinary gifts of the Spirit or the external manifestations of such gifts. As well as the proper author of these affections, the Spirit is the seal (2 Cor. 1:22; Eph. 1:14), that is, the very existence and atmosphere of eternal life in the saints. These affections, therefore, are not merely natural, such as may exist in a high degree in natural men in certain relations and situations. This involves a new inward perception or sensation of the mind, a principial foundation laid in the nature of the soul that informs the understanding and activates the will.

Second, the first objective ground of gracious affections is the "transcendently excellent and amiable nature of divine things as they are in themselves; and not in any conceived relation they bear to self or self interest." Edwards gave full exposition of this idea in his posthumously published work *The Nature of True Virtue.*

Having given exposition of the nature and manifestation of self-love, Edwards wrote, "The first foundation of the delight a true saint has in God, is his own perfection; and the first foundation of the delight he has in Christ, is his own beauty . . . and then they have a secondary joy, in that so excellent a Saviour, and such excellent grace is theirs." This spiritual grasp of the loveliness is complemented by a true sense of the vileness and deformity of themselves. While this is distressing in some ways, it also serves to "purify their affections" as well as "sweeten and heighten them."

Third, true affections are founded on the "loveliness of the moral excellency of divine things." Edwards discussed the relation of natural evil to moral evil and natural good to moral good. For example, angels possess natural good in the capacity of their understanding, their great strength, and their honorable circumstances; their moral good consists of "their perfect and glorious holiness and goodness, their pure and flaming love to God, and to the saints, and one another." While the infinite greatness of omnipotence, the awe-inspiring attribute of omniscience, and the decretal purpose combined with sovereign wisdom to execute all things as God sees fit should bend all creatures to awe and wonder, the pervasive presence of holiness in all of these prompts holy affection. Edwards highlighted the point: "A holy love has a holy object: the holiness of love consists especially in this that it is the love of that which is holy, as holy, or for its holiness; so that 'tis the holiness of the object, which is the quality whereon it fixes and terminates." Edwards distinguished between *bonum utile* and *bonum formosum*, the one that serves my interest thus suiting self-love, and the other a good in itself, such as the "moral and spiritual excellency of the divine nature."

Fourth, these holy affections "arise from the mind's being enlightened, rightly and spiritually to understand or apprehend divine things." Gracious affections are not "heat without light." They arise from some information in the understanding. Instruction as to the meaning of biblical texts is essential for gracious affections, those aspects of delight and praise that are founded on divine truth. To cognition must be added spiritual enlightenment. The savory goodness in a text, or a composite synthesis of biblical truth that evokes increase of love and intelligent praise, depends on the special operation of the Holy Spirit. God "has shone in our hearts to give the light of the knowledge of the glory of God in the face of Jesus Christ" (2 Cor. 4:6). Unabashed in his assertions of divine sovereignty in this matter, Edwards said, "If the Scriptures are of any use to teach us anything," then it is absolutely certain that "a spiritual, supernatural understanding of divine things" is a peculiar blessing to the saints "which those who are not saints know nothing of." The worshipful grasp of a text comprehended easily by natural intellect "is entirely different in nature and kind, from all which natural men are, or can be the subjects of." In a memorable pungency of phrase, Edwards summarized that "it consists in the sensations of a new spiritual sense, which the souls of natural men have not."

Fifth, "gracious affections are attended with a reasonable and spiritual conviction of the judgment, of the reality and certainty of divine things." The truths of the gospel cease to be a matter of probability or capable of dispute but are empirically pressed on the conscience and the mind so that "they are points settled and determined." God does this by removing prejudices of reason, by positively helping the reason to embrace the abundance of existential and historical evidences as certainly determining the credibility of the Bible's narrative, and by impressing immediately on the senses the reality of biblical truth. The character of God, the sinfulness of man, the beauty of the person of Christ, the disarming loveliness of the provisions of the gospel, and the truth of final judgment all become certainties of both reason and sense. The Bible demonstrates human sin from its origin and shows its pervasive presence. We feel its devastating nature. The Bible presents the glory and ineffable wonder of Christ in His Sonship, His work as Savior, and in His mediatorial glory, and we live in the sensate reality of it. "The truth of these things revealed in the Scripture, and many more that might be mentioned, appear to the soul, only by imparting that spiritual taste of divine beauty." This being given and the number of biblical truths being expanded to the consciousness, "the soul discerns the beauty of every part of the gospel scheme."

Sixth, these genuine religious affections, or, as Edwards consistently called them, "gracious affections," are attended with evangelical humiliation. He defined this as a "sense that a Christian has of his own utter insufficiency, despicableness, and odiousness, with an answerable frame of heart." Edwards distinguished between legal and evangelical humiliation. He gave extensive discussion of the manifestations of legal humiliation and the false confidence that it produces. Though it might be useful as preparatory to true evangelical humiliation, it has a tendency to deceive, create a spirit of eminence, produce self-righteousness, and hide from the eyes the true glory of the gospel. True saints in a state of the greatest awareness of their sin, with an attitude of deepest humility and reverence, still sense that their present humility is small and "their remaining pride great, and exceedingly abominable." As opposed to a person under impressions that are only the legal working of humility—those who "think highly of their humility" and are "forward to put forth itself to view"—a truly grace-filled person "is not apt to think himself eminent in any thing; all his graces and experiences are ready to appear to him to be comparatively small; but especially his humility."

Seventh, gracious affections "are attended with a change of nature." All exercises of grace come from the true presence of Christ, through the Spirit in the soul of man. This does not mean, however, that the soul itself does not partake of the holy influences that Christ brings by His presence. The grace that is shed abroad in the heart imparts a savor of Christ in the soul itself, "so that the soul, in being indued with grace, is indued with a new nature." Such grace through the personal presence of the Spirit does not leave the soul so that it returns to its carnal domination, but actively seeks to mortify those remaining principles to which it was once captive. The soul has been transformed and educated permanently so that from deadness it is quickened, raised up, created in Christ Jesus to good works, made a habitation for God by the Spirit, and seated with Christ in heavenly places.

Eighth, gracious affections "tend to, and are attended with the lamblike, dovelike spirit and temper of Jesus Christ." Since true saints are indwelt by Christ in the same Spirit that vindicated Him in His incarnation (1 Tim. 3:16), their new nature will express itself in the increasing dominance of a Christlike spirit, even as the saints are predestinated to be conformed to the image of Christ. Even their boldness for truth will push away those fierce, violent, sharp, and bitter passions to which they have been so susceptible. Edwards, as is usual in each of these points, gave relevant catenae of Scripture support, emphasizing meekness, humility, love, condescension, forgiveness, mercy, submission, patience, kindness, holy fortitude, pity, compassion, benevolence and beneficence, and suffering for righteousness' sake. In virtually every section, Edwards made a point to affirm the authority of the Bible in the discussion. So it is here: "But this I affirm, and shall affirm till I deny the Bible to be anything worth, that everything in Christians that belongs to true Christianity, is of this tendency [for] the Scripture knows of no such true Christians, as of a sordid, selfish, cross and contentious spirit."

Ninth, "gracious affections soften the heart, and are attended and followed with a Christian tenderness of spirit." Each reader of this work sees the depth of Edwards's biblical concern to drive home the truth that genuine religious affections arise from divinely wrought transformation of the soul (as defined earlier). Each section also includes a discussion of the way that hypocrites seek to mask their being void of such humbling and holy transforming power and to imitate by carnal and worldly means those Christian graces that Edwards described. In this section, Edwards delivered a sad warning: "He that has counterfeit repentance, and false comforts and joys, is like iron that has been suddenly heated and quenched; it becomes much harder than before. A false conversion puts an end to convictions of conscience." He closes this mark with a description of the person who has such tenderness of spirit.

> The less apt he is to be afraid of natural evil, ... the more apt he is to be alarmed by the appearance of moral evil, or the evil of sin. As he has more holy boldness, so he has less of self-confidence, and a forward assuming boldness, and more modesty. As he is more sure than others of deliverance from hell, so he has more of a sense of the desert of it. He is less apt than others to be shaken in faith; but more apt than others to be moved with solemn warnings, and with God's frowns, and with the calamities of others. He has the firmest comfort, but the softest heart: richer than others, but poorest of all in spirit: the tallest and strongest saints, but the least and tenderest child amongst them.

Tenth, gracious and holy affections have "beautiful symmetry and proportion." Joy and comfort are attended by godly sorrow and mourning for sin. The confidence of true faith is, at the same time, penetrated with repentance. Testimonies of love to Christ will find expression in benevolence toward men. Their affection for some men is not countered by bitterness toward others. Their care for the bodies of the destitute includes a preeminent care for their souls and their access to gospel truth. Likewise, where genuine care for the eternal well-being of sinners exists, so does compassion for their temporal welfare. True Christian affections will not be plagued with a "monstrous disproportion" in the complementary elements of any biblically warranted affection. Hatred of sin and zeal for righteousness will be manifest toward themselves, in the first place, before any judgment of others. True Christian affections produce love for the pleasant joys of social religion but "in a peculiar manner delights in retirement, and secret converse with God." If a person is "little moved when they have none but God and Christ to converse with, it looks very darkly upon their religion."

Eleventh, the raising of such gracious affections increases the spiritual appetite for even greater and more pure affections. They do not rest satisfied in themselves. Some who seem earnestly to seek salvation and cry after it and implore God to save them find satisfaction in a particular display of emotion, and thus conclude that God has answered their prayers. This satisfaction ends their seeking after God and they rest in a carnal security, thinking that they have obtained the goal of their exuberant seeking. True seeking under the converting influence of the Spirit of God issues in a fulfilled desire to find a gracious God and increases the earnestness of their desire to know Him and show forth His holy character and love. True grace comforts but never fills; the appetite is increased and, like the apostle, they press forward to those things that are ahead. Hypocrites may at times press after more discoveries of truth and grace, but they do it so that they may be more satisfied and secure in their own souls—that is, for self-interest. The saints desire the sincere milk of the Word for its intrinsic beauty and for the moral excellence and holy sweetness that comes by earnest pursuit of the propositions of revealed truth.

Twelfth, gracious affections have their fruit in Christian practice. Edwards gave an extended amount of space to this discussion. Such practice is the best evidence of saving faith to others as well as to one's own conscience. An earnest pursuit of "good works" as described in Scripture, throughout and to the end of life, is the biblical evidence of transforming grace. Though salvation comes not by works of righteousness that we have done, nevertheless we are to maintain good works. Though it is only by the sovereign granting of regenerating grace that we are saved, "not of works," nevertheless this grace is not only a forgiving and justifying grace but it establishes a workmanship that creates good works in the true believer. After giving six biblical arguments for this twelfth sign, Edwards affirmed, "Now, from all that has been said, I think it to be abundantly manifest, that Christian practice is the most proper evidence of the gracious sincerity of professors, to themselves and others."

Edwards closed this discussion of good works with a forceful and succinct defense of its consistency with the doctrines of justification by faith and the sovereignty of grace in the salvation of sinners. His final sentence concluded a discussion of the great benefits of good works as a practical demonstration to the world of the reality and excellence of the religion of the Bible: "Thus the light of professors would so shine before men, that others seeing their good works, would glorify their Father which is in heaven."

REVIVE OUR SOULS

Based on Psalm 85

By your great grace, O sovereign God,
To You we were restored;
Transgressions covered with Christ's blood,
Our sins that You abhorred.

Since You have saved us, stay Your wrath,
Forsake Your indignation.
Show us, O Lord, a holy path,
Complete our restoration.

Revive our souls to love Your truth,
Increase our joy in You.
Forsaking all, may we like Ruth
Hold only You in view.

I look upon Your Word and hear
Reconciliation.
True glory comes to those who fear
The Lord for such salvation.

Since justice found a way to love
And righteousness bred peace,
O Holy Wisdom from above,
Let holiness increase.

Please heal our land, remove its strife.
We die that we might live.
May Jesus' resurrected life
Give hope, make pure, forgive.

Scripture Index

ABOUT THE AUTHOR

Tom Nettles is one of the founding faculty of the Institute of Public Theology. He served as the Professor of Historical Theology at The Southern Baptist Theological Seminary. He previously taught at Trinity Evangelical Divinity School where he was Professor of Church History and Chair of the Department of Church History. Prior to that, he taught at Southwestern Baptist Theological Seminary and Mid-America Baptist Theological Seminary. Along with numerous journal articles and scholarly papers, Dr. Nettles is the author and editor of fifteen books. Among his books are *By His Grace and For His Glory; Baptists and the Bible, James Petigru Boyce: A Southern Baptist Statesman, Praise is His Gracious Choice, Remember Jesus Christ, and Living by Revealed Truth: The Life and Pastoral Theology of Charles H. Spurgeon.*

FOUNDERS

M I N I S T R I E S

Founders Ministries exists for the recovery of the gospel and the reformation of churches.

We have been providing resources for churches since 1982 through conferences, books, The Sword & The Trowel Podcast, video documentaries, the Founders Study center (*www.study.founders.org*), online articles found at www.founders.org, the quarterly Founders Journal, Bible studies, International church search, and the seminary level training program, the Institute of Public Theology (*www.iopt.org*). Founders believes that the biblical faith is inherently doctrinal, and we are therefore confessional in our convictions.

You can learn more about Founders Ministries and how to partner with us at *www.founders.org*.

FoundersMin

FoundersMin

FoundersMinistries

FoundersMinistries

Other Titles from Founders Press

Prayer and Politics
By David Mitzenmacher

> How should Christians engage in politics? This is one of the hot-button issues of our day, with different opinions abounding. But there is one thing that all Bible-believing Christians should agree on: Christians must pray for our government leaders. This booklet looks at the Apostle Paul's exhortation to pray for government authorities in 1 Timothy 2:1–4 and explores the underlying political theology. By better understanding the role of government within God's created order, we can better understand how to pray for our leaders and engage in the political process in the fear of our Lord and the love of our neighbor.

> — David Mitzenmacher
> Associate Pastor,
> Grace Baptist Church, Cape Coral, FL

What Is A Reformed Baptist?
By Tom Hicks

> Knowing and understanding wholesome theology is essential for the Christian life. Right living must be based in right believing. Tom Hicks has produced an excellent survey of many of the key doctrines upon which a holy life may be built, faithful to the Word of God and the Baptist Confession of Faith. This is a wonderful book for church members, for those seeking church membership, for study classes and for new believers. I am grateful that we now have this important resource.

> — James M. Renihan
> President, International Reformed Baptist Seminary

Serious Joy: Reflections and Devotions on Jonathan Edwards' Seventy Resolutions
By Joey Tomlinson

> Joey Tomlinson has written a wonderful introduction and guide to Edwards' Resolutions, wisely expounding and pressing them into the corners of our lives. I'm glad to commend this little book in *Serious Joy*.

> — Joe Rigney, Fellow of Theology,
> New Saint Andrews College

Dear Titus: Letters on Church Planting
By Nate Pickowicz

At a time when defection from the truth is rampant and many in ministry have lost their nerve, this book provides the needed encouragement and clarity to remain steadfast in gospel ministry. Additionally, as church planting efforts struggle to keep up with population growth in many places worldwide, this manuscript serves as a crucial tool to prepare and equip leaders for the task. Nate Pickowicz's labor to produce this volume will arrive right on time.

— Chris Larson
President & CEO, Ligonier Ministries

The Revolutionary Reading of Romans 13
By Timothy L. Decker

Pastors need tools in their belts as they help Christ's people lead godly and honorable lives under the civil government. Decker's work will be one such tool, contributing to your thinking as you prepare to lead the people entrusted to your care.

— Daniel Scheiderer
Pastor of Grace Baptist Church, Chambersburg, PA

A Pastor in Revival
By Kurt M. Smith

This new study of Edwards' experience and vindication of revival is rich in historical context, primary source material, and footnotes (which I love), but also spiritual lessons for today. It is eminently readable and I am extremely happy to commend it as an extremely helpful precis of Edwards' involvement in the Great Awakening.

— Michael Haykin
Chair & Professor of Church History
The Southern Baptist Theological Seminary

Suffering with Joy
By Thomas K. Ascol

Suffering has been our constant companion since the Fall. It is a great equalizer that eventually comes calling at the door of every family and is never a welcome guest. In this helpful book, Tom Ascol serves as companion, model, and teacher as he helps his loved ones, and us, navigate the deep waters of suffering and loss. This book is a timeless treasure to be shared with those inside the church as a guide to suffering well, and with those outside the church as a guide to knowing the one who is our only source of true and lasting hope.

— Voddie Baucham
Founding Dean, ACU
Founding Faculty, The Institute of Public Theology
Author of Fault Lines

Additional Titles

Dear Timothy
Edited by Thomas K. Ascol

Striving for the Faith
Alex Kocman

As the Darkness Clears Away
Tom Ascol

God In His Beautiful Greatness
Baruch Maoz

Just Thinking about Ethnicity
Darrell Harrison & Virgil Walker

The Beauty of the Binary
Luke Griffo

A Primer for Conflict
Josh Howard

By His Grace and for His Glory
Tom Nettles

Getting the Garden Right
Richard C. Barcellos

The Law and the Gospel
Ernie Reisinger

Teaching Truth, Training Hearts
Tom Nettles

Just Thinking: about the state
Darrell Harrison and Virgil Walker

Seeds and Stars
E.D. Burns

Missions by the Book: How Theology and Missions Walk Together
Chad Vegas and Alex Kocman

Order these titles and more at press.founders.org